Hel~~ping Teachers Develop~~
Through Classroom Observation

Helping Teachers Develop Through Classroom Observation

2nd edition

Diane Montgomery

 David Fulton Publishers

David Fulton Publishers Ltd
Ormond House, 26–27 Boswell Street, London WC1N 3JZ

www.fultonpublishers.co.uk

First edition entitled *Positive Teacher Appraisal Through Classroom Observation*, published 1999

This edition published in Great Britain in 2002 by David Fulton Publishers

Note: The right of Diane Montgomery to be identified as the author of this work has been asserted by her in accordance with the Copyright, Designs and Patents Act 1988.

Copyright © Diane Montgomery 2002

British Library Cataloguing in Publication Data
A catalogue record for this book is available from the British Library.

ISBN 1–85346–872–X

Typeset by Textype Typesetters, Cambridge
Printed in Great Britain

Contents

Introduction

Since the first edition of this book (*Positive Teacher Appraisal Through Classroom Observation*) was published in 1999 events in the field of performance management have moved on quickly and in a more positive direction. The DfEE (1999a) consultation document focusing on linking pay and performance management, in particular threshold assessments for experienced teachers with nine spine points relating to qualifications and experience, drew a large amount of critical comment and this does appear to have been heeded. The main objective is retained but more supporting information is given on how schools may achieve the results, with some autonomy in the approaches being permitted.

Following these consultations, in September 2000 the DfEE introduced a performance management system which replaced the statutory appraisal system (DFE 1991) because the former arrangements had failed to improve teaching and learning in schools or to raise pupil standards.

The three general purposes of appraisal – promotion, reward and professional development – are once again centre stage. This time perhaps with more likelihood of success – for there is now a strong link between methods of classroom observation and school and professional development. These, in a system of performance management, are linked to the school development plan and target the raising of pupil performance.

In this book the main emphasis is upon the ways in which classroom observation can serve performance management and school development by helping teachers improve their teaching performance and, through this, their pupils' learning. This should all take place in a cycle of continuing professional development (CPD).

A range of performance management techniques are reviewed in Chapter 1 to illustrate their effects on teaching performance and the issues and problems which can surround their use. Questions are raised about whether the strategies and 'instruments' used for assessing performance for promotion and reward can be the same as those to be used for teacher development and raising teaching standards.

In Chapter 2 the range of techniques available for classroom observation are discussed and evaluated, and in the final section of this chapter a professional development method is described which can be used to consolidate and affirm the performance of good teachers and retrieve the performance of failing teachers or those in difficulties. This is an evidence-based system – a rarity in this field. It is formative and uses a coaching system linked to classroom observation.

The observation method and evidence for its effectiveness are presented in Chapter 3 in both quantitative and qualitative terms and then illustrated through a series of primary and secondary school case studies. The method has also been used successfully with minor modifications as a staff development system in higher education. An outline is given of how a case example school uses this method of classroom observation in its performance management and school development strategy.

In Chapters 4 and 5 an analysis of effective learning and teaching is undertaken and shows how the needs of able and slower learners can be met when schools incorporate notions of learning strategies and styles and the 'cognitive curriculum' in their teaching across the curriculum. In these chapters a range of examples are given to show how modest changes in method can improve motivation and raise pupil performance through inclusive teaching methods. These strategies are also those which can help underpin the work in the Excellence in Cities initiatives, the gifted and talented, and reverse lower attainment in underachieving learners. *Reversing Lower Attainment* (Montgomery 1998a, also published by David Fulton), is the companion volume to this book and illustrates the applications of the teaching and learning strategies to different curriculum areas.

CHAPTER 1

Performance Management

Introduction

In September 2000 a performance management system was introduced into English schools with the purpose of strengthening the links between the school development and improvement plan and pupil performance. This system would directly link individual teachers' performance with their pupils' attainments. This time the system emphasised the links with professional development so that the satisfaction and motivation of teachers could be enhanced and thus produce the desired outcomes.

The reasons for this new development were that the appraisal system previously established (DFE 1991) had fallen into disuse (again) in some schools and was perfunctory in others. However, some had established useful models which, if linked to performance management strategies derived from the business world, could have led to the raising of standards in schools. As a result of the consultation following the Green Paper (DfEE 1999a) significant improvements in the strategy were achieved, marrying best practice in both fields and, by providing supporting materials, research and guidance.

The specific concerns identified in the White Paper *Excellence for All* (DfEE 1997) were that the appraisal arrangements then in operation did not provide an adequate check on students' performance. The targets set often failed to focus on improving teacher effectiveness in the classroom and were not specific or measurable. The Office for Standards in Education (OFSTED 1997) identified five main weaknesses in the appraisal systems operating in schools. They were lacking in rigour; there was poor evaluation of the impact on teaching quality and the pupils; there was unrealistic target setting; there was infrequent or ineffective classroom observation; and there was a failure to link appraisal to training. In effect, appraisal in the majority of settings had become a perfunctory exercise.

In the same year the National Union of Teachers (NUT 1997) reported that teachers feared that the results of appraisal would be used against them. This indicated a lack of trust between the appraisers and the appraisees. The NUT insisted that appraisal must be linked to professional development and not to pay, promotion or capability procedures – shades of the debate which had raged more than a decade earlier when formal appraisal was first introduced (Joseph 1984). In other words, all the attributes which good appraisal schemes might be expected to offer had somehow been bypassed, and appraisal had become a paper-and-pencil exercise in keeping with the worst predictions.

Research by Wragg *et al.* (1996) in 400 schools found that only 28 per cent of teachers were observed teaching, and this occurred only once instead of twice as in the appraisal regulations. In many cases the observation lasted for less than the 30 minutes' minimum recommended span. There were also doubts over what was being appraised and it was left largely up to the teachers to decide on the focus for the observation. The foci chosen were teaching methods in 28 per cent, curriculum in 7 per cent, and assessing children's work in 4 per cent. Of those who had been appraised, only 60 per cent thought that it had improved their work performance (Baron *et al.* 1998). Whether or not it was more than a 'Hawthorne Effect' or a 'feel good factor' was not tested.

With the intended publication of the Green Paper (DfEE 1999a) schools across the country began, in advance, to reappraise their appraisal procedures and prepare for the new regime. Thus it was that following a workshop on Positive Classroom Observation and School Improvement at the Secondary Heads Conference (SHA 1998) several hundred schools signed up over the next two years to learn more of the system described in this book. It was part of the Learning Difficulties Research Project (LDRP), Programme Four on the Evaluation and Enhancement of Teaching Performance begun in 1983 to support appraisal in schools when the initiative was first announced (Joseph 1984).

Although appraisal schemes had, to all intents and purposes, lapsed or become attenuated since 1991, the clear exceptions were in relation to the appraisal of Newly Qualified Teachers (NQTs) and to capability procedures.

In schools in the LDRP, where full appraisal schemes still operated, staff usually chose the focus for the lesson observation with differentiation – equal opportunities, special educational needs, provision for the more able, classroom management, questioning techniques and curriculum being the most popular. The choice of focus tended to depend upon the areas of competency and interest of the observer, recent in-service training inputs, as well as the expertise of the person observed.

Experienced and expert teachers still reported being unsure of their competencies in appraising the classroom performance of others. They were clear about being able to recognise and deal with failing performance but less secure about how to retrieve it or about how to appraise with some exactitude the broad range of competencies which they might meet. Senior teachers were often concerned about their distance from the classroom, the role which they brought to any observation and the effect it might have upon pupils, as well as their lack of subject expertise except in their own domain. Devolving appraisal to subject leaders and heads of department equally did not fill them with confidence. Others who were involved in the appraisal of NQTs and in capability procedures often relished the negative powers that their new role could bring and some enjoyed the title of 'axeman-woman'. This did not contribute to the health and wellbeing of a school as a developing organism.

In the new scheme performance management is closely linked to threshold assessments which are based on the new standards introduced for head teachers, subject leaders, SENCOs (Special Educational Needs Coordinators) and NQTs, and induction standards.

In addition to these standards and courses of specific training at approved centres for head teachers and aspiring heads, the Government has introduced a National Literacy Strategy (NLS) (DfEE 1998), a National Numeracy Strategy (DfEE 1999) in primary schools, with pilot projects on literacy and study skills in Year 7 for secondary schools. This, of course, returned primary schools to the situation they had been in before the introduction of the National Curriculum ten years earlier when every primary school spent most of each morning on 'Basic Skills' often in application in subject areas. The result has been that literacy standards have risen to previous levels but the overprescriptive and narrow approach adopted to literacy through reading has left spelling and writing behind. The Numeracy strategy has proved to be more responsive and less subject to criticism.

Since these core skills have been addressed to some extent, other priorities have emerged such as the underachievement of boys in writing (OFSTED 2000) and Black Afro-Caribbean groups (OFSTED 1999). There have also been a flurry of initiatives such as Excellence in Cities (DfEE 1999d) and the establishment of training programmes for Gifted and Talented Coordinators in schools, and associated funding of 'Summer schools', Master classes' and World Class Tests, for all of which there is no evidence for their value or effectiveness (Freeman 1998).

Teachers are once again weighed down by the welter of initiatives and a continuous round of bidding and funding. Performance management, however, has its most serious side for it touches at the heart of teaching and learning and the personal performance of teachers. This time we must get it right. This time more opportunities for local initiative have been permitted, and with their focus on development they have the potential for success.

Performance management

The performance management system now in place is one which provides for the reviewing and agreeing of priorities within the context of the school development plan (Bubb and Hoare 2001).

The main points of the current system are:

- to agree annual objectives for each teacher to include objectives relating to pupil progress and ways of developing and improving the teachers' professional practice;

- to undertake, within the year, monitoring of progress and classroom observation of teaching;
- to hold an end-of-year review meeting which includes an assessment of the teacher's overall performance – this should take account of achievement against objectives and agree objectives for the next year – the discussion should cover development opportunities and activities;
- to use performance review outcomes to inform pay decisions as appropriate; and
- for head teachers the objectives agreed should relate to school leadership and management and general pupil progression.

Fundamentally, these are no different to those which were established in schools which operated well-structured appraisal systems. They now have a harder cutting edge in that SATs results, public examinations, OFSTED assessments and other measures such as reading and spelling test outcomes must be built into the assessment procedures. Teachers reaching the spine point nine on the salary scale are eligible to receive an extra increment of £2,000 if they have met the objectives agreed. Failure in one or two out of five lessons in an OFSTED inspection, for example, would prevent this increment being awarded until the teaching performance shortcomings had been identified and remedied.

There were many teachers who had reached scale point nine when the scheme was introduced and so performance management suddenly had a wide and strong impact which the appraisal forerunner did not have because there were no such incentives.

Performance related pay – accountability

The accountability movement began in 1872 when a system of 'payment by results' was introduced. Over time, it lapsed until the Education Act of 1902 formally discontinued it. It re-emerged again with the Ruskin College speech of the then Prime Minister James Callaghan, in 1976, and now, again under a Labour Government, in 1998. Callaghan launched the 'Great Debate on Education', arguing that a section of the economy that consumed such a large proportion of public money, £6 billion (now £16 billion), should be more accountable to that public for the way in which the money was spent and the value which resulted. He wanted value for money. Accountability was linked not only to costs and value for money but to standards and the questioning of autonomy in the education system. Professional autonomy was no longer to be sacrosanct.

There had been a move from a selective tripartite system of education in 1970 to a mainly comprehensive style of education. This had raised concerns in many quarters about standards. It fuelled public concern about education, and appraisal was seen as a method for ridding the profession of failing teachers. This of course made all teachers feel somewhat threatened as there were considerable differences of opinion about teaching methods, styles and contents (Bennett and Jordan 1975). This gave rise to a central concern about the credibility of the appraiser and the process in the pursuit of accountability.

At that time 'appraisal by walking about' was the most common method in operation. Few schools had instituted formal appraisal procedures, although there were some notable exceptions (Samuel 1983; Trethowan 1987). In many small primary schools, heads and deputies joined in the classroom work with staff and so were able to claim that they had observed their staff teaching. The same could not be said of secondary school heads and college principals, however. In addition to this, a wide range of teachers helped in the training and appraisal of students in their own classrooms by contributing to the college assessments. This participation slowly increased until the present, when mentors in school may be the prime teaching practice supervisors and assessors. Despite the requirements for the profession to be made more accountable and the institution of a system of independent inspections by OFSTED, no special money was put into appraisal itself.

In the current performance management system, in addition to threshold payments and sums of money to attract new members into the profession ('golden hellos'), governing bodies can also make discretionary pay awards (performance related pay (PRP)), and there are a host of initiatives (Beacon Schools, Investors in People, Specialist Schools, Excellence in Cities, etc.) to bid for, which can bring extra funding, so that many schools now have a more flexible budget to promote initiative and development.

There have always been divided opinions in the teaching profession about PRP and incentive driven systems. Noticeably, it was the younger members of the profession who favoured PRP. Shortage of money, promotion being blocked by senior colleagues whose jobs they felt they could do or were doing, and inexperience and lack of knowledge of the underlying issues might have contributed to this perspective. On the other hand, those disputing the value of PRP held that a true professional is just that, a professional, and this means that they seek to do the best job they can whatever the circumstances, and thus financial incentives can do little to improve their performance. They should, however, be paid at a level befitting their professional status. Such incentives can be seen as bribes and may actually demotivate and dissatisfy when they are small and when staff given them are not perceived to have been given them fairly (and this is at times inevitable despite best efforts). All staff on the whole will think that they deserve and must be awarded the PRP and it can be difficult to bring some to see the reasons why they may not be awarded it.

PRP was introduced into higher education in 1991 on a limited scale, in the first place for senior managers, and each had targets to meet which were established in an appraisal review. The targets were usually written by the individual, tinkered with by someone senior and then assessed at some later period by the senior on a five point scale in an undisclosed, unevidenced manner, without consultation. The 'pot of money' set aside for the purpose was then shared out. At the time, the more external funding a tutor acquired the higher the PRP. All sums were undisclosed. An attempt to roll the system out to all members of staff to all intents and purposes failed as there was insufficient money to fund it adequately, and experiments were tried where two or three tutors who had consistently demonstrated excellence in teaching during the year were awarded sums of £500. Faculty approaches to this varied in who was put forward and why, from the system of sharing the £1,000 out between all, to selecting two on the basis of 'Buggins' turn this year' to systematic internal and external validation of appraisal of teaching. The new system of performance management in schools is far more complex and rather more subtle and has avoided some of the major flaws, not least that a significant sum of money has been made available and that teachers are competing with themselves rather than with others, and this is tested against nationally established criteria with local agreement on their application in practice.

Higher education institutions now do have in place systematic appraisals of staff and in June 2001, Sir Howard Newby, incoming president of the Higher Education Funding Council for England announced that ministers were taking seriously the funding gap of nearly £1 billion in higher education but that the new money to be made available must be linked to a system of appraisal which was performance related so that poor performance was not rewarded. No doubt a similar system to that which operates in schools will be devised in which a significant sum of money is available as a 'carrot', or bribe, to opt into the system and set the whole thing in motion.

The performance management structure and implementation

The implementation of a performance management scheme has meant that heads and deputies have had to broaden the management structure to strengthen it and delegate responsibility down through the school system to teams of middle managers. This has inevitably led to a hierarchical system of management. It can work well where it is served at each level by good or inspirational leaders. However, the system does not work in an easy and fluent manner as yet, for there is a history of promotion and reward in schools which has never been evidence based in this way. It is also true that teachers are still appointed to post on the basis of interview, which is only 25 per cent reliable! They should be seen teaching, even if they are to lead a department, for their quality in teaching can help them promote it in their team and at least gain respect for their professional skills.

The new structure has thus strengthened the staff development responsibilities of team and subject leaders. It also requires that there is a system for feeding this information into the system so that staff development undertaken is linked to the school development plan and funding acquired for the purpose. There may also be individual professional development needs identified or raised in reviews and classroom observation discussions that fall outside this plan. Encouragement to pursue these personal goals for updating, professional career development or career change are important and small amounts of financial support or study days can help this.

Many schools had begun to plan ahead of the performance management initiative and were ready to implement it straight away. However, leeway was given so that the whole process in the initial round should be completed in at least 18 months, and thereafter annually. For some it was yet another initiative placing further demands on teachers' time and requiring more detailed paperwork creating further stress particularly in small primary schools which were already in overload mode. At this point some heads left the profession, having decided that the antagonisms which could be generated by being unable, in all good conscience, to give experienced teachers their threshold payments, would be too stressful. In secondary schools the chain of command can be longer and its more difficult aspects shared or delegated.

To help schools, the DfEE (2000b) published an explanation of how performance management could directly underpin the production of the school development plan and the collection of data for the threshold assessment, and as a tool for raising standards.

The system itself has had some benefits in, for example, a case where the teacher could raise performance sufficiently to pass the OFSTED inspections but would not be able to maintain this. The comparative statistics of the within-school GCSE results where colleagues teaching in a mixed ability, inner city school that achieved 49, 56, 59 and 63 per cent A to C passes, but where he obtained 14 per cent, could not be denied. It might be questioned why on earth this data had not been presented to this particular teacher before. Here we see the lack of support for capability procedures and processes in some schools and LEAs and the likelihood that the head of department would, because of initiating and managing the process, become the subject of an extensive grievance procedure. Such procedures in the past have often taken 18 months to two years to complete and can spawn other investigations, numerous and various.

Although reliance on statistical data can never be absolute, it can now be taken into account and the reasons for low or high results can be investigated. The data can provide threshold information against which objectives for the following year are set and then reviewed at the end of the year to explore what has happened and why. Alternatively it can bring about immediate attempts at remediation against a timetable in which the performance must be improved or capability procedures entered into.

As increasing powers have been delegated to schools and governing bodies away from LEAs so we can see schools operating more as businesses as in the private school sector. We can also observe the immense power to 'hire and fire' that has been delegated to heads. With this comes great responsibility to lead, manage and administer such a system fairly and honourably. In these mini kingdoms such power can also deter and corrupt.

All of this has meant a substantial change in ethos in much of the teaching profession, for the head has become the chief executive supported, or not, by the governing body. The head's responsibilities are largely delegated down a hierarchy of departmental and year group teams in secondary schools. However, in primary schools the organisational structure was never large enough to support this Doric and net structure. (See Figure 1.1.)

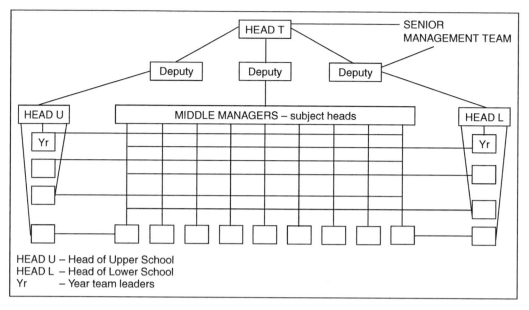

Figure 1.1 Doric and no structure

The Doric organisation of head, head of faculty, heads of department, down to subject staff has seldom operated in schools without the cross weave of deputy heads and heads of year, team leaders, the pastoral head and system, the curriculum deputy, the deputies or senior teachers variously responsible for boys, girls, finance and so on. There was always a conflict of interest, responsibility and allegiance at the interstices between the year heads and subject heads. Now they can be appraisers as well as their deputies all feeding up through a chain of line managers finally to the head.

The primary sector organisation seldom had enough staff and funded posts to operate such a system and in small primaries in particular operated a web system with the head as spider at the centre connecting directly to all staff along the radii. The concentric rings of the web were the sites from which 'stars' or the prime members of the 'social club' operated in closer and closer proximity to the head and the seat of power. The deputy, if one existed, very often had a class more or less full time and may or may not have been in a significant place in the web or have had any power at all.

Those in these web structures will have had to make the most changes in attitude. If these heads do not learn to delegate they will quickly be in overload mode, and finding to whom to delegate in the absence of extra scale points, or even more important teacher time, is quite a problem. In addition to these problems of time and recompense is the most important one of finding the right people to do the classroom observation appraisal part of the work (Montgomery and Hadfield 1989).

Now this comes as part of any senior teacher's and middle management role and is still a problem. As will be seen even with systematic training in classroom observation and the schools' assessment criteria and processes, it is still difficult to carry out this function well, but to use it as part of staff and school improvement plans is particularly problematic. Quick fixes in this field still do not work and the results may still disappoint when reviewed in a few years' time. The reasons for and around this will be explored in subsequent chapters.

Middle managers and team leaders are now responsible for the classroom and subject teacher. They have the most important role of all in that they are charged with the responsibility for helping teacher colleagues improve and become confident in their teaching performance. Some enjoy this role immensely as it is certainly intellectually and personally challenging. Some have become quite expert at it in relation to working with NQTs. However, establishing similar relationships with often older and more experienced colleagues can prove daunting. They have never been trained for this. This is one of the major inbuilt problems of the system and it is based on the mistaken notion prevalent in all levels of the bureaucracy which controls education. This is that teachers simply teach a subject to their pupils rather than teach pupils to learn subjects. The implications of this are wide ranging and profound. It undermined the previous system of appraisal so that it fell into disuse and will do the same for much of performance management if we are not careful. These issues will be addressed in Chapter 2.

In sum, for many teachers, teaching had become an isolated and isolating activity, occasionally penetrated by OFSTED inspections. Now they must readjust to making their classrooms freely available to colleagues for assessment, staff development, training, collaboration, monitoring and so on. Where schools had established peer support systems and peer appraisal strategies – these changes have been made smoothly and easily. These were the establishments where following the appraisal movement and its demise they had continued under the school improvement ethos to build staff skills. In the performance management system the best features of these two have been amalgamated and the two cycles operate in tandem to give good results. An excellent summary of these two cycles is illustrated by Bubb and Hoare (2001: 9) and is copied here with their kind permission. (See Table 1.1.)

Monitoring

Monitoring of necessity is built into performance management systems and, as can be appreciated, it would be wrong to wait for a whole year if the teacher's behaviour was not improving and pupil results were not improving on interim measures. Another whole group of pupils must not be allowed to be disadvantaged again.

The teacher may need special help with teaching strategies, class management or subject knowledge development. Here, investment of time and money may bring about the desired results and some schools who have had NQT managers have used them to convert to staff mentors or coaches to support these teachers. Helping a more experienced teacher out of difficulties is much more complex and may be beyond the abilities of colleagues. There are, as will be seen in later chapters, a number of reasons for this and ways of remedying the situation. On occasions the

Table 1.1 Two cycles operating in tandem (from Bubb and Hoare 2001: 9)

School Improvement Cycle	Performance Management Cycle
AUTUMN TERM **1 How well are we doing?** **2 How do we compare with similar schools?** *Team/Subject Leaders* • Analysing/interpretation trends in whole-school data • Sharing outcomes of analysis with staff *Class Teachers* • Participating in discussion of whole-school performance data **3 What more should we aim to achieve?** *Team Leaders* • Coordinating individual end of key stage target setting • Arriving at whole school end of key stage targets each year from individual end of key stage targets and from analysis of whole-school performance data • Agreeing statutory targets with Governing Body *Subject Leaders* • Participating in individual end of key stage target setting for subject area • Arriving at whole-school targets for subject area each year from individual end of key stage targets and from analysis of whole-school performance data (in conjunction with management team and class teachers) *Class Teachers* • Participating in end of key stage target setting **4 What must we do to make it happen?** *Team/Subject Leaders* • Reviewing/amending long-term curriculum plans and School Improvement/Development Plan to support progress towards end of key stage targets • Implementing Performance Management Cycle across school *Class Teachers* • Participating in reviewing long-term plans and School Improvement Plan **THROUGHOUT YEAR/SUMMER TERM** **5 Taking action and reviewing progress** *Team/Subject Leaders* • Monitoring progress of year groups towards end of year pupil progress objectives (Performance Management Cycle) and towards end of key stage targets (School Improvement Cycle)	**AUTUMN TERM** **Agreeing objectives** *Team Leaders* • Identifying pupil progress objectives (end of year targets) with individual staff for each class • Agreeing professional development objectives with individual staff *Class Teachers* • Identifying pupil progress objectives (end of year targets) for their classes • Identifying professional development objectives for coming year **Agreeing a work and development plan** *Team/Subject Leaders* • Agreeing medium-term plans with each teacher to support progress of each year group towards their pupil progress objectives (end of year targets) • Agreeing plans to achieve professional development objectives with each teacher *Class Teachers* • Identifying learning objectives in medium-term plans that reflect progress towards pupil progress objectives • Reviewing/amending medium-term planning to support progress towards pupil progress objectives • Agreeing plans to achieve professional development objectives **THROUGHOUT YEAR** **Teaching and Learning – Monitoring Progress in Year** *Team/Subject Leaders* • Monitoring progress of year groups against pupil progress objectives and progress of staff against professional development objectives *Class Teachers* • Identifying short-term learning objectives from medium-term plans and from strategies as basis for on-going teaching • Using assessment information from on-going teaching to monitor progress towards learning objectives in medium-term plans • Adjusting teaching in the light of this monitoring **SUMMER TERM** **End of year review of progress** *Team Leaders* • Reviewing progress towards pupil progress objectives and professional development objectives with each teacher *Class Teachers* • Reviewing progress towards pupil progress objectives and professional development objectives, identifying issues that may need to be addressed in the coming year

teacher may just not be putting full professional effort into preparation, teaching and marking. There is an absence of obvious signs in the classroom except that insufficient work is set and there is a lack of feedback through marking. It may be called laziness by some or it may just be that culturally there is a lack of understanding of what must be involved in teaching and learning. If the teacher lapses again into coasting mode after the interventions are removed, this can be picked up in the monitoring period and taken into account in the annual and subsequent review cycles. Thus it can be seen that the monitoring of performance is a crucial part of a performance management system but it is not without its difficulties.

Monitoring has been until recently an informal, essentially private, trouble-shooting process. It was found to identify the problems but then the monitors failed to deal with them successfully (Eraut 1990: 21). Eraut considered monitoring unnecessary for the identification of poor performance. In a sense such performance identifies itself by the raging noise from the classroom and the poor results when the pupils' progress is assessed and compared with peers.

However, lazy or marginally effective teachers can boost their classes' performance by selective revision for internally set examinations and tests and by going sick at critical intervals so that concerned heads of department take over the classes and boost the results. Monitoring must include such records.

Eraut's criticisms of annual appraisal, that it was so frequent that it would lapse into tokenism and it was unlikely to address issues needed to be raised in the OFSTED review cycle, have been proved to be correct. He said it would also be unlikely to be intimately related to curriculum evaluation. All these problems would mean it was lacking in cost effectiveness. The process was expensive and would divert money away from staff development. With this new system of performance management it can be envisaged that induction of new teachers, threshold assessment, new staff recruits and teachers in difficulties will be the major focus of concern after the initial two annual cycles of review. Steadily good performers will have their appraisals attenuated and this may be necessary to reduce the overload; perhaps thought should also be given to re-establishing their appraisal cycle on a three-year basis. The civil service style can still be felt in this one-size-must-fit-all structures in which only a desk-based review system operates and the issues are much simpler and clearer.

These examples show that monitoring must be carefully built into the system and take account of the widest range of processes and outcomes of teaching and learning. The Autumn Statistical Package (DfEE 1999b) shows how to convert SATs data to a points system for finer analysis and permit comparisons with other standardised data from schools. In addition, pupils' work can be sampled, marking can be sampled, and so can teachers' records, minutes of meetings, displays and exhibitions as well as the results from standardised tests such as Cognitive Abilities Tests (CATs, Thorndike et al. 1986), YELLIS and reading and spelling screening tests. Surveying events within and outside the school may also be monitored as part of planning monitoring and development. In any cycle not everything will need to be or can be monitored, so that fitting these into a three-year cycle may be a good plan.

Standards in teaching

In order to become a teacher the individual must have passed the Qualified Teacher Status (QTS) standards. These have been drawn up by a committee of 'experts' who one suspects had really never had full responsibility for actually training a teacher to teach throughout a three- or four-year course. They may have had responsibility for a subject or a practice or been an advisory teacher but none of this, I would argue, necessarily equips them for the job of defining realistic standards for NQTs. The result is a checklist of some 98 different attributes called 'competencies' which the intending teacher must be deemed to have passed and which the supervising teachers/tutors must assess. Funded for one hour's lesson observation per week plus travel, they are seldom paid for the one hour or more of paperwork which this engenders or the extra time for the discussion with the trainee. The validity of the exercise is highly questionable, as it ever was in the hands of untrained higher education tutors. Delegating it to training schools is equally fraught with difficulties of reliability and validity. Being a professionally qualified and experienced teacher does not automatically confer the ability to teach someone to teach for contained in this are a much higher order set of skills and competencies.

As the standards for QTS currently exist, no NQT could possibly meet them nor any supervisor be able to assess even if they sat in the classes full time. Checklists were ever subject to such abuse and misuse.

What results is a paperwork exercise which no one can complete adequately and which still leads to students being passed who are not suitable for the profession or who have not the requisite range of skills for their first post. This by default permits courses to be endorsed which are not fit for the purpose and tutors continuing within employment who cannot teach a student how to control a class and which puts the supervisor in a difficult legal position in terms of accountability.

Thus it is that the notion of the probationary year which had been discontinued has been reintroduced as the induction year which must be successfully passed, linked with the compilation of the Career Entry Profile for each new teacher.

One of the main routes into teaching, it has to be remembered, is by way of a subject degree which may have no more relationship to the National Curriculum (NC) than in name. This is followed by a one-year Postgraduate Certificate in Education programme consisting of 24 weeks' practice in school – teaching practice – interspersed by 12 weeks' or its equivalent learning in the college about teaching and professional matters. Most of this time is of course taken up with teaching the students to teach the NC, leaving the odd hour for matters such as teaching and learning methods and issues, classroom management and control, child abuse issues, bullying, needs of the gifted and talented, and special needs. In the practice in schools, they gain experience of working with small groups and hopefully the class under the supervision of the teacher mentor who likewise is a qualified and experienced teacher but not of course trained in teaching anyone to teach. There is thus a huge variability in the skills and abilities of these mentors and the student experience. It is a bad situation simply transferred from the college to the school. Fortunately there are still a significant number of trainees capable of learning from watching others and who can then by a process of experimentation and reflection on practice improve their own performance. They are active self regulated learners, learning to learn on the job. Others can be trained on the job in the induction year by the subject on year leaders and the SENCO. Supplied with lesson plans, packages, suggestions, strategies and tips, the NQT can gradually make the transformation from trainee to competent teacher.

The first six weeks of the new teacher's role are the most testing as discipline and class management are strained and gradually improve, or not as the case may be. In two to three years the NQT who survives this rite of passage will have developed a stable pattern of teaching behaviours, classroom knowledge, subject knowledge with working value and a wide range of professional knowledge and skills. Much more is dependent in schools these days on teachers' interpersonal skills and the ways in which they encourage and support pupils in the constantly changing dynamics of lessons. Hard workers with good subject knowledge but lacking in interpersonal and group skills and personal insight cannot expect to survive in the profession today.

Induction

The induction year, as can be appreciated, is a very necessary process and the NQTs must meet not only the QTS standards consistently but also the ten induction standards. These are organised under the same three main headings as in the QTS standards of perfection but do not require more subject knowledge and understanding. They are set out below:

1. **Planning Teaching and Class Management**
   a) sets clear targets for the improvement of pupils' achievement, monitors pupils' progress towards those targets and uses appropriate teaching strategies in the light of this including, where appropriate, in relation to literacy, numeracy and other school targets;
   b) plans effectively to ensure that pupils have the opportunity to meet their potential notwithstanding differences of race and gender, and taking account of the needs of pupils who are:
      ● underachieving
      ● very able
      ● not yet fluent in English

   making use of relevant information and specialist help where available;

c) secures a good standard of pupil behaviour in the classroom through establishing appropriate rules and high expectations of discipline which pupils respect, acting to pre-empt and deal with inappropriate behaviour in the context of the behaviour policy of the school;

d) plans effectively where applicable to meet the needs of pupils with Special Educational Needs in collaboration with the SENCO, makes an appropriate contribution to the preparation, implementation, monitoring and review of Individual Education Plans;

e) takes account of ethnic and cultural diversity to enrich the curriculum and raise achievement.

2. Monitoring, Assessment, Recording, Reporting and Accountability

f) recognises the level that a pupil is achieving and makes accurate assessments, independently, against attainment targets, where applicable, and performance levels associated with other tests or qualifications relevant to the subject(s) or phase(s) taught;

g) liaises effectively with pupils' parents/carers through informative oral and written reports on pupils' progress and achievements, discussing appropriate targets, and encouraging them to support their children's learning, behaviour and progress.

3. Other Professional Requirements

h) where applicable, deploys support staff and other adults effectively in the classroom; dealing with bullying and racial harassment;

j) takes responsibility for their own professional development, setting objectives for improvements, and taking action to keep up-to-date with research and developments in pedagogy and in the subject(s) they teach.

DfEE (2000c)

What can be seen is that there is no frame of reference established to show how these standards are to be interpreted and more importantly how they are to be assessed. What does constitute a pass or a fail? Without such criteria it is very much up to each school to decide on the success or failure of an individual NQT on the basis of the practice in a particular school. It may promote a willingness to accept into the profession someone who is weak but likely to improve. This is a risky decision often more based upon empathy and support than harsh realities, despite the fact that DfEE insist that NQTs must pass all the standards – they cannot compensate by meeting nine very well and and not meeting a tenth. Having advertised three times for a teacher in a shortage subject and with pressure from staff and parents to fill and maintain posts, it is likely that efforts will be strongly targeted to the weak area and getting the NQT over the borderline and even giving them the benefit of the doubt rather than losing them.

It is easier to succeed in a well-run school with good standards of discipline and academic work or with a supportive team and department and where care and attention are given to the NQT, rather than in the case where they have the most difficult sets or classes dumped upon them to sink or swim if they can. A teacher operating successfully in the well-run school may soon fail in a challenging one, unless given the right sort of support.

Threshold Standards (DfEE 2000c)

Knowledge and Understanding
Teachers should demonstrate that they have a thorough and up-to-date knowledge of the teaching of their subject(s) and take account of wider curriculum developments which are relevant to their work.

Teaching and Assessment
Teachers should demonstrate that they consistently and effectively:

— plan lessons and sequences of lessons to meet pupils' individual learning needs
— uses a range of appropriate strategies for teaching and classroom management
— use information about prior attainment to set well grounded expectations for pupils
— monitor progress to give clear and constructive feedback.

Pupil Progress
Teachers should demonstrate that, as a result of their teaching, their pupils achieve well relative to the pupil's prior attainment, making progress as good or better than similar pupils nationally. This should be shown in marks or grades, in any relevant national tests or examinations, or school based assessment for pupils where national tests and examinations are not taken.

Wider Professional Effectiveness
Teachers should demonstrate that they:

— take responsibility for their professional development and use the outcomes to improve their teaching and pupils' learning
— make an active contribution to the policies and aspirations of the school.

Professional Characteristics
Teachers should demonstrate that they are effective professionals who challenge and support pupils to do their best through:

— inspiring trust and confidence
— building team commitment
— engaging and motivating pupils
— analytical thinking
— positive action to improve the quality of pupils' learning.

Assessing the effectiveness of teaching

Assessment may be formative and developmental, summative and corrective or diagnostic and interventionist. However, according to Borich in 1977 there was no agreement on a definition of the criteria that could be used to assess teaching performance or to establish competency. Elliott (1990b) found that the LEAs whose advisers and inspectors had for many years been appraising teaching performance of school staff on a regular basis emphasised different aspects of teaching in their checklists, so that a core understanding of the process either did not exist for them or was not shared by them. This is not surprising since advisers and inspectors were most often experienced senior teachers seeking a particular kind of power and responsibility that inspecting gives. It is a career route for those wishing to leave the classroom but who do not wish to become heads and deputies. If there was no coherent theory of teaching in 1983, according to Wragg, (at a public lecture in 1983) then it is not surprising that these senior ex-teachers were not in agreement, trained as they were in earlier decades. If lack of definition was and still is true then it certainly poses a problem for appraisers.

The Suffolk Report (Graham 1985) announced that effective teaching was at the heart of teacher appraisal but at no point did it define what was meant by 'effective' or 'good' teaching. It also referred to 'below par' performance without describing what was meant by that. This attitude belongs to the school of 'we all know what we mean by good teaching' and 'when I see it I know it' or it's 'just intuition'. Such appraisers can judge as good teaching a range of performance from indifferent to downright bad. Teacher educators will recognise these viewpoints put forward in the defence of students on teaching practice from both teacher mentors and college staff.

The 1983 DES document on *Teaching Quality* welcomed the recent moves towards self-assessment by schools and teachers and thought that these should help to improve school standards and curricula. It went on to state:

> But employers can manage their teacher force effectively only if they have accurate knowledge of each teacher's performance. The Government believe that for this purpose formal assessment of teacher performance is necessary and should be based on classroom visiting by the teacher's head or head of department, and an appraisal of both pupils' work and of the teacher's contribution to the life of the school.   (p. 27)

Clearly the managerial model is in mind but the content and purposes of the appraisal are missing. It was not surprising that the assumption made by the media was that it was Sir Keith Joseph's intention to use it to get rid of failing teachers.

In *Better Schools* (DES 1985a) there was little about the process of appraisal except to say that it involved the collection of information that is 'reliable' and 'up to date through systematic performance appraisal' (p. 55). On quality in schools, DES (1985a) gave the following definition:

appraisal emphasises the forming of qualitative judgments about an activity, a person or an organisation . . . it may start as self appraisal . . . it will normally involve judgments by other persons responsible for that teachers' work – a Head of Department or Year, the Head Teacher or a member of the senior management team or an officer of the LEA.   (p. 7)

As can be seen, it considers who but not how to get reliable and valid data nor what constitutes such data.

In a second volume by the Suffolk group – *In the Light of Torches* (Graham 1987) – they considered the implications of appraisal in terms of time for negotiations, training, implementation and money. It discussed head teacher appraisal procedures; classroom observation; training in appraisal interviewing; resourcing an appraisal system; and the report of a study visit to California, featuring in particular the San Diego Instrument. This was a set of checklists, rating scales and criterion-referenced scales for appraisal of head teachers and teachers as a whole. This time 'effective teaching' was defined but the lack of a common set of guidelines is to be bemoaned. The characteristics of effective teaching were summarised in the report as follows:

Effective teachers
- believe that *all pupils* can learn, and such teachers take responsibility by organising and assigning appropriate tasks and by other means to see that pupils do learn;
- keep pupils 'on task', use unambiguous cues and provide evaluative feedback that is clear and instructive;
- use a variety of teaching methods ranging from 'whole group' to 'individualised' teaching, from didactic teaching to discovery approaches. Skill level, subject matter and the aims of the lessons determine the method chosen;
- use direct teaching when basic skill acquisition is the aim;
- are good managers of the teaching/learning process and of people. They use a variety of good management practices including setting a classroom 'tone' or 'climate' conducive to learning, preventing disciplinary problems through planning, eliminating disruptions and delays; monitoring pupil attention, i.e. keeping all pupils involved, and establishing clear rules and expectations for each lesson and for the class;
- develop a leadership style which is essentially democratic yet authoritative (not authoritarian). They view their role as helping the development of potential and assume that a sense of responsibility is inherent in every pupil.
                                                                              (pp. 22–3)

The report announced that good teachers are both born and made, but mostly made, and that effective teaching was both a science and an art. It went on to give the above summary list of the characteristics of the effective teacher who was 'characterised by some or all of the following' (p. 23). There then followed a list under three headings – *Planning and Preparation; Classroom Management;* and *Evaluation.*

For the purposes of this book a closer look at the Classroom Management list will prove interesting if not helpful.

The teacher
- makes clear the rules, consequences and procedures on the first day and adheres to those rules consistently throughout the year;
- provides for a sustained rate of success by using a range of learning activities which are appropriate to each pupil's ability;
- keeps pupils on appropriate activities and promotes necessary content coverage;
- works to improve individual learning deficiencies with specific transferable skills;
- provides a role model for pupils by a business-like approach to teaching;
- uses direct teaching with the whole class or small groups when teaching basic skill mastery;
- creates a supportive learning atmosphere by showing concern and respect for each pupil. (p. 23)

From this list a later prompt list was derived, which the authors stated was 'neither prescriptive nor exhaustive' (p. 25).

Once again it can be seen that there is a lack of a coherent and shared theory and practice of teaching. There are descriptors which have been agreed. They describe what are the observable OUTCOMES of what are perceived to be effective teaching characteristics. They do not deal with the HOW by which these outcomes are to be achieved if we are to improve performance. This is particularly well illustrated by item three above. Precisely how does the teacher keep the pupils on task? What are appropriate activities and how shall they be defined? Showing concern and respect for each individual can be shown to be a necessary but not a sufficient condition for establishing a supportive climate. Some best teaching is not necessary or businesslike and so on. We have to resolve these problems if an effective classroom observation appraisal system within the performance management structure is to be set up and guaranteed to work. It needs to specify not only the nature of effective teacher behaviours but how these are to be achieved. Thus although summative assessments are required, there needs to be some formative structure as well to achieve improved outcomes.

In the section of *In the Light of Torches* (Graham 1987) on classroom observation, a range of different types of checklist are illustrated. These include prompt lists, profiles, rating scales, formative observation checklists, behaviourally anchored rating scales (BARS) and criterion-referenced scales. For example in 'Torches' we find:

Domain 3 – Instructional Organisation and Development
3.1 Efficient Use of Time:

a. Begin classwork promptly
b. Organise class to keep the lesson going
c. Shift systematically from one subject to another

d. Control interruptions
e. Organise efficient distribution and collection of materials
f. Provide structure for those students who finish classwork early.

In this system three different observers – principal, vice principal and a peer – all rate the teacher as satisfactory (S) or needs improvement (I), based on their different observations. In 'Begin classwork promptly', what does the teacher need to do if after calling the class to order and be ready to start the lesson they do not comply or even refuse to do so? Starting promptly might then be wrong. If the observer then steps in and tells the pupils to be quiet and they are, what lessons are there then for the pupils when the observer leaves the room?

In this framework of a 'good lesson' what happens when the teacher does not and cannot control the interruptions? It is of little help to be told that this is what must be done for the lesson to be effective. The teacher probably already knows this but cannot find a way to do so and unless he or she does they are on their way towards a capability procedure. It will be necessary for the observer to explain to the teacher how this can be achieved, in other words, an element of teaching professional skills is required. After that in a further observation coaching in the particular strategies may need to be undertaken. It is in this area that most appraisal systems have failed because teachers and principals seldom know how to set these matters right. They can do it themselves but do not have the vocabulary and the constructs to describe what they do which makes them effective. Until this 'nut' is cracked, performance management of teaching in the classroom of a genuinely valuable kind will not be developed in schools.

One of the reasons for this problem is that the appraisal method selected is summative and quantitative for auditing and accounting purposes. It is thought that in having defined something or described it this is in itself explanatory and can then be used as a formative tool to intervene and improve performance. If this was so, books such as this would not be necessary and 20 years ago the matter would have been resolved and teacher and pupil performance raised. All students in initial teacher training would emerge as good and effective teachers from college. Unfortunately learning to teach and evaluating teaching is not as simple as this and administrators, bureaucrats and industrialists cannot help in resolving this core issue. The answers have to be sought within the field of teaching theory and practice itself by teachers and teacher educators who have researched the problems.

According to Burgess (1990), no national or local appraisal initiated by administrators has been based on criteria from systematic teachers' research into their own practice. He states: 'Instead adaptations of researchers' observation schedules and items from findings of experiments on learning are preferred by administrators. They then claim objectivity and fairness' (p. 37).

The observation schedules were devised for research and not teacher appraisal. To then make an amalgam from various checklists as schools do without researching them is equally unacceptable. Burgess makes the important point that research reviews of the past 60 years of process-product studies of teaching have shown meagre returns, citing the following authors:

> . . . 'teaching that attends to the set task, giving students the opportunity to learn what is later tested, is weakly correlated with learning achievements' (Rosenshine 1979).
> . . . 'Learning has but a contingent and not a causal relationship to teaching' (Borich 1977).
> . . . 'The extent of teachers' knowledge of the topic being taught is not correlated to learning outcomes' (Borich 1977).

Tom (1984) on teacher effectiveness stated that: 'So far no powerful concepts have emerged out of the data. All we have are some low level empirical claims such as direct instruction or academic learning time, which are masquerading as conceptual models.'

In competency-based teacher education there is doubt whether skills practised and then tested transfer to the real classroom, according to Burgess (1990), McIntyre (1980) and Elliott and Labett (1974). The connection between the checklist summative system and competency-based approaches is clear.

The Cambridge Institute of Education (Dadds 1987) was commissioned to evaluate the findings of the six LEA pilot appraisal schemes. The researchers asked six questions:

- In what ways had the appraisal improved the quality of induction of Entry grade teachers? Has it made assessing their performance easier and more reliable?
- Has appraisal changed the way in which teachers participate in INSET?
- Has appraisal led directly to new or modified roles for teachers and how have those involved perceived the process?
- Has appraisal successfully identified potential for career development? Has the related support been made available?
- Has appraisal helped those teachers who are experiencing performance difficulties? What relationship with disciplinary procedures has emerged? How is this difficult area perceived by those involved?
- What relationship, if any, has emerged between the records of appraisal and appointment procedures and references?

There were a number of methodological problems with the analysis which the researchers had little chance of overcoming. For example, it would be expected that the results would necessarily contain the 'Hawthorne Effect'. This famous study in the Ford factory in 1929 found that people just being observed improved their performance and this was maintained after the observations ceased. The pilot studies also were based in LEAs already interested in appraisal and dealt with volunteers who are a special sort of sample and likely to 'show' improvements. In addition when someone takes an interest in you and your work this also inevitably engenders the 'feel good factor', especially when the interest is a positive and supportive one. It could only be concluded that appraisal of whatever sort the LEAs employed with their volunteers would be seen to be 'a good thing'. Some of the real benefits would be more accurate records, references and reports, and the ACAS scheme would be duly endorsed and was.

Scriven (1986) proposed four dimensions of merit for summative teacher evaluation, these were:

- quality of content taught (not the quality of content known)
- success in imparting or inspiring learning
- mastery of professional skills, e.g. class control
- ethics seen in the avoidance of racism, sexism, classism and so on.

He found that good lesson plans were not critically related to these dimensions but they were often in evidence and that poor teachers could not make up in subject knowledge for their inability to control a class.

In 1990, McIntyre's summary of the situation was: 'there are no general theories of teacher competency which could provide a basis for summarising accounts, and it is not plausible to expect any such theories will be developed' (p. 71). I do not happen to agree with this and would suggest with Snow (1973) that research undertaken is defined by the theories held and the experiences which reinforce them. As with the Suffolk group, the literature research will be defined by the key words entered or not entered in their case and by the literature with which the researcher is familiar. It is only when we look across the vast domains within education that new theories and research to support them can be found. Coherent theories of teaching and learning do exist but often do not appear in mainstream educational literature. They arise in Instructional Psychology, Gifted Education, Moral and Philosophical Critiques, Cognitive Psychology, Special Education and so on.

To help in the assessment of teaching for performance management and to underpin the evaluation of standards, the DfEE commissioned research by Hay McBer (2000) into the factors which teachers control that affect pupil progress. In their analysis they came up with three main factors: Professional Characteristics, Teaching Skills and Classroom Climate. No surprise there! They then subdivided these into levels of competence which might be expected, level one being the basic level.

Under 'Professional Characteristics' they detailed challenge and support, confidence, creating trust and respect for others; analytical thinking, conceptual thinking; planning and setting expectations and so on. They go on to describe levels within these categories which can be used as scale attributes to assess or to work through with teachers.

In relation to 'Levels for Managing Pupils', they gave descriptors and examples as follows:

1. **Gets pupils on task**

   Quickly gets pupils on task, beginning lessons by stating learning objectives. Recaps and summarises points covered. Provides clear instructions about tasks and focuses pupils' attention.

2. **Keeps pupils informed**

   Makes quite sure pupils understand why they are doing something. Describes how the activity fits into a programme of work. Keeps pupils up-to-date by providing information and feedback on progress.

3. **Makes every class effective**

   Consistently makes any class or group effective by getting the right pupils working on appropriate things. Removes barriers which are preventing the class or groups working effectively together.

4. **Takes actions on behalf of the class**

   Speaks positively about the class to others and builds up its image. Goes out of his or her way to obtain the extra materials and resources the class, group or team needs; for example by engaging in support of parents, the community or commercial organisations.

5. **Takes the role of leader**

   Ensures the class and groups fully achieve their objectives at all times. Fully motivates *every* pupil and gets everyone wholly involved in achieving what needs doing. Always establishes a positive, upbeat atmosphere and takes pupils forward together.

One wonders if the researcher(s) had spent any time in classrooms or had qualified to teach anything. Level one – quickly gets pupils on task – describes a good end of level performance. Playing advocate and taking the role of leader may or may not be higher levels. They certainly are of minor consideration when dealing with marginal performance. At level five we note the word 'every' appears in italics, emphasising each and every one is engaged. This is a council of perfection but even in an excellent lesson pupils' attention flags, they take time off task and have rests. Are we to deny this teacher a grade five? With some assessors the answer will be 'yes' as minor infringements by pupils are magnified and criticised, or there may always be one pupil less diligent than the rest (perhaps this one is ill).

What we see here too is the inherent weakness in all checklist, rating-scale and competency-based systems, even when the scales are in an appropriate increasing order of competency. The checklist, however well or poorly constructed, is only a composite description of performance which enables a *summative assessment* of the performance to be made. A wide range of teachers can learn to use them, good or bad, with a reasonable degree of accuracy. However, having identified an area of weakness, the checklist system does not necessarily enable the unwanted behaviour to be changed. It does not indeed identify those behaviours which are inappropriate. For this we have to rely upon the assessor's interpretation of these runes and the knowledge and understanding of how to teach someone to teach. In other words a summative assessment strategy or instrument is being used for an entirely different purpose, diagnosis and intervention. This is an area in which the *formative assessment* is more appropriate and we must question whether we should be using the one for the purpose of the other.

This controversy has been evident in the teacher education field since its inception at the beginning of the twentieth century, as it soon became apparent that experts in subject knowledge with the highest qualifications were not necessarily the best people to teach others to teach. It therefore became necessary for methods tutors to be appointed. In the primary sector these were practitioners moulded in the form of Froebel, de Lissa, Montessori and the Macmillans setting up training on the basis of their theories of early childhood education needs. The secondary school sector languished without these sorts of influences and adopted a model of academic teaching theory of education disciplines from the universities of psychology, philosophy and sociology. As these were often taught by academics who had never taught in schools, the applications to classrooms only arrived in the 1980s as their students were confronted by classroom teaching issues and problems. Since then there has been a vast base of knowledge relevant to teaching building worldwide. Anyone wanting to improve performance cannot enter the debate without being knowledgeable about both theory and research in practice and having practised it or else tested it in practice.

So how do teachers learn to teach? They will mostly aver that 'they did it themselves'. Now we can only assume from this that it is mainly true or that they were trained by those best leaders whose followers always say 'we did it ourselves'. In the course of training there is no doubt that students learn examples of what to teach and are exposed in college and in schools to different examples and models of teaching. What they seem to have to do, though, is to construct their own theories and practices of teaching and learning from a somewhat inchoate programme. Some are better than others at this. The ten quick tips to teaching which someone invariably gives them is like water off a duck's back as they blunder through their early lessons repeating all the mistakes of generations of teachers before them. As long as they are not confined to one practice school for long and can recover or leave their mistakes behind them they can start afresh, hopefully at one step advanced from before. The students and the teachers who do not learn from their mistakes on a continual basis and who keep repeating them will be the unsuccessful ones who finally leave the profession or finish up on capability procedures. They need to be helped to break this cycle of feedback blindness.

In my experience in the detailed observation of over 1,200 lessons there is a cycle of disconnections which can be healed in the majority of cases, except where the person has a particular form of perseverative neurotic personality problem. The successful professional teacher has learned to become a reflective practitioner. In many instances these processes are implicit but where they have been made explicit they can lead to enhanced performance. However, reflection on practice alone cannot necessarily lead to the identification of transferable skills underlying good teaching. Teachers may think they do but they need the opportunity to research these in practice. Thus it is that Adelman (1990) estimated that a consortium of teachers working on this will take at least three years to come to a conclusion. Teacher reflection and research on practice must be an integral part of any performance management and appraisal system but it too is not sufficient for purpose for the situation can be envisaged where good practice is defined by describing current practice and in such a situation we can argue that what exists is not necessarily what should be going on.

It is important to note that none of the classroom observation schedules and scales thus far except the LDRP scheme (to be described in Chapter 2) have been evaluated in a research programme. This needs to be done in context to see if they achieve any of their aims, such as assessment and the enhancement of performance. Such a system must demonstrate that it can work with teachers in general and those with marginal performance and on capability procedures. The evidence for any resultant decisions should be public and verifiable. It may be that two instruments are necessary for such intended outcomes.

Some other key issues

Credibility

It is important that the procedures selected are fair and are seen to be so. Inextricably linked to the notion of fairness is that of credibility. Lack of credibility can quickly undermine any system of appraisal. It is therefore necessary, before embarking on appraisal, that these issues are fully explored. This exploration demonstrates the necessary commitment to the process by all concerned. It is vital that all the staff share an understanding of the criteria to be used and the processes to be experienced. It is thus better if they share in the development of the criteria and processes rather than having them imposed. This problem is implicit in any national scheme for it is important that there should always be some autonomy at the local level. If there is not then people do not identify with the aims and purposes and do not feel that they have ownership of the system. It is then in serious danger of becoming a paper-and-pencil exercise.

Appraisal schemes tend only to flourish where there is a tradition of self evaluation. Then it is seen as a natural development of a process already in operation. It is also important that any results from appraisal are linked to appropriate action such as training, development or career enhancement. If they are not then the procedure will have been an empty one, soon to be discounted.

If the appraisee is given feedback and advice from a mentor whose teaching they do not respect, this can create a great deal of frustration and cognitive conflict and it can undermine the school's performance management system and sour the ethos of the school, which is bad for everyone. Thus considerable care and training must be given to those who are to fill the appraisal and observation roles. Here, leaving the individual with some choice of mentors can help overcome some of these problems.

Eraut (1990) suggested that the credibility of the appraisers was questioned because they did not know the subject. As the appraiser in most schemes was a more senior member of staff, this also created a credibility gap because promotion to senior rank was perceived as being based on qualities and qualifications other than good teaching (p. 22). He concluded that the cost of appraisal of teaching was higher than for other jobs because of its complexity and that annual appraisal was too infrequent for monitoring – which he distinguished from appraisal.

It will be shown in subsequent chapters that knowing the subject content is not the most relevant dimension. Most important is to know about classroom management, what creates interest and cognitive challenge across subjects, and pupils' learning needs.

Subject content is largely determined now by the NC and a subject specialist can always be consulted afterwards to check on content. However well teachers know the subject, this is no guarantee that they can teach it or can make pupils want to learn it.

Capability

It is most important that when a monitoring system has picked up that a teacher has a problem, frequently one of class control but not always so, that the appraisal, including classroom observation first concentrates on staff development. There need to be several classroom observations and feedback interviews. After each one, targets for change and improvement should be identified and after a period for practice another observation can take place. This should identify any progress which has been made and set new targets and strategies for further development. After a cycle of such appraisals, conclusions can be drawn about whether the person is capable of development or improvement. It is extremely difficult for a failing teacher to retrieve the failure with older classes. It may be necessary for there to be time for a new intake and a change of classes to take place to get the necessary degree of improvement. When this does not occur then capability procedures need to be entered into and this point should be very carefully marked and made quite clear to the teacher.

The first verbal warning can then be followed by a new appraisal cycle which starts the capability procedure. At this point a summative instrument is needed which can be used again during and at the end of the agreed period to measure improvement or otherwise. The formative input can still take place in between to try to retrieve the situation if this is required. Thus it is important to act very quickly once monitoring procedures identify a problem or otherwise the process can become too prolonged, to the detriment of the pupils and the school as a whole. Six months is the maximum time now that this procedure should take. Even so, a term would be a better target for the pupils' sakes.

Not all failing teachers fall into this category, and a very small minority exhibit a quite different problem. They can maintain discipline – albeit in the quieter backwaters of a disciplined school, perhaps a girls' school. There they rest, making very little effort of any kind in terms of preparation and marking. On inspection days they can always pull out the stops and put on a creditable performance. However, if one were to compare the results achieved by their classes with those of the rest of the school, the problem is revealed. Pupils during these sessions are often heard to remark, 'We never do this sort of thing, usually.'

Headteachers in the past have often been unwilling to enter into capability procedures over such cases for a variety of personal and other factors. Not least of these factors is the vilification to which they themselves or the school may become subject. They choose to 'carry' such an individual and 'bury' the evidence of the incompetence (this is considered quite feasible in some of these cases). For example, in some subjects, hard data in comparative terms is not readily available.

However, under the performance management regulations these problems must be resolved.

Role issues

The appraiser thus far in formal schemes has been the head teacher, a deputy or one of the senior management team. Additionally heads of department have also been involved in appraisal in some secondary schools. It is thus essentially a 'top down' process such as envisaged in the DES/DfEE documents. What is found is that the higher up the school hierarchy the appraiser is then the more difficult it is for them to leave this role at the classroom door. When the head is there, for example, the pupils usually behave much better. If they do not then the head is put in a difficult position and may 'take a hand'. Often the observer sits at the front or perches on a desk to be informal but then stands out like a beacon. If at the back the pupils can 'feel' the eyes boring into their backs and behave differently from usual.

Of course, in small primary schools these problems are not so apparent as the head is often teaching and working with the teachers as one of a team.

The role problems can be diminished if the observer is in the room in advance, is seated at the back out of sight of most pupils, perhaps at one of their tables at the back, makes no eye contact with any of them, keeps a very low profile and just writes and writes. This is the 'fly on the wall' method and after a few minutes the pupils forget about the visitor and start to behave in their normal way. If this gets no overt response then they will continue as usual. The same result is achieved when they are being video taped – within a few minutes they ignore it.

A critical issue is that the appraiser is collecting and analysing a large amount of qualitative data derived from the techniques of classroom observation and interviewing. The appraisers are therefore thrust into a key role. The theories and ideologies held by these persons and the sophistication in their research skills will direct the way in which they collect, manipulate, interpret and present the data they collect.

In the many appraisal training sessions which have been run in the LDRP, a practice video extract and feedback session starts the course. It enables the way in which would-be 'appraisers' mangle and remould the data to fit their favourite themes to be made explicit. It can call forth some horrendous statements and assertions and the whole frequently presents a very negative picture of failure in a session which is not bad but could be better.

In addition to this, other role problems are carried into the sessions. The head or senior teacher carries with them role authority and pupils may well not behave in their usual ways and so biased data is collected. Similarly in the feedback session the authority of the role may cause what is said to be accepted and acted upon when in fact the advice is not of good value and works only with the backing of the role status. Evidence from teacher job interviews by these same senior personnel would lead us to have little confidence in their interviewing skills because they appear to be far from skilled when using evidence to evaluate teachers. Add to this the range of personnel now at these interviews in the form of school governors – and it makes the interview a very unreliable device for employing or redeploying staff.

Video observation?

All methods have been tried such as video and audio recording, sitting in the prep room, or cupboard or the next room with the door open. But the 'fly on the wall' method has been shown to be the best for gathering all the data. A video can never filter out the ambient noise nor see the changing focus of disruptive events. It cannot follow critical multiple interactions and still catch others at the periphery of vision. A video or audio record can be useful for the teachers to see themselves as others see them. Some can learn from the experience of watching themselves; others need tutoring with the video. This was the method selected by Marilyn Hunter outlined in the Suffolk Report (Graham 1985). She used a behavioural approach, taking a small video extract and analysing it in detail with the teacher. This method has also been used successfully by Norma Hadfield following our research programme. She reports it is particularly effective where teachers select their own section of video to discuss. Hunter interviewed for the Suffolk Report (Graham 1985) reported it as an effective method but the evidence for effectiveness was never clarified. After such an event it is very likely that a teacher will have learned something but can this be converted into improved performance in the classroom? How is this improvement quantified or assessed and is it externally validated?

Process and models

Target output model

In the target output model a set of objectives is agreed with the teacher and then the teacher's work is compared with them (ACAS 1986: 4). The objectives may arise from the job description or from attainment targets for learners. An attempt is then made to measure how far the targets have been achieved. It is a productivity contract – a quota fulfilment model. There is no necessary analysis of how the objectives might be achieved. This is because teacher objectives are frequently vague:

- offers a well-balanced curriculum
- makes provision for different levels of ability
- shows evidence of good classroom organisation
- shows evidence of enthusiasm for the subject

and it is very much a matter of opinion rather than fact as to whether the objectives have been achieved. Putting a scale of numbers on these and recording 3 out of 5 is wholly arbitrary and scientifically illiterate. Now that pupil attainments are to be the target this could prove to be even more threatening and just as arbitrary. Already teachers are being accused of focusing on A, B and C graders at GCSE so that the school's rating is increased. This has produced a wider gulf between the higher and the lower achievers, with more of the latter failing (GCSE results, August 1998). Another interpretation of the same data could be that the methods of teaching promulgated by the former Chief Inspector for Schools (Woodhead 1997, 1998) known as interactive teaching is disadvantaging the less able, focused as it is upon verbal learning and memory techniques.

The current *Threshold Standards* (DfEE 2000c) provide a strong inducement and structure for adopting the Target-Output model linked through a checklisting system.

Performance criteria model

The teaching model is skill based and the performance is analysed into a list of competencies represented by indicators. However the DES (1985a) writing on appraisal of teaching performance in *Better Schools* state that 'Research has not unearthed any simple or comprehensive indicator of effective teaching' (p. 70). Nevertheless they then proceed to give examples of performance indictors which could be used, for example:

Communication with learners:
Indicator 4: Gives directions and explanations related to lesson content.
Indicator 6: Uses responses and questions from learners in teaching.
Indicator 7: Provides feedback to learners throughout lesson.
Indicator 8: Uses acceptable written and oral expression with learners.

(DES 1985a: 75)

If these criteria were applied to work I recently observed in two classrooms by teachers on capability procedures, the honest response would be that they performed each of these activities satisfactorily. However, the classes were out of control. Boring and mundane lessons might also pass on these indicators as well as very good ones. There is redundancy in such items. It is of note when they are not present, but even so I have observed some very good lessons in the absence of indicators 4, 6, and 7. Performance criteria such as these can pose problems for they can impose a set of procedures on lessons and a teaching process which assumes interactivity and teacher dominance which is not always be appropriate.

Performance criteria such as these usually require another set of criteria before they can be used. These would specify such notions as: acceptable, related, satisfactory, feedback and so on. The use of checklists incorporating such items is therefore equally problematic: they merely lend a spurious air of scientific exactitude to a bad procedure. It does not matter how many staff put their heads together to produce such a list.

The diagnostic model

The ACAS (1986) document linked appraisal to the diagnosis of potential as an agreed principle. The process of classroom observation should be used to identify training needs and career potential. In practice the problem is that the appraiser may not have the necessary skills or knowledge to do this – whether head of department, coordinator of special needs or head teacher. For example, diagnosing more differentiating by input as needed for some underachieving boys conceals the fact that the 'chalk and talk' teaching method was at fault.

The appraiser and appraisee may have different ideologies, each of which may be successfully used by the individual. If the appraiser diagnoses a need for change and development it may not be relevant – it may even be the appraiser who needs the development. The resultant career advice and development plan would in the circumstances be most unwelcome. In addition, needs might be identified which the school does not have the budget to fund. It is also possible to fail to identify important needs and perhaps even more problematic, to find a lack of development and career potential in an ambitious individual.

The bureaucratic model

The bureaucrat draws on authority from superiors and carries out procedures to the letter. There therefore has to be a considerable detailed attention to the paperwork and its various specifications. This model is concerned with products and procedures in which information travels up the system and decisions travel down. The information collected has to be at a simple level, preferably convertible to number values and statistics. It can then be used by any official for a variety of purposes, usually to do with resources and expenditure.

We can see in the Performance Management (PM) system devised by the DfEE (2000b) linked to pupil attainments targets in the school development plan that we have a national scheme in which the teacher's performance can be converted into numerical values for accounting purposes.

The process model

In this model the professional possesses a personal licence to practice (Winter 1990). Here there is a special responsibility and relationship to the client, the patient or pupil. Thus the allegiance is downwards and reference is to an internally specified set of professional theories, practices and criteria.

> Client cases . . . cannot be decided upon by the application of general rules (given from above) but only by the discretionary interpretation of specialist knowledge . . . This means that professional workers are continually learning (increasing knowledge and enhancing their skills) through the actual practice of their profession.
> (Winter 1990: 50)

Winter goes on to explain that in the process model of appraisal the value is in the process itself. It is this process which will result in professional development or the effective learning by the teacher. Thus the contradiction is revealed of a bureaucracy presiding over a profession, a situation which does not exist in medicine or the law.

The system to be described in the next chapter is formative and set within this process orientated approach.

Systems for feedback

Maier in 1976 made an interesting analysis of the systems which appraisers used to structure the appraisal interview and these can still be found in use today. They were as follows:

Tell and sell method

In the telling part of the session the appraiser tells the appraisee how he or she is getting on. Here immediately we might question the authority and credibility of the teller. Having given an opinion on the performance, selected aspects of that performance might be described to illustrate the points made. If a checklist is part of the procedure the appraiser may simply go through the list and even indicate a score if rating scales are attached. Other appraisers compile a list of seven or eight problem points to tell the appraisee. Sometimes it can be difficult to find some problem points and areas for improvement and then the appraiser may focus on trivia or raise issues not present in the session as omissions for something to discuss. All this can have a highly demotivating effect on the recipient. The 'selling' part is where the appraiser has to persuade the teacher to accept the evaluation and feedback as valid and then to implement the proposed remediation.

Experienced teachers may simply not accept the evaluation or the procedure as valid and see the source as lacking credibility. NQTs and teachers in difficulty may have to simply accept what is handed down and implement it until the pressure is off. Easy-going staff may simply uncritically accept the authoritarian leadership which this method embodies and this can lead to docility and conservatism rather than development.

In this system of 'top down' appraisal, the implicit assumption is that the appraisal will be fair, accurate and acceptable to the appraisee who will want to carry out the improvement plan:

> This approach relies on the interviewer having the skills and knowledge necessary to persuade and motivate the appraisee to change in the prescribed manner, and, to gain acceptance of the evaluation, without appearing to dominate the interview or 'preach'.　　　(Montgomery and Hadfield 1989: 20)

According to Maier, there are two possible outcomes in using this method. One is that the evaluation is rejected and the other that it is accepted with little enthusiasm. In either case the results offer a poor prognosis on the health of the organisation.

Tell and listen

In this style of interview, the appraiser presents the evaluation in full to the appraisee without interruption. In the second half he or she sits back and listens to the appraisee's response, acting as a non directive counsellor to enable the teacher to express feelings and opinions openly. The idea behind this is that if people are allowed to express their feelings and frustrations the defensive mechanisms will be removed or diminished and there will be an opening up to change.

The appraiser in this situation does not always expect the appraisee's agreement and needs some very good counselling skills in accepting and understanding the often aversive responses. In a successful interview, misunderstandings can be clarified and communication and feelings of support and understanding enhanced.

Despite this apparently more open system it is still in the 'top down' mode and if mishandled, can cause just as much strife as the 'tell and sell' technique. It can also lead to the appraiser feeling much abused by aggressive and personal critical responses. Because of the non directive nature of the 'listen' section, it can cause the appraisee to regard the appraiser as knowing nothing helpful to pass on. This can lead over time to lack of credibility in the appraiser and the process.

The problem solving system

This is a form of negotiated appraisal in which over a period of time appraiser and appraisee discuss problems and issues in performance and ways in which these might be tackled. The purpose is to come to a shared view of the way forward in a mentoring relationship and it is aimed to increase motivation and job satisfaction. It enables the teacher to analyse the performance constructively rather than defensively and so own the process and the outcomes. In Maier's view, this system can have far reaching and beneficial effects. It is a positive system of staff appraisal. However, the extensive skills required for this individualised form of appraisal are not widely available and require extensive training and experience. In the hands of a skilled person, any system of appraisal can be expected to work.

Difficulties can arise if neither of the participants has any ideas on ways to resolve a problem identified or if the needs of the individual do not match those of the institution.

The counselling approach

Although Maier does not mention this approach, it was one commonly adopted in the earlier rounds of appraisal interviews. A number of teachers had undertaken counselling courses to help them in the pastoral work and one of the counselling approaches is to get the teacher to talk about the lesson and identify the issues and problems.

None of their concerns may be addressed but the teachers are encouraged to find resolutions for themselves facilitated by the 'counsellor'. When teachers were working with difficult classes they found this approach, to say the least, frustrating and time wasting. It did not give them confidence in their appraiser as knowing anything about teaching.

Summary and conclusions

ACAS in 1986 identified the stages in the appraisal process as follows:

- self appraisal and preparation
- initial review discussion centred on a prompt list
- classroom observation
- the appraisal interview
- appeals
- records.

This cycle is incorporated into the performance management system in schools.

In the same year Nisbet (1986) observed that appraisal would strengthen the mechanisms of power and control over teachers. The model proposed was a 'top down' one with the classroom observation undertaken by an immediate superior. Dadds (1987) commented that it was a process thrust uncritically upon an already overcrowded agenda. Fifteen years later we can see that these predictions have indeed been borne out in the new system.

In this chapter, a review of the performance management system in operation in English schools has been discussed and some of the more important issues have been examined. The system is designed to identify and reward effective teaching where it promotes the learning and standards of pupils in schools. This is directly linked to the school development plan.

However, it has been argued in this chapter that effective teaching may not always lead to directly measurable and intended outcomes. How effective teaching is constructed is not defined in the various official documents and related research but is only defined by its outcomes. Thus it is suggested that raising standards by the methods of classroom observation and review proposed may not be achievable except in a marginal fashion and with less experienced teachers.

The system which promotes senior managers to take an interest in a structured way can of course be expected to be motivating and beneficial and create a 'feel good' factor. But as the structure of the NC, performance-led management and centrally directed teacher education is finally locked in place, we can see the emphasis on a bureaucratic system which has encouraged a didactic teacher-led form of education such as might have been typical of the old grammar school system from which successive ministers of education and civil servants emerged.

Increasingly we have seen this original design has had to be retreated from as many pupils do not find their education a fulfilling experience and do not respond in the required manner – they still leave without qualifications and without any desire to ever connect with education again. In fact there has been an increase in disaffection from school and an increase in learning difficulties created by the curriculum and pedagogy such as was originally reported in the Scottish Education Department's Report (SED 1978) in 50 per cent of learners in Scottish primary and secondary schools.

The main forms of appraisal and classroom observation under discussion are *formative* or *summative* and some claim to be both, although with little justification. The formative approach is very much concerned with staff development and giving feedback on performance. In the latter, the appraiser compares the performance with external criteria and judgements are made about pass or fail. Sometimes levels of attainment and rating scales are incorporated into summative scales to make them more sensitive. These checklists are then often used to identify where performance improvements should be made. It is suggested that there may be no logical connection between these two and this would account for the failure of managers to improve poor performance.

It would appear to be necessary to have both formative and summative forms of appraisals in a PM structure but according to Scriven (1986) the criteria for summative personnel evaluation should have either a logical or a legal connection to teacher performance and they must be necessary for good teaching. The popular focus, for example, on questioning techniques selected for a classroom observation may be neither necessary nor sufficient for good teaching to be taking place and therefore avoids the central concerns of teaching and teachers.

Following the analysis of effective teaching research, the three major issues of credibility, capability and roles were discussed, followed by an outline of models and systems for collecting and presenting the results of an observation to a teacher.

The most common reason for declaring a teacher incompetent was (Wise *et al.* 1984) an inability to control the class. That this is still true today is evidenced in the annual reports issued by the DfEE on behalf of the Chief Inspector for Schools. However, it is mostly in the classrooms of NQTs and those heading for capability procedures that classroom management is a major concern. It is frequently addressed by using the school's summative appraisal strategy with little success. What will be described in the subsequent chapters is a method which has been shown in evidence-based research and in qualitative terms to improve teachers' performance. It has also been shown to have the power to retrieve the performance of failing teachers.

Essentially it is a system in which appraisal means to prize and value a colleague's performance for we grow from having our strengths identified and developed.

CHAPTER 2

Classroom Observation Methods

Introduction

The Further Education Unit (FEU) commissioned a review by Tuxworth (1982) of competency in teaching. The report described and discussed performance-based (PBTE) and competency-based teacher education. PBTE is consistent with a reductionist view of teaching. It serves to break it down into a series of discrete parts, the teacher performances or competencies. Once these are established it is then assumed that if teachers are trained on these parts this will build towards the whole and result in effective teaching. This behaviourist view of teaching can be criticised for its lack of cognitive input in an essentially cognitive, dynamic and interactive activity.

The FEU report also criticised PBTE from the point of view that it had a very weak research base to support it. It had not been widely demonstrated that the approach improved either the pupils' learning or the teachers' performance who had been trained in it. The report cited an example from the USA in which 30 training modules were drawn from 100 possibilities covering 83 teaching skills and put together to make a teacher training course. At the cost of two million dollars the scheme was put into operation with a cohort of teachers. What was discovered was that although teachers might gain a 'good' pass on all the 30 modules and have received training on all 83 skills, it was no guarantee that any of them could successfully teach a class of pupils.

It was ever thus! It is only surprising that such a project could attract funding. Research on skill development has shown for decades that training on the separate parts does not lead automatically to competent performance. For this the learner has to practise putting the whole lot together. During this period the feedback on performance of the 'coach' can significantly contribute to high levels of performance. The better the coach, the higher the levels that can be achieved, even by the less skilled. Experience in youth as a springboard diver and later as a coach confirms this in practice. Coaching skills are extremely important in the development of skilled performance and a significant part of teaching is about teaching skills.

However, the appraisal 'instrument' has arrived. We have *Threshold Standards* (DfEE 2000c) which simply demanded to be converted into lists of competencies. Schools up and down the country cross referenced their own lists with these *Standards* and the OFSTED criteria. A whole system of further education had been redesigned on the basis of competency-based courses for National Vocational Qualifications and none of it has taken place because of evidence that it works. However, this all creates items to be measured and in the assigning of numbers or scores we so often think we have assessed the item both reliably and validly. Questions have already been raised in Chapter 1 about using a summative instrument for formative purposes.

These assessment schemes are most frequently 'validated' in use and they can easily be seen to have face value – the items are associated with performance perceived as good teaching or good 'ground work' (digging holes). However, we must not assume from this that these instruments and capabilities are thereby legitimate and valid. The critical test of validity is seldom, if ever, made. In other words, to use the appraisal checklist with a failing teacher and after one or two sessions to be able to convert them into a successful one. Instead the instrument is used with these teachers and on numerous occasions they fail to improve. Strangely enough, this is never taken as invalidating the instrument. Instead, the teacher is failed and capability procedures are entered into. Can this be fair?

Scriven (1986) said that the criteria must have a logical or legal connection to teacher performance and must be necessary for good teaching. If the feedback on the performance showing the strengths and weaknesses does not result in change even when the appraisee accepts the verity of the information, can the items be necessary? As early as 1982 Clift's research had led him to conclude that the schemes and instruments then available were incapable of raising the quality of education, and that self evaluation was probably a necessary but not sufficient condition for professional and institutional improvement.

It is therefore surprising that CATE (1991) drew up a list of competencies for students in ITT and the DfEE encouraged by subsequent Governments are still pursuing these approaches (DfEE 1998a).

If the checklist- and competency-based summative system is not fit for purpose, then we must design methods which are. This must involve some reference to the theory and practice of teaching and learning. For, as Kant concluded, practice without theory is blind. Theory of education is a subject which successive governments have banned from teacher education courses and thus it is not surprising that teachers themselves are not in a position to argue with those imposing their views on the profession from outside. Teacher educators' views and experiences were ignored in this debate.

Those imposing the competency-based agenda are using models from other fields and ignoring the special nature of teaching as a dynamic interactive system full of complex substructures and processes. It is only by identifying the factors which can influence change in teaching behaviours and also those which at the same time influence learning in both teacher and pupil that teaching and learning can be improved. It has already been argued that the process is made more complex by the fact that teachers do not actually teach subjects but that they teach pupils to learn subjects – a much more complex scenario and a situation where *process analysis* is much more important than product analysis. Product analysis – summative assessment – can be made at any point but would appear to have little influence on process.

Methods of classroom observation

Naturalistic observation and ethnography

Observation in its specialised sense is not a set of comments or thoughts of a person looking at a lesson. Observation is the act or practice of noting and recording facts and events as they happen. Psychology has borrowed the term 'naturalistic observation' from comparative studies in which biologists observed animals in their natural habitats to learn about their habits and behaviours. In sociology the term used is ethnography, which has been taken from social anthropological studies.

Naturalistic observation has played a significant role in child development studies but psychology in general until recently has favoured the experimental procedure of testing hypotheses by comparing performance of experimental and control groups. The criticism is that because of the overemphasis on the experimental paradigm technique, we have never truly established what is usual in human terms by systematic observation. Perhaps this is also true of this field – teaching.

A number of different techniques of observation have been developed because even in the simple case of observing one individual child there can be far too many behaviours to record. For this reason video or audio records are frequently made to enable an observer to go over the events many times to collect all the available data. However, even a video recording of a class lesson spanning the whole room cannot 'see' all the events which happen. An alert and experienced observer, however, can see most of what goes on. The problem is of course that it cannot all be recorded. It is for this reason that there has to be a careful selection of methods.

By gazing about

The observer usually sits with the pupils and looks at the teacher teaching the lesson. When the pupils are settled down to a particular task the observer may get up and walk around, looking at what the pupils are doing and perhaps giving some help.

After the lesson the observer and the teacher retire to a quiet area and the observer shares thoughts on what was seen, using sell and tell, for example, or any of the methods already outlined. At the end of this session the observer may write a summary report of the main views on what was seen, not always modified by the discussion which took place afterwards.

There are a number of problems with this technique. One of the main ones is that there are no factual data afterwards to discuss. Anything written is *ex post facto* observation or historical recall which may in the process have been changed or manipulated. The whole procedure may be very idiosyncratic and unreliable and it cannot be proved. It is very often used by observers to conceal a lack of knowledge and inexperience about what to do and say.

Participant observation

In this system the observer records at intervals whenever feasible and at other times is engaged with the pupils or the teacher as a participant in the lesson. Team teaching can give rise to this form of mixed data. The observer may also actually sit with the pupils as a participant in their discussions or may engage in individual or small group teaching following up the teacher's work.

In each instance it is difficult to participate and record at the same time and so the data is somewhat limited. Standing back from the situation and looking at overall patterns is not really possible in this method. As a participant the observer is also responsible for creating and changing some of the data and is thus responsible for the success or failure of the lesson with the teacher.

To help ITT students it is often necessary for the supervisor to sit with a difficult group and help control them in order to enable the student to have the experience of teaching the rest of the class without too much interruption. It can also provide small lessons in behaviour management afterwards for the student to try out later. Taking over a class even when it dissolves into chaos is not a good strategy. The students never appreciate it because the control, however tenuous, has passed from them. The next time they will find it even harder to maintain discipline. Taking over control from a colleague in difficulties is also not recommended for the same reasons. This is often difficult for the observers as they can feel that they are condoning the misbehaviour. They then often engage in non verbal and covert strategies to stop the bad behaviours. This is in effect assuming control and changing the data.

Diary description

It is often recommended that the observer makes a running log of all that is seen. As can be imagined, it is impossible to do this on a continuous basis for a whole lesson or for that matter to record all of what was seen in any case. Too much is going on. The observer is thus obliged to select from all the rain of data what will be recorded. Having once started recording, the observer can still be writing about that event when others have followed in rapid succession, until there ends up being a lag of five or ten minutes in the record.

Observers are also idiosyncratic in what they record. They are obliged to be selective in these circumstances and they tend to target their preferred items. They may often have decided what the teacher's problem might be before they enter the room and are looking for signs to write down which will support this.

Many simply begin recording the pupil entering behaviours and start of the lesson strategy. 'Beginnings' are considered crucial to getting a good start to the lesson. Thus they branch out into classroom management procedures and this can colour the whole record. Their own preferred strategies may also be in evidence.

Time and event sampling

Sampling is frequently used in formal observational studies and has been tried in classroom observation studies. However, it gives a somewhat fragmented record because recordings are made, for example from 30-second observations – looking – and then three minutes of recording. In the recording period events happen which invariably the observer would like to record. Sometimes the record is 'fudged' to include these critical incidents.

It is probably best used as a research tool when observing many lessons to adduce general patterns rather than as a technique in appraisal.

Problem points lists

This used to be a favoured technique used by college supervisors with students in initial teacher education. Thus all teachers will have experienced some version of this. They may indeed adopt it as their own favoured method.

It involves the minimum of effort on the part of the observer. Observation is still conducted by gazing about and in this method when points for improvement are identified these are noted down. Examples might be:

1. Try to get your class in more quickly.
2. Why not let two monitors give out the exercise books?
3. Don't let Trevor M shout out answers.
4. The revision of last lesson's points went on too long.
5. There were several pupils at the back playing about when you were doing the explanation of the task.
6. Quite a number still did not know what they had to do, although you explained it twice.
7. Some of the homework had not been marked correctly.
8. Don't let them take over the ending of the lesson and rush off.

They usually seem to try to find seven or eight points. Occasionally a positive statement might be inserted by some tutors. As can be imagined, such lists can be demoralising and demotivating. This is especially so if they are left in the file and the tutor has disappeared without comment. In addition, what is not always appreciated is the anger and frustration such a strategy can engender. It is also extremely difficult to learn from a negative. The person knows what not to do but not necessarily how to put it right.

Teaching is such a complex interactive and dynamic activity that while attending to one aspect the novitiate invariably misses out on several others that were originally going well.

Checklists

Checklists are in a sense a proposed sampling frame. However, the categories or titles under which the observer records are usually established on the basis of experience in classrooms and discussion, rather than naturalistic observation narrowing down on patterns and categories.

It is not surprising that there has been a general move in the observation of teaching to focus upon the checklist as an answer to the criticisms. It is usual for the school to collect a number of examples of such lists and then to produce a composite one which represents what can be considered to be their committee's view of items relating to good teaching. To these they may attach the rating scales, behavioural outcomes or criterion references. They then try this instrument out on a few NQTs and perhaps in some peer appraisal sessions. After minor changes, it becomes part of the agreed policy of the school that they will use it as their appraisal instrument.

Because the checklist has been agreed with the staff there is then a general acceptance of its use. It also gives teachers who have no experience of classroom observation a tool to use and boxes to fill in, and things to look for that, left to their own devices, they might not have thought of. It helps prevent those with 'bees in their bonnets' about particular things distorting an observation and feedback session. This is perhaps an important interim phase in school development work where all teachers begin to understand the methods and then verify them or otherwise in use. In practice as long as the feedback is presented in a supportive atmosphere and there is an opportunity for a dialogue on the contents, it is likely that targets for the following year can be agreed. However, these may bear little relationship to what was observed in the lesson(s) and how aspects of that lesson can be improved. More often the aspects that need to be improved are identified and agreed but not *how* to do it. Where how-to-fix-it methods are suggested, they frequently do not work because they are only a part of something else more powerful and important but not overt that needs to be addressed.

The targets set according to OFSTED (1997) were also on the whole too general to be of much value. Hence the new 'Standards' for NQTs and for Threshold Assessments (DfEE 2000c). These have already been discussed, as have the limitations of checklists. An excellent summary and sets of pro formas for checklisting in all its various forms may be found in Bubb and Hoare (2001) and Jones (2001). If they are used as summative instruments, they will be found to be helpful but they should not be used formatively as well.

Sampling frames

The final instrument which was devised for classroom observation was a sampling frame. A sampling frame is really only a set of categories under which the observer records. It is, however, based upon research and usually begins with diary description and time sampling to evoke patterns and clusters in the data.

The records in the frame or table may be simple tallies and ticks. An early example of this was a table for recording levels of play observed in young children, e.g. solitary; looking on; parallel; and cooperative play. Because all teaching behaviour in an observation cannot be recorded, the checklist can also be regarded as a form of sampling frame.

In the system of classroom observation to be described, a conceptual sampling frame for classroom dynamics was evolved by the methods just described based on many hundreds of lesson observations and feedback sessions. However, it is not a summative system in which boxes are ticked; the frame is a theoretical one based upon teaching interactions known to have the power to change the behaviours of teachers and learners. The method of recording is continuous writing about the processes observed. It is a description of critical events in the classroom in a continuous, timed, running record. If it is used as a tally system it reverts to checklist, summative status.

The development of this observation system

There are a wealth of qualitative data thrown up by classroom observation, however it is collected. The following framework to be described is based upon the formal observation of over 1,200 lessons. It began with the search for helpful methods of observation of teacher education students on their various teaching practices. More or less every technique just described was tried out. Because the students were talked through the observations and invited to give their own thoughts on the process, it was possible to begin to identify what worked and what did not. At the time there were few guidelines to help in this process. It was research grounded in classrooms. At the same time these studies were set in the psychological research context. Here data from the USA were beginning to suggest that positive approaches to discipline with individuals (Becker *et al.* 1967; Scott MacDonald 1971; Blackham and Silberman 1971), were working, at least temporarily. These studies in behaviour modification became very popular in education training courses (Harrop 1984; Wheldall and Merritt 1984) but lacked the wider application to general classroom management until recently (Canter 1976, Canter and Canter 1999; Rogers 1994a, b, 2000).

Over time it was possible for me to begin to form a set of strategies which could be taught to students based on lesson observations which would enable them to improve their performance on classroom management as well as in lesson planning and implementation.

The key problem identified in failing teachers is their poor classroom control and behaviour management of pupils. Any appraisal and staff development procedure must thus first take account of this. It is of course a major problem for ITT students who are always told that until they get class control they will not be able to teach anything. It was quite clear that the research in psychology could be used to suggest indicants and cues which might be relevant to this problem of classroom management. However, in developing a theory about what were key behaviours to bring about change and improvement, successful class management techniques would need to be identified and defined.

The research process

Over time, in hundreds of lessons, a hierarchy of steps in which the qualitative data has been brought into some kind of order can be identified, as follows:

1. Counting: words, items, occurrences, indicants, cues – frequency counts.
2. Patterning: observing and noting certain recurring patterns in the data in successful and failing lessons.
3. Clustering: groups or categories of activities, settings and so on with similar characteristics are brought together, e.g. behaviour management strategies, questioning techniques, cognitive challenge and motivation.
4. Factoring: cluster groups are reduced to a number of factors with some explanatory power, e.g. CBG, 3Ms, and PCI.
5. New relationships – may be sought between factors. These factors were used to help students in training become more effective in classroom management in addition to subject tuition and management. Tactical lesson planning was outlined to help structure the time span of the lesson in relation to the learning needs of learners posited in theories of learning.
6. Causal networks: The above may aid in building causal networks particularly if findings relate to already established general and theoretical frameworks. The developing teaching skills model is now being used as a model for retrieving poor performance with success.

This process over a period of about five years resulted in what is called the 'process sampling frame'. This enables the observer to attend to and record a limited range of potent items in the observation period. Once the sampling frame was established it was possible to use it as a formative hypothesis and test out whether it was indeed capable of improving performance. During the development period for the instrument a range of techniques for using it were also tried. It can be used as a checklist itself, a frame in which counts are recorded and so on. None of these produced the supportive atmosphere and the factual record which the appraisee would find beneficial. From this evidence the final form of the record was produced.

Recording

The technique which evolved with the process sampling frame over time was the *continuous running record*. By this is meant that the observer simply wrote continuously everything that could possibly be recorded in relation to the three variables of the sampling frame. Times were noted at intervals down the side of the page. Everything written had to be a factual statement or record of what was seen. This did not preclude asides and comments and questions as the record ran on but this needed to be made clear either on the record or afterwards in the debriefing. In addition when wrong things were seen the way of dealing with them was to try to restate them in a neutral or even a positive way, e.g. 'Did you notice that when you lowered you voice they became quieter too?' instead of,

'Don't shout.' The one essential was very rapid writing often while looking at ongoing events.

Until 1983 the technique had only been used with students in initial teacher education. However, the student feedback showed that it did work and that they could go on developing after the supervision period was over by referring back to it and using the strategies they had learned. It enabled them to become self regulated learners because they could have internal dialogues with themselves about their own teaching. They could hold 'learning conversations' (Thomas and Harri-Augstein 1984) or tap into their metacognitive processes (Flavell 1979). Flavell found that this could increase a person's intelligence and problem solving abilities. With this system it was found that teachers could improve their teaching by reflecting on it with the help of the process structure. It was found to produce a language of teaching which the then Chief Inspector for teacher education, Pauline Perry (1984), had found lacking in education

The Classroom Observation Sampling Frame: CBG, 3Ms and PCI – all within a Tactical Lesson Plan (TLP)

Changing the learning climate and changing the behaviour using CBG

The overall purpose of CBG and its constellations of constructs is to improve the learning and classroom climate. This involves changing the climate, if necessary, from negative to positive. There is a vast body of research and practice which underpins this and some recent exponents are Rogers (2000) on positive classroom management and Canter and Canter (1999) on assertive discipline.

The initials stand for Catch (them) Being Good. There was a considerable amount of early research which has shown that teachers spend most of their time attending to pupils when they are off target, not working and being disruptive (Kounin 1970, Scott MacDonald 1971, Wheldall and Merritt 1985). When pupils are working and being constructive, they received little positive support. These early studies have formed the basis for the subsequent recommendations for practice by Rogers and others, linked to their own experience in classrooms.

Pupils who receive little attention, support and approval at home will tend to seek it at school from teachers, or failing them, from peers. If they cannot gain this attention and recognition that they crave through their work they will find other means to satisfy their needs.

The strategy CBG is one which every teacher thinks they use but when they are recorded the number of desist and negative unsupportive behaviours and comments outweigh the positive and supportive ones. The less successful the teacher the fewer the positive responses and failing teachers gave none (Scott MacDonald 1971).

The CBG strategy requires that:

- The teacher positively reinforces any pupil's correct social and on-task responses with nods, smiles, and by paraphrasing correct responses and statements and supporting their on-task academic responses with such phrases as 'Yes, good', 'Well done'. Incorrect responses should not be negated but the pupil should be encouraged to have another try, or the response should be. 'Yes, nearly' and 'Yes, and what else . . .', and 'Good so far, can anyone help him or her out?' (and so on).

- It is very important to remember CBG behaviour as well as answers to questions. It needs to be done more discreetly. It consists of going to children when they are on task and working, and making quiet supportive statements and comments. They may not choose to respond immediately but over time they will be found to increase their time on task, even if they laugh off any praise.

- When pupils are working and it is not a good idea to interrupt them at that moment, simply standing near them and looking at their work and smiling is very supportive. Detailed looking at work as they are doing it and moving on shows them you are interested in it and them. They know or feel you will intervene if there is a problem even if you yourself are just looking and murmuring 'Good'.

- It makes them feel that you are actively involved with them and the work they are doing for you and that you consider it to be important enough to give it and them your attention. If a teacher sits at the front and marks the books of another class it demonstrates an 'us versus them' attitude with tasks handed down to the lower orders without them having any intrinsic worth. Even if the teacher is marking that class's work and is calling individuals up, it is far better to be out and around the room doing the marking.

- At its simplest CBG is one form of behaviour modification technique in which the teacher positively reinforces desirable behaviours emitted by the pupil, gradually *shaping* them towards desirable ends determined by the teacher, without the child being aware of the goal towards which they are directed. There is no cognitive input in this technique.

- When supportive discussion about the work and the behaviour takes place, this moves it into the cognitive sphere and the behaviour changes and CBG comes under cognitive regulation and is more likely to be sustained. This places it in the constructivist realm of theory and research.

In the original researches (Becker *et al.* 1967) the teachers were told to ignore any undesirable behaviour and only support those behaviours directed towards the target ones. This of course had deleterious effects on the other children who saw the target child getting away with misbehaviour and so the behaviour of the whole class could deteriorate. To avoid this situation it may be necessary to tell the pupil to stop talking, sit down, open a book and start reading but then *immediately* he or she does, give attention support and encouragement for the on-task behaviour.

Children learn vicariously how to behave in classrooms as much from what happens to other children as from what happens to them and thus it is important to stop unwanted behaviours at the outset and when they are in their earliest stage. This may be compared to the strategy of 'nipping things in the bud' described by Lawrence *et al.* (1984). Where a child is very disturbed it is possible within these parameters to ignore a significant proportion of the unwanted behaviour for the other children identify him or her as a special case. In some circumstances it may be necessary to seek the support of the rest of the children in helping an individual gain mastery over unwanted behaviour.

3Ms – Management, Monitoring and Maintenance

3Ms represents a series of tactics which effective teachers used to gain and maintain pupils' attention whatever teaching method or style they subsequently used. When teachers with classroom management disciplining problems were taught to use these strategies in observation and feedback sessions, they became effective teachers (Montgomery 1984, 1989).

Management – phase one

The teacher makes an *attention gaining noise* such as 'Right!', 'OK, class 3', 'Good morning, everybody', 'Uhummm!' or bangs the door or desk, claps hands. Some teachers simply wait quietly until the noise subsides as the pupils notice they are present. Next the teacher gives a *short verbal instruction* such as: 'Everybody sit down', 'Get out your English folders', 'Come and sit on the mat', 'Sit down and listen carefully' and so on. At this point 20 of the pupils will do as requested and ten will not. The effective teacher pauses, looks round, spots those who are not doing as requested and quietly *names* these pupils and individually instructs them to stop what they are doing and to listen. This is usually quite sufficient if a *check back* look is given to bring the whole class to attention. The mistake that the ineffective teachers make is to begin to shout 'Be quiet' and 'Sit down', as a general instruction to all pupils. The raising of the teacher's voice and the general command to those who are already behaving as requested begins to engender hostility in them. Some who were attending now begin to chat, causing the instruction to be repeated louder still, thus contributing to the general level of classroom noise and seeming to transmit the information that the teacher is not quite in control and can surreptitiously be disobeyed by an even larger group. Thus in a short period of time the class has become out of control. The teacher at this point usually becomes very exasperated and red in the face and shouts the class into submission. These 'shock tactics' become less and less effective the more they are used and it takes a considerable amount of time and effort to reconstruct this teacher's behaviour to make it effective, allowing for the opportunity to actually teach something (Montgomery and Hadfield 1989, 1990). Many give up the struggle and 'teach' over the noise so that the level of attention and achievement of all pupils is low.

The effective teacher, having gained the pupils' attention and silence, will immediately launch into the introduction to the session or begin reading the story.

During the teacher's talk or story it is necessary for a range of attention gaining and maintaining tactics to be employed, for example:

- pausing in exposition to look at pupil talking until they stop
- walking to pupil and gently removing tapping pencil or note
- asking the talking or inattentive pupil a question
- repeating the phrase just given
- insert 'and Goldilocks said to the three bears!' in the middle of the story, looking hard at the miscreant
- use hand signal or finger on lips cue to quieten
- use 'stink look'.

The main point about this phase of the lesson is that if there needs to be a lot of controlling techniques used, then the material and the mode of delivery need to be reconsidered and wound up as soon as possible.

Monitoring – phase two

As soon as there is an activity change from pupils' listening to getting out books and writing or going back to places to work, this is when disruption can and does arise. The monitoring strategy needs to be brief, perhaps lasting no more than 30 seconds. As soon as the pupils are at their places the teacher should move quickly round the room to each group or table, very quickly and quietly settling them down to work. It is essential not to linger to give detailed explanations at this point but to say that you will come back shortly to help, going to the noisiest group first but making sure that all are visited. If there is not a lot of space to move round then a vantage point should be selected and the monitoring directed from there by means of calming gestures and quiet naming.

In addition to activity change, monitoring should be used when pupils are engaged with tasks and the noise level and attention seems to be slipping. This can be noted at any time by the well-attuned ear and usually only requires that the teacher looks up and round the room to the talker. A pointed look may well be all that is required or very quiet naming. The important thing is not to nag and be noisy about criticism and having told a pupil to be quiet for the teacher to look up and check back on the pupil within 3–5 seconds.

Maintenance – phase three

Once the pupils have been settled by the monitoring techniques to the task, it is then advisable for the teacher to move round the class to each individual to find out how the work is progressing. In the maintenance period all the requests and queries of individuals can be dealt with. During a lesson period or period of study within a curriculum area each pupil should expect to receive some form of individual constructive and developmental comment on the work – PCI. This has been called *positive cognitive intervention* (Montgomery 1984, 1994, 1996). In this steady move round the room the teacher should look at the work with the pupil and offer *developmental* advice which makes a positive statement about progress thus far and then offers ideas and suggestions for extension or through constructive questioning helps the pupils see how to make the work better or achieve the goals they have set themselves. When the work has been completed, again there should be written or spoken comments as appropriate and further ideas, for example:

- 'Jason, I enjoyed your story very much. The beginning section was good, it set the murky scene very well. I think you should look at some of Roald Dahl's quirky characters – your style at the moment reminds me of some of his better books. You might have a gift for story like him. If you look up one or two I will show you what I mean.'
- 'Chrissy, the contrast colours and the texture you give them in your picture are good, next time I want you to explore the effect when you use a palette of three.'

At intervals during the maintenancing period the noise will fluctuate. As soon as the level goes above 'interested work' or an individual's voice is clearly audible and does not stop after a few moments then a quick monitoring session should ensue. This may only need to be the raising of the teacher's head to look in the direction of the noise to cue the pupil to silence or it may again involve the 'stink look' and quiet naming. If this does not suffice then it may be necessary to go over and settle the problem. A noisy pupil who continually causes the teacher to go and attend to them needs further consideration for this is an attentional problem which is gaining illegitimate satisfaction which will in itself maintain the unwanted behaviour. At this point it may become necessary to institute some behavioural modification procedures to cause the pupil to spend more time on task in seat. There may well be a learning difficulty which underlies this behaviour which needs direct and individual teaching to overcome. In addition the lesson/session plan and pedagogy needs to be reviewed to assess whether these can contribute to restoring general good classroom behaviour.

PCI – Positive Cognitive Intervention

During the steady move round the room the teacher should look at the work with the pupil and offer *developmental* advice which makes a positive statement about progress thus far and then offers ideas and suggestions for extension or through constructive questioning helps the pupils see how to make the work better or achieve the goals they have set themselves. This involves the *cognitive approach*. When the work has been completed, again there should be written or spoken comments.

In addition to this form of developmental PCI there is also the need to design lessons which do offer some cognitive challenge. Although open questioning is a favoured method this is not sufficient. In addition there needs to be a system of differentiation and the use of cognitive process teaching methods if all pupils are to be more motivated and challenged. These latter will be explored in Chapter 5, Effective Teaching.

Some individual behaviour management strategies

Building the causal network and the EBD policy

Just a few pupils are serious problems and disruptive with most staff. They are of course at their worst with teachers in difficulties. The following outline strategies are those which schools may have to adopt to help such pupils retrieve their problem behaviour. It may just have gone too far with the problem teacher and so it may be helpful to have these strategies in mind and written into the EBD policy to support all teachers.

Shaping: Behaviour modification strategies are most frequently advised upon by the School Psychological Services and they may also offer training courses to help the management of particularly difficult, often disruptive pupils. BATPACK courses (Wheldall and Merritt 1984, 1985) and their books on Positive Approaches to Teaching are all based on the principles of reinforcement established by Skinner (1958) in his studies of Operant Conditioning and most books on classroom management and managing difficult behaviour include this (Cheeseman and Watts 1985; Chisholm *et al.* 1986; Luton and Booth 1991). The pupil emits unwanted responses which the teacher learns to ignore but reinforces the closest opposite and desirable response. By a process of continuous positive reinforcement the behaviour is gradually 'shaped' towards more 'desirable' ends.

Elements of all of this have been described in the foregoing as well as some of the problems which can result if it is not used well. The difference in the case of a disruptive pupil is that close observation and identification of the target behaviour is needed together with the drawing up of a reinforcement schedule and school behaviour management plan. Even so it is impossible to reinforce each occurrence of the desirable behaviours and it may be better to put the pupil in a much smaller class – a group of 8–12 with a specially trained teacher while the main part of the programme is being implemented. Rogers (1994a) suggested withdrawing disruptives for regular 20-minute sessions to give social skills and behaviour management training from trained teachers.

Other colleagues, including playground and canteen helpers, need to be made aware of the main elements of the 'therapy' if all the work in the classroom is not to be undone. Many of the studies in the USA used positive reinforcements which not only included giving merit points for good behaviour but also enabled such points to be saved up to spend time on hobbies, games or to buy candy, paints and even make-up. As a rule it is not surprisingly found that when the novelty has worn off the pupil decides not to work for more credits. This is supported by the work of Deci and Ryan (1983) and Ryan *et al.* (1985) who found that extrinsic rewards such as these actually cause a decline in motivation over time whereas intrinsic motivation is raised by a *positive supportive learning* environment. It is thus the teacher who is the real source of motivation and it is the teacher's smile and genuine support and praise which is the all-pervading and prime motivator. Younger pupils like to earn stars and merit points but it is mainly because these are the tangible expression of the teacher's appreciation that they are so effective.

Modelling. This is another strategy the teacher may use (Blackham and Silberman 1971). At its simplest level it involves the teacher saying such things as 'Very well done, the Green table is ready', 'Show me who is ready', 'Michael was really listening so he is doing it well', 'Sharon has a good idea, watch how she does it', 'I like the way Gary helped him' and so on. Other children vicariously learn by watching the reinforced model (Bandura and Walters 1963). In more sophisticated versions the model is reinforced and then the pupil watching is reinforced for any approximation towards the good behaviour of the model. A range of different models need to be selected so that one child does not become a 'star' for the others to dislike and even bully.

Time out. From reinforcement (Blackham and Silberman 1971), this is another recommended strategy. Where pupils have become overexcited or distressed, are upset or having a tantrum, 'time out' with head down on arms on desk, eyes closed, can be very useful. Pupils can give themselves 30 seconds' peace and quiet to recover or they can be sent to a quiet area of the room (if possible), knowing no other pupil must look at them or speak to them until they look up or it is agreed that they can come out now they are calm. It is not advisable to send them out of the classroom for they may run away and be involved in an incident outside. If the pupil is unmanageable it is wisest to send another responsible pupil to the head or deputy to summon help.

Disruption on this scale is serious and of course the parents would need to be consulted about underlying difficulties and joint efforts to help the child. For a period of time it may be essential to draw up a *behaviour contract* with the pupil and parents stating attainable goals (Rogers 1994a) and the ways in which the pupil will behave and this will be signed by all the parties. The class teacher and any specialist teachers will sign the record at the end of each session or write a comment on the pupil's conduct. At the end of the day the record is inspected by the head or deputy and commented upon. This should only need to be kept up for two or three weeks and then the pupil should be officially signed off for good behaviour and the record filed. Such periods can give an opportunity for attitude change and a review of the child's needs in more detail and may be enough to deal with the problem. The contract may have to be redrawn at a later stage as some new factor arises. It is so often found that the counselling relationship which is established between the pupil and the person to whom the daily report is made can develop strongly enough to make the pupil want to work for the good opinion of that person. The pupil will then seriously try to iron out what may have before seemed to be insuperable difficulties.

Mentors are now helping with disruptive and excluded pupils, and counselling them in small groups is emerging as an effective technique.

Coping with confrontations and disruption

These are most often explosive episodes involving an individual pupil and teacher or pairs of pupils in a fight. Little may appear to have happened to provoke the outburst or it may be the end of an episode of noisy disruption ending in verbal abuse which the teacher in desperation seeks to stem and which causes the final outburst. The teacher may already have tried calming strategies and may have asked the pupil to stop the tirade or to sit still and get on with their work. The pupil has thrown down the gauntlet and challenged the teacher verbally or physically. The teacher has a range of options to select from:

- summon help if necessary;
- offer choices (Rogers 1994a, b);
- recover the situation (Montgomery 1989) by:

- *deflecting* (the confrontation) – putting it on *hold* (give time for things to cool down and for brains to be engaged);
- *normalising* (continue with the lesson as though nothing had happened and support the work effort);
- Keeping pupil behind at the end of the lesson and then *counselling*.

Assertive Discipline (AD)

AD was developed by Lee and Marlene Canter in the USA in 1976. It is a method of disciplining based on behaviour modification. It consists of a highly structured and administered system of rewards and punishments. Rewards may be stars, merit marks, play time, and even tangible rewards such as prizes and gifts earned by the collection of tokens or merit points. The most recent edition of their work was published in 1999. Gifts are less popular in this country than in the USA. The punishments or consequences are at no more than five levels of increasing severity: having one's name put on the board, keeping in for five minutes at playtime, isolation for a short period, reporting to the head, informing parents. At the first infringement a warning is given. Having the name put on the board five times leads inevitably to the next stage of punishment and the penalties are non negotiable. It can ensure a quiet, calming discipline. Canter insists that no child's name should be put on the board or the list until two others have been praised. The system is graded according to individual schools policies and the staff team must agree to implement it systematically. Teachers learn to establish no more than five clear rules, for example: follow instructions the first time they are given, put your hands up to answer questions, keep noise level low, keep your hands, feet and objects to yourself, do not talk while the teacher or other pupils are talking.

Behaviour Management Products Ltd was set up in the UK in 1991 to carry out the AD training and claimed that over 2,000 schools were using the system. Makins (1991) reported that schools adopting the system were able to see the difference within a day. Schools adopting the system have had some difficulties in maintaining it, especially in secondary schools where the commitment of all of a large staff is more difficult to secure and where as pupils grow older they do not respond to the incentive system. These courses and those of Rogers who comes regularly to the UK to run them are always oversubscribed.

Tactical Lesson Planning

In the work with students in ITT it was usual for the supervisors to meet with their individual students to go through their Teaching Practice plans in the week before the practice. This included the general curriculum to be followed in each subject or topic area to give a broad and balanced curriculum. It had to follow on or develop from where the class or subject teacher had left off and in consideration of what they wanted the pupils to do next. The students had TP notes issued by the college that insisted that they must write up schemes of work and prepare their first week's lesson plans on the model: Title; Objectives; Content; Method; Materials.

It quickly became apparent in observing lessons that the model was not in fact a Lesson Plan. It was a way of helping the students organise their thoughts about the lessons they were to teach. It resulted in a general title and sometimes some relevant objectives, often repetitive, two or three pages of teaching content and one or two lines on the method, followed by a list of materials sometimes including 'toolbox' items such as pens, pencils rulers etc. to fill up the space.

It was quite clear that, when the students were in the classroom, many of them were focused on the content. Much of it might have been new to them as the English specialist with history subsid. was grappling with the geography in environmental studies and the secondary physics student with the biology of the fish from studies long past. Now they are having to learn the intricacies of the NC before having to teach it. Learning it and teaching it are two very different activities. It became clear that for the teaching side of things a different sort of plan was helpful.

It began with a concern for what the pupils were going to do in any situation. The students' plans really focused on their own learning and not on their teaching. Given that the content was determined, the Lesson Plan should show clearly what the pupils would be doing in relation to it at any point. Thus content and method need to be more closely linked. When this was done with the focus on pupil learning the pupils were found to be much more absorbed with the content. Thus the notion of a Tactical Lesson Plan evolved. It was found to be particularly successful for helping students who were experiencing difficulties with their teaching. Those who were successful were in fact phasing their teaching on a tactical basis and so these observations reinforced the plan.

It proved difficult to get students to change their habitual ways of writing up their Lesson Plans until they experienced the effects of doing so with tutorial help. The bureaucracy could not be caused to change the system. It had approved and had the method written down. It was a method probably going back 50 years. The tutors themselves had probably been asked to write it that way.

The Tactical Lesson Plan has the following pattern:

Central objective. Formulate the central objective as a single statement about what the pupils are to learn. This is the main point of the lesson or series. It can form the title of the lesson or the title can be a separate item which indicates the subject content.

Introduction (3–5 mins). This occupies the first few minutes of the lesson when the teacher

– outlines the main purpose, states the objective of the lesson;
– and/or revises previous related work;
– and/or revises by questioning the pupils.

Phase one (about 10 minutes depending on age and concentration span of the pupils). Presentation of the first part of the lesson content including where possible any visual/auditory stimulus or concrete examples. Probably mainly teacher talk, pupils *listening*. If things are going well a dialogue can be extended to 25 minutes, then it must be realised that slower pupils will need more help and structure for the follow up.

Phase two (about 5 minutes depending on task requirements). This must present an *activity change* for the pupils so that from listening in phase one they can turn to writing, drawing, practical work or to discussion. Making a legitimate opportunity for pupil talk at this point, e.g. pairs discuss . . . can be a very useful tension release for them. Otherwise they talk through the next activity to compensate. Pupils *talking*.

Phase three (about 10–20 minutes). This should present another activity change for the pupils so that they now settle down to something such as writing or recording. This will quieten them down.

Phase four (about 5 minutes). At intervals as pupils become restive this phase can be introduced where perhaps some of the pupils read out what they have done or there is some more Question and Answer. The teacher may offer some additional advice or input. Pupils *talking and listening*.

Finishing activities. In short lessons the finishing activities might be those described in phase four. The whole class are brought together for a brief summing up or concluding activity before being dismissed.

In double lessons or long sessions, the number of phases can be increased. The additions might be *practical work*, including role play. Even in art and design lessons there should be opportunities to bring the group together to rest briefly from the individual concentrated effort to think and listen and perhaps discuss points and techniques.

Very often the cue to the need for an activity change is increasing restlessness among the pupils and an inability to settle for long when asked. This restlessness is frequent where the content is unstimulating or difficult. This should easily be picked up during the maintenancing periods when pupils are getting on with written work, for example.

Too long a period on written work can in itself lead to fatigue and pain for some, so introduce legitimate periods of relaxation by giving an activity change such as hearing some pupils read aloud what they have written; by introducing additional material; by going over the main structure; by discussing some further ideas; or by revising material already presented etc.

In lessons where there is extended practical work, it is advisable to set methods and tables for recording data so that practical work and recording on task take place in the same period. At any point it is then possible if the class is becoming noisy and inattentive to settle them down to check the data collected so far and reorganise the work to its conclusion.

Tactical Planning thus involves activity change based on the attention span of the class from, e.g. *listening* to *reading* to *writing* to *practical work* to *speaking* to *writing* and so on. In many subjects *group problem solving* would replace practical work. In Tactical Planning it is important to realise that *it is the acitivity which changes but the content remains the same.*

The validation of the sampling frame as an appraisal instrument

In February 1983 after 'shadowing' a pupil in Heathside school in Surrey whom the school were concerned about the project in appraisal began. The day had been spent observing the pupil's experience. The feedback illustrated the kind of experience to which the pupil had been subjected. As he had a mild language difficulty it was of concern that for the whole eight lessons no teacher had spoken directly to him and he had not answered one question or spoken more than once or twice to ask another pupil for a rubber. The language development, study skills and learning strategies in which we had jointly planned and shared training days might not have been. This was despite the positive feedback received by the trainer after two linked training days and a series of curriculum development follow up meetings by the school.

Today this might be a thundering glimpse of the obvious. However, training days, cascade models and such like are still in operation in schools. Seldom are they evaluated six months later in practice observations.

After the feedback session, discussions ranged over a wider frame with the two deputies and the head teacher. They were worried that they had several teachers whose classroom discipline they were concerned about, as were the teachers themselves. The school had already spent considerable time and effort trying to help them. It was found that when the deputies went in, the role appeared to modify the situation and prevented them seeing as much as they might. Even so the strategies they suggested, the counselling and video review sessions, were not working in these specific cases to bring the teacher up to satisfactory performance.

It was at this point that the gauntlet was thrown down. It was basically – 'You are a teacher trainer, you are supposed to know how to train a teacher, sort this one out.' This was regardless of the fact that these were experienced teachers trained in other institutions and that the school had been supporting the teachers, often for more than six months.

Nevertheless the challenge was an interesting one and was picked up. The method the tutor used had never been written down in a formal way. Now this had to be done as part of the project if other people were to be enabled to learn how to use it. At the preliminary stage the deputies were invited to accompany the tutor to experience the method with some postgraduate students in training from a variety of colleges in the area while the procedure was formalised. Before this programme began, another secondary school close by also joined the project.

The notes for the sampling frame given above remain substantially unchanged from their first publication in the pilot project (Montgomery 1984). They are in continual use in consultancy appraisals and the most recent revalidation was undertaken in 1998–2001. The data from these studies was analysed in functional, qualitative and quantitative terms and these results are reported in the next chapter.

Appraisal: The ten point plan

From the original studies in the two pilot schools an appraisal plan was drawn up. This was then tested out and applied in the next stage. In 1985 a research assistant called Norma Hadfield was recruited to join the project for three years. Her role was to test the system out in a wider range of schools and do a comparative evaluation of it against other methods. Thus a number of other schools in the area, both primary and secondary, joined the project. The method had been developed and used in the full range of schools, from nursery classes to sixth form colleges. It was therefore transferable to each of these situations and could also be used across all curriculum subjects. Thus the user did not have to be a subject expert to appraise the lesson. Where there were content concerns, these could be discussed later with heads of department. In the case of students in training this was more often necessary than with teachers who were already trained. The appraiser should follow this protocol:

1. The teacher should voluntarily agree to be observed.
2. The appraisee selects a time and lesson which will show a typical performance unless otherwise agreed.
3. Observer and teacher must agree the focus, terms and nature of what is to be observed, in this case classroom management.
4. A complete lesson must be observed as though by the 'fly on the wall'.
5. The observer makes a continuous, timed, running record based on the agreed sampling frame.
6. Every record must begin with a positive statement and all 'negatives' should be couched in positive terms.
7. Immediately after the session both should retire to a quiet room for the feedback in a comfortable, relaxing setting.
8. The observer first asks the teacher how the session went. This permits tension release and to put right all the imagined wrongs.
9. The observer does not enter into discussion but next reads aloud the running record, stopping at intervals to give and receive comments, clarifications, develop suggestions and ideas.
10. At the end of this, two or three targets should be developed and agreed. These should be noted down and a copy of the whole document given to the teacher.

Both should feel satisfaction and that it has been a worthwhile and in-depth experience. At intervals news of developments can be exchanged in the more informal setting of the staffroom until the next observation. A review interview might be the appropriate follow-up in the next round.

NQTs and teachers experiencing difficulties will benefit from a second observation and feedback session. This should not occur before three weeks have elapsed for the consolidation of skills to take place but should be within six weeks so that improvements can be reinforced and consolidated. After this the teacher can be expected to go on developing the techniques. Opportunities to start again with a new class are also important so that the newly learned techniques can become part of the automatic response repertoire.

If there is no improvement at all, then a third observation session can be entered into. In this case it will probably be necessary for the observer to step out of role into that of trainer and coach during the lesson. This means that at critical points the teacher is drawn to one side so that whispered suggestions on monitoring and maintenance strategies can be made. On a few occasions it has been necessary to move round the class demonstrating the PCI strategy to show how it can calm and motivate the students.

The debriefing interview

It really is important for the debriefing interview to take place immediately after the observation session. Lessons, lunches and days should not be allowed to intervene. The reason for this is that the appraisee is in a most anxiety-inducing position which is not helpful, especially if improvement in performance is wanted. It is also important to make the feedback immediate if the nuances of performance are not to be lost.

Immediate feedback should be given despite the needs of the appraisee to think through their responses, or reflect on the experience to present some useful points. These can all be given later as afterthoughts and follow-ups. They can all too easily, if delayed, detract from the central issues in the frame and be distorted into personal hobby horses.

The setting

The setting for the debriefing should be a small comfortable room with coffee or tea available and an opportunity to eat sandwiches if necessary. Corridors, class-rooms and the staffroom are definitely unacceptable – we have tried them all. The setting needs to contribute to the relaxed and comfortable atmosphere and not destroy it.

There should be two armchairs with a space and an angle of about 30–45 degrees between them for the participants to relax into. A small coffee table should be placed in front. It should be possible to reach the cups on the table and for the appraiser to read the sheaf of notes forming the observation to the appraisee. The appraisee should also *be able to see the notes* and, if necessary at points, to read them as well. This is crucial as it sets the sharing tone and has a marked relaxing effect on the appraisee. Face-to-face positioning would be confrontational.

Beginnings

It is crucial at the outset for the appraiser's first statement to be to ask the teacher *how he or she felt about the lesson.* The reason for this is that during the lesson there may have been a series of things which concerned the teacher and this is the opportunity for them to get these off the chest.

While the situation does not worry some teachers, those who are more anxious may have a stream of concerns which they must pour out and things they feel they must put right first. Until they have done this, they cannot really hear anything that is being said to them.

It is then helpful for the appraiser to establish *how typical the session was.* As soon as this is done, it is useful to simply state what is going to happen next, e.g. 'I am simply going to read the record that I made to you and will stop at intervals so we can discuss or clarify points.'

Middles

This is then what happens. The running record is read to the appraisee. It is helpful if *times have been noted down* the side at intervals so that time spans of sections of the lesson can be looked at in the summing up stages if relevant or in relation to the Tactical Lesson Plan which is illustrated in Chapter 3.

Every record should start with a positive statement because this sets the emotional tone of what follows and because people can learn to grow better from their strengths. The record should be descriptive and specific. It should refer where necessary to things that can be changed. This can be in the form of asides, suggestions and questions, either written into the record if possible and if not raised in the debriefing.

If suggestions are offered, the appraisee should have options to try where possible, rather than just one thing that must be done. This gives more autonomy in selecting the courses of actions to apply. These can be monitored in the interim or checked up on in the next observation session.

During the reading of the record, it is possible to stop and discuss points, broadening the ideas and explanations. It is also possible to check the record, and to delete anything which is incorrect or not well articulated. Some events may be seen differently and such things can be negotiated and ideas shared as well as any suggestions made for intervention. The teacher may well know individuals in the class much better than the appraiser.

At suitable intervals in the record, the main points established should be summarised. The record can then be resumed. It should seek to affirm the strengths of the teacher and the interview may do more of this if it is too short in the record. At the same time there can be counselling and guidance, as in any helping interview.

Endings

When the final section of the record has been read then the two or three main targets need to be discussed. With teachers in difficulty the main targets will be CBG and the management and monitoring in the 3Ms. With successful teachers tactical planning and the higher ranges of PCI may be discussed. The teacher may have more ideas to improve the performance here than the appraiser.

Because teacher educators not only contribute to students' planning but also see such a wide range of lessons and classrooms, they usually have a rich repertoire of suggestions. Teachers who have only worked in a few schools and seen very few lessons and rarely those of other departments may be hard pressed to come up with ideas. It is in this respect that SENCOs are building up a wider repertoire as they do support teaching across the curriculum. Thus it is that interdepartmental observations are important in school development plans for building teaching and learning skills.

At the end of the feedback interview it is a good idea to summarise the main points again and to identify several areas and aspects which can be singled out for genuine praise for all appraisees. Those who find it hard to praise anyone should not be engaged for this work.

Feedback can say as much about the appraiser as the lesson and it is helpful for the question to be raised – 'How did you feel the appraisal went?' From this, even if the teacher is in difficulty there should be *very positive and satisfied feelings about the appraisal* itself. The teacher should feel helped and motivated, willing to try to gain mastery of the techniques and the situation.

Administration

When the interview is concluded the running record can be photocopied and the appraisee given a copy. The original should be kept for reference by the appraiser and should not be shared without the explicit agreement of the appraisee. The targets once negotiated and agreed need be the only paper item which is kept for the record.

In this way massive files do not need to be stored. In the second observation session it is possible to record which targets have been met and which need further work. The time span for this can then be indicated.

When capability procedures have to be entered into it is then possible to use an entirely different instrument which has a summative scale attached.

Summary and conclusions

This chapter has considered the nature of types of classroom observation which can be undertaken with some of the problems which are involved. The technique which it was found had most to recommend it was based on research in hundreds of classrooms was a naturalistic record involving rapid writing of factual events as they occurred.

In order to cut down the amount which needed to be written, a process sampling frame of three key types of classroom behaviours and one planning framework were identified. These were subsequently referred to as CBG; 3Ms; PCI; and TLP. Details were given of each. It had been found that it was these which had the potency to improve ITT students' performance. When used with experienced teachers in difficulties they were also able to benefit. The extent of their improvements and the work with other teachers will be discussed in Chapter 3.

Other wider frames of theory and research were consulted in support of this sampling frame, in particular behaviour management and learning theory. A theory of teaching was constructed and developed over the intervening years (Montgomery, 1981, 1983, 1990, 1996, 1999, 2000). Those relating to learning and teaching and frameworks will be explored in Chapters 4 and 5 in more detail.

Case Studies in Appraisal using the Formative System

Introduction

In the pilot study (Montgomery 1984) which represented the first use of the sampling frame and the observational method with qualified teachers, one of the first quantitative studies of performance enhancement was undertaken as well as qualitative appraisal based upon the sampling frame. The procedure was that after the first and second feedback sessions a summative criterion referenced rating system or checklist was also completed.

There were eight categories: Personal and Professional Qualities; Verbal and Non Verbal Skills; Planning and Preparation; Relationships with Pupils including Class Control and Organisation; Presentation of Material; Achievement by Pupils (differentiation); Recording and Evaluation; Pupils' Learning. These were based on the Kingston Polytechnic Criteria for School Experience designed by the School Experience Committee circa 1980 and trialled and validated over a number of years. Each category had four levels (0, 1, 2, and 3) assigned to it and was illustrated with several criterion references for each level. A 'Pupils' Learning' criterion had been added because the category Achievement by Pupils actually referred to differentiation provided by the teacher. For example:

Level 0: Does not provide sufficient material. Presents material which is unsuited to the attainment of the pupils. Uses material unselectively.
Level 1: Prescribes tasks which are generally appropriate for the rate of progression of the class. Allows sufficient time for them.
Level 2: Prescribes tasks which are adjusted to the range of performance among pupils in the class. Provides for feedback.
Level 3: Meets the needs of a mixed ability class.

When the teacher's level of performance was compared with the scale a level of functioning could be identified. It was therefore possible to obtain a summative score and a profile of a teacher's performance before and after the intervention based on this checklist. The total score which a good teacher could achieve was thus

24 points. Because a deputy head from the other school was also in the lesson there was the opportunity to look at inter-observer reliability in the use of the checklist. There was no training given on the use of the checklist although its concepts and use were discussed in some detail.

This summative checklist has now been redeveloped by Kingston University and cross-referenced with the TTA Standards for students in initial teacher education training. It is published annually for guidance for supervisors, schools, mentors and students. As the before and after data (repeated measures design) is very hard to come by in field research, the original criterion referenced summative scale is used in the subsequent researches during 1986–9 and 1998–2001. This ensures that the measurements are on the same basis and the small sample can be grown as each new opportunity for intervention comes along. The inter-observer reliability quotients were high, most assessments varying between 0.5 and 1 point, giving correlations of +0.95 and above.

What usually occurs is that training days and sessions are arranged for the school and then they like to pursue the practice themselves. However, some schools want to become more involved with the development and coaching skills which this system entails and then request demonstration classroom observations with feedback for selected members of staff. These members of staff then do the follow-up session so there is consequently no guarantee that the procedure has been followed or that the feedback was appropriate. They are also reluctant to share their recordings. Thus this specialised research data comes in slowly, especially when there is no funding to back it and as appraisal moves on and off the schools agenda.

The summative results from the programme

Table 3.1 Results of the research programme

a. Unsuccessful teachers

Subjects	Before	After	Subject	Difference B from A
A.D.	9.0	16.7	19.0	7.7
B.G.	7.25	10.25	16.0	2.25
C.S.	4.75	11.5	19.0	6.75
D.F.	9.2	13.05	15.0	5.8
E.A.	5.0	9.5	12.0	4.5
F.J.	8.0	12.0	14.0	4.0
G.P.	4.0	17.0	8.0	13.0
H.S.	5.0	13.0	12.0	7.0
B.N.	12.0	17.0	16.0	5.0
N = 9 Means:	7.13	13.33	14.55	+ 6.22 (Signif. 0.01)

b. Successful teachers

Subjects	Before	After	Subject	Difference B from A
L.S.	20.0	23.0	21.0	3.0
M.T.	17.0	21.0	19.0	4.0
P.S.	24.0	24.0	20.0	0.0
L.T.	19.0	23.0	20.0	4.0
D.P.	24.0	24.0	24.0	0.0
C.P.	17.0	20.0	19.0	4.0
D.S.	24.0	24.0	23.0	0.0
N = 7	20.71	22.71	20.85	2.14

The mean performance of the failing group was 7.13 before intervention and 13.33 afterwards. The difference between these sets of scores was significant at the 0.01 level of confidence. As can be seen, there is considerable variation between the original scores from a base of 4 out of 24 to what is a marginally poor performance at a score of 12. In relation to the successful teachers the pre- and post-test results are not significant and this is accounted for by the fact that we were looking at some excellent teaching and the instrument was not sensitive at this end of the scale. In fact any instrument that I have looked at would put D.P. and the other two top scorers as ace on any scale. However, what she and the others were intrigued by (and many were very experienced teachers) was how their excellence and their success was constructed. They had never had this revealed to them before and were not only pleased with the result of the observation but delighted with a self improvement and continuing professional development strategy which they now knew how to share with others.

In addition to this form of quantitative analysis it was also possible to quantify item improvements in relation to the sampling frame recorded in the pre- and post-records. This enables the summative scale to be used to give feedback on performance. Of course what it could not do was to improve that performance.

The observers and the teachers in the pilot study also recorded their summative assessments of the pre- and post-intervention lessons. This evaluation showed that before the intervention one teacher was in serious difficulties across the board, the other three were having some serious problems particularly with discipline. After the intervention it was recorded that each teacher was seen to have made a significant amount of improvement. All their performances had improved to a basic satisfactory level. Several years later all were functioning satisfactorily. The NQT had passed the probationary year comfortably and the one with the most serious difficulties had become the school's 'star' teacher. In the case of the art teacher who made improvement but only to a marginal satisfactory level, it was necessary to return for a third and fourth visit to give coaching on the job in the classroom. His performance then did rise above a score of 12 and was maintained so that capability procedures did not have to be entered into.

The inter-observer reliability was very high in the use of the checklist – 98.4 per cent in the Before condition and 95 per cent in the After condition. The teachers (subject) in each case rated themselves considerably higher than the observers. This is not untypical and their misperceptions are contributing factors to their problems.

In the next phase of the research (Montgomery 1988, 1990; Montgomery and Hadfield 1989, 1990) a range of primary and secondary schools were recruited to take part in the three-year research programme. It had already been shown that other appraisers could be trained to use the system and that this was most effectively done with at least one practice demonstration. The new researcher went through a similar training programme and also had supervised practice.

The programme was set up to produce public verifiable evidence of the improvements in performance which can be achieved by the system through videotaping of lessons and pre- and post-feedback interviews. The feedback was frequently given without the video as this was not found to be necessary to the method. The tapes were also made so that data mining could be undertaken as well and so that they could be used in training sessions. In this research programme a range of local schools were invited to participate and although the schools through the heads were volunteers, most of the subjects had not volunteered. The input was used as additional support to the schools' system of appraisal and this time dealt mainly with successful teachers and NQTs.

In one series of evaluations, experienced teachers on inservice training courses were shown unedited extracts of the before and after lessons and were asked to judge in which extract the teacher had been more effective. The order of presentation was varied. In 99.5 per cent of cases they were correctly able to identify which was the more successful lesson and this correlated precisely with the second lesson after the appraisal feedback (Montgomery and Hadfield 1989).

In a separate study Hadfield (unpublished questionnaire returns, part of the research project, Montgomery and Hadfield 1989) also looked at the relative effectiveness of the sampling frame method compared with the use of checklists and personal construct strategies as feedback in obtaining improvement. Controls in this field work were difficult to achieve. It was not as in the perfect laboratory design. However, it was shown that the sampling frame method was significantly more effective than the other two methods in producing positive improvements in teaching performance. In relation to the other two there was also a general 'feel good factor' in operation as they were both positive methods in their approach, but there was no detectable change or improvement in teaching performance.

It became clear during the research that as in all consultancy there needs to be a necessary element of teaching (Dare 1982) if change for the better in performance is to be achieved. The extent to which a consultant has the necessary developmental teaching skills therefore becomes crucial. This is no doubt why many teachers engaged in appraisal have difficulty in carrying it through as they do not have mastery of the disciplines which contribute to and underpin teaching and learning, nor the breadth of experience in classrooms. Specific curriculum subject knowledge is necessary for being a subject adviser but is not sufficient for the role of appraiser. In this particular method there is a significant amount of 'coaching' involved in relation to teaching and learning and thus the relevant frameworks for this is spelled out in the next two chapters.

One of the deputy heads (James 1984/1989) in the pilot study went on to become an advisory teacher with responsibility for probationers in the LEA secondary schools. The work involved disseminating information and setting up training groups for deputy heads who were in most cases the probationers' mentors. She decided to compare the probationers' feelings about the methods of appraisal which they had experienced. There were two types. The appraisal and feedback given by the LEA inspectors and the appraisal and feedback given by the researcher trained in the method discussed here using the sampling frame. There were considerable differences between the two experiences, not all of which could be ascribed to fear and anxiety induced by the title of 'inspector'.

In the sampling frame method the probationers valued being made to feel relaxed and at ease; the classroom observation was felt to be supportive and unobtrusive; there was a general feeling that the experience was positive and helpful; they welcomed the detailed observation and the time given to offering specific feedback.

In relation to the appraisal visits of the inspectorate the probationers felt nervous, uneasy, on edge, apprehensive and uncomfortable about being observed by the inspector. Some probationers had found it difficult to manage an inspector's visit, particularly when the inspector interrupted or wanted to take over the lesson, arrived unannounced, or after 10–15 minutes wanted to discuss the lesson there and then. Some were disappointed with the negative feedback or, in other cases, no feedback at all.

When the probationers were asked what they had learned from these experiences of classroom observation, it was found that from the researcher/adviser they had an awareness that they were doing well and of the skills they were using; they learned of the importance of developing positive relationships with pupils; and they achieved an understanding of the importance of positively reinforcing pupils' work and behaviour. They also had a greater awareness of classroom management strategies.

In relation to the visits of the inspectorate, 50 of the 78 probationers felt they had not learned anything as little or no feedback was given. Those who had learned something now displayed more pupils' work; tried to be more effective in the use of the voice; and had developed some classroom management strategies.

Inspectors were obviously on a tight schedule and unable to give time to this work among other priorities. In the event it may well have been sensible to have relinquished this work to several trained specialist advisers. The inspectors had themselves been the recipients of a three-day LEA training course on appraisal. The feedback from OFSTED inspections is similar. Because they give no feedback to the individual teacher after the session, little respect is afforded to the outcome, especially if the observation has only lasted ten minutes, as has been frequently reported to me by teachers.

Difficult cases

There are a tiny minority of cases in which a teacher is in serious difficulties and finds it extraordinarily difficult to change their habitual behaviours. Most teachers will have relapses, of course. But in these particular cases where they have been given the feedback on the first and then the second lesson with the three-week interval or more in between, only a tiny amount of progress is seen. It is episodic as suddenly they remember to CBG or use the quiet naming and monitoring techniques. One male teacher was actually drawn out of the Art room cupboard for the whole lesson by use of the system. Another actually came out from behind the wall of books which he had erected, much to the surprise of the head who was using the system but did not believe that it could work, having tried many other strategies.

With the agreement of the teacher, a further stage of intervention can be engaged in based on the system. At no point must the observer take over the lesson but instead at appropriate points can draw the teacher to one side and murmur strategies in the ear so that the teacher can move off and implement them and then come back and discuss and be CBG'd.

To this procedure can be added a further exercise in modelling and reinforcement. The observer accompanied by the teacher moves round and does small demonstrations of CBG, Monitoring or PCI and then follows as the teacher goes off and does likewise. Each time the teacher successfully uses the technique the coach is there to murmur praise. The pupils must not become aware of any of this – only that there are two teachers working in the room.

Once the habit barrier has been broken and the pupils start responding well, they give the teachers the feedback that is necessary to encourage them to keep going and keep working on their technique. Monitoring progress should then be enough to keep them going until the next classroom observation cycle.

The system of classroom observation is thus process based, a naturalistic observation system using a running record which samples specified behaviours in a sampling frame. The feedback is a readback session of the record with shared dialogue on the text, the issues and events. Here there is a problem-solving-based approach, including teaching and coaching as necessary, especially where improvement has been hard to achieve.

Two examples of postgraduate appraisal records

The reason for including these will show the difference in the records that sometimes have to be made for students in training. There is a far greater element of teaching that needs to go on especially in relation to the subject content. This is of course not entirely surprising although these are graduates who have completed a degree programme. There is always a mismatch between the degree coverage and the pupils' needs in the school curriculum.

Mrs G.   A Staines Secondary School
Biology with 4th Year/Year 10   (Mixed class of 23 pupils)

Topic: The structure and function of the kidney

1.30 Good, when we arrived you had a nice working atmosphere and reasonable noise level.

Large room always poses problems for projection of voice especially science laboratories.

Notes on board – did you consider and reject giving them the first word cues for them to write the rest in their own words? Might have been useful to use as a check immediately afterwards to confirm they had grasped the essentials. Of course they do like to copy, it's comforting to have the correct answers straight away but it lacks the cognitive thrust (i.e. Piaget's accommodation is not likely to occur).

Good, nice clear instructions but when you give them make sure that you have the attention of *all* the group, e.g. the table at front were quietly chatting still, with backs to you. Need to take account of this as a slight undermining of authority in insidious ways. Probably not important here – but it did mean you had to go back to two of them and get them to join the rest.

Some good phasing of the lesson, e.g.:
Introduction: Q/Ans, Recap.
Stage 1 Some copying (writing)
Stage 2 Practical work.

I wonder whether you might have been advised to give your instructions for the dissection for them to list first so that they could try to follow these. (Following written instructions quite difficult task.) As it is you are dissecting the kidney, issuing the instructions, and trying to control them – three things.

'Will you be quiet when I am talking!' This was issued loud and strong but in some desperation. It shows in your voice that you are somewhat under threat, they can sense it. I suggest that you think about saying things in a series, e.g.:

1. 'Listen when I am talking' (not 'will you' as if it is a question, rather than an instruction). Say it firmly but not pleadingly, then pause and say:
2. 'Listen Joanne'
3. 'Turn round Allison' [Pause]
4. 'Good, now . . . I want you to . . .'

When they moved the desks around it was an opportunity to create a row – try saying:
(a) 'Move the desks quietly.'

Drop your voice to give them the cue. Then you can say:
e.g. (b) 'John, I said quietly.'

Consider whether

(a) It is worthwhile not putting all the desks together have them gathering in groups round the tins with their written instructions which you can move round and monitor.

(b) You might put the desks together for the lesson before they come in.

In this instance (a) might have been the better bet as the dissection session was so short, i.e. 2 or 3 minutes.

Good – encouraging attention, now saying 'Come on'.

Good, you are ensuring that all are quiet and listening. I think that you could use some names – not, 'You three on the side', but, 'X turn round please for a minute'. Good try – useful effect.

When you say, 'I want you all to listen', you introduce a pleading note as though you are not absolutely convinced that you will succeed; e.g. you say 'List – ern' try 'List'n' all on one note.

One or two nice bits about 'kidneys and your tea' *nice smile*. Try to move round now that they are drawing and say something to each group, if possible each individual, but in particular find something *positive* to say, e.g. *Catch (them) Being Good*. A lot of your contribution while going round is *control statement* and *information* plus the odd *nag*.

e.g. 'If you can't see the board move closer' tone of voice is nag/control. It seems as though you are really implying – 'You ought to be able to see it if not you must do something you do not possibly want to do, move closer.'

To go back to the practical:

Are you a scientist?! How do scientists study, discover, investigate?

Don't they do dissections, experiments etc. and then very closely and in detail observe what they dissect. Is this not how discoveries are made. Part of teaching biology is teaching about scientific method as well, so this is best done by getting them to draw *what they have dissected*, don't allow them access to the books to copy yet. Make it an exciting voyage of discovery. When they have drawn what they see *then* let them check with the book – even let them score points for the observations correct, marking their own.

' *Will you* listen, you won't be able to answer the questions otherwise!'

' *Will you* list ern!' 'Yes' (pupil). You are back to this habit.

3Ms

While you are going round *maintenancing* – i.e. working with individuals – and *this is good*, it is keeping these more difficult girls at the back going, but the three boys in the middle have been switched off for 5 minutes or so.

2.25 Most of the class now sitting back relaxing because so much of your time is being devoted to the girls at the back. Move round faster. Boy with missing pencil, always have a spare, try not to get into a confrontation over something so small however irritating.

'Miss, I've done it!' 'Good, hold on.' Nice response. They like the attention you are giving them but again try to intersperse some smiles, some 'goods', some positive comment.

End of lesson, you are getting tired, don't weaken and talk over them.

The one or two little bits of baiting from the girls at the back you handled quite well, i.e. you did not get angry; you could also smile and say 'Concentrate' quite pleasantly.

Some general points (While you are clearing up)

1. Positive support, smiles – non verbal control, CBG.
2. 3Ms Management, *monitoring* and maintenance; do more monitoring.
3. Cognitive aspects – e.g. observation can contain cognitive challenge – in the exploration of the tubule bit, you may ask them to listen to your explanation and then get them to try to pick up the story of a molecule of urine round the class. You could also introduce a few bits about when things go wrong in kidneys and what is happening to them, e.g. 'why do people need transplants?' Morbid facts do tend to absorb them and help them remember even: e.g. why do some people persistently have to go to the loo; when should this be used as an indication of illness other than nerves, when should they check with the doctor? Types of urine test, diabetes insipidus, indications of liver and/or kidney failure in their pets etc. You could even get them to collect newspaper and magazine cuttings to stick in their exercise books. Such things will gain their interest and help them remember the more formal aspects of the lesson.

Summary

1. I think you have some good potential which it will take a little while for you to realise. If you could gain some more practice in easier control of your voice this would be very helpful under stressful conditions. It could involve simple things such as perhaps practising singing in the bath or round the house and then inventing and singing control statements such as you might use in the classroom. Practice in reading aloud will help phrasing and breath control. Also try sitting in front of a mirror and shouting at yourself practising vocal control techniques. If you have a friend who will help, sit opposite each other and speak crossly at each other in random numbers, e.g.:

   43, 52, 61, 98!
   1, 3, 7, 21, 9!
   32, 54, 9, 68, 31, 2, 49, 64, 68, 38!

2. Concentrate more on trying to put cognitive challenge into the lesson as indicated and giving more time to structured practical work. You were particularly successful when you did this.

Plan your lesson like a military strategy and do not talk too long Q/A e.g. Introduction to lesson . . . revision Q/A. Then:

Listening	Stage 1	Teacher information giving, story telling
Writing from head	Stage 2	Pupils writing main points
Talking	Stage 3	Check facts by pupils telling part of this round class
Writing from dictation	Stage 4	Dissection instruction, dictated
Practical	Stage 5	Practical work
Drawing	Stage 6	Pupils drawing dissection
Checking	Stage 7	Checking and marking drawing from text books or board
Listening Q/A	Conclusion	Revision of the main points, homework.

(The left hand column represents activity changes for the pupil phased throughout the lesson while the content remains the same. Be careful not to spend 25–35 minutes just in teacher talk at the beginning.)

3. Keep on moving around the class as much as you can to help and support individuals. Good effects when you do this.

Mr W.   PGCE Student   Guildford Secondary School
2nd year/Year 8 History   (Class of 30 mixed pupils)
Castles – Scottish History

11.00 Good, you lined them up outside insisting that they went in quietly. Good use of the pause and waiting for silence at the beginning. Good, you altered the strong voice and once it was quiet you dropped the pitch and spoke very quietly. Very effective use of contrasts. Well done.

After giving out the books which was done well, the 'Listen then please', 'Look this way without talking' very good effect. But if not entirely effective after two general statements use the names of one or two individuals. One boy two desks in front of me at the window was still 'refusing' to attend, i.e. by body attitude had shouted to you. Watch out for this – make eye contact and gesture him to turn round.

Good, nice smile, nice use of questioning.

Good, lots of reinforcement – e.g. you say 'Yes' and smile after their answers or you paraphrase them. Good techniques.

Nice use of voice and good tone making it interesting. Good, during introduction on Scotland used opportunities well to ask questions relating this to previous knowledge.

These pupils appear *very* well behaved, any little misdemeanours are quite subtle, e.g. flicking over pages of another's book, quiet asides, gazing out of windows.

Good use of the gurgles about the 'Wallace', nice smile, gentle humour, made pupil feel significant, and not put down, the others were being a bit derisory (e.g. his surname was Wallace too). I think that you could not always expect such a quiet and attentive audience, i.e. you have been story telling for ten minutes without interruptions from barracking, distractions, comment or question. Unusual these days. It used to be typical of the old Grammar school settings 20 years ago. I expect you realise this.

By the way, did you know that the girl Michelle whom you asked to read it was able to do so reasonably or was prepared to? Such a request can send some pupils into paroxysms of fear and make a slight difficulty in reading become magnified so that others deride and ridicule.

There is now perfect silence and all the pupils are concentrating in some good measure. Not entirely due to intrinsic interest in content or your control I think. Our presence, the school and environmental ethos. Do you know which? How far is this typical of them and other classes?

Good, while Michelle was reading you were looking up and watching out for any potential difficulties; it is at these points with difficult classes that you need to use the eye contact and gesture to exert class control. So keep this up. Not always necessary to say anything in these circumstances, if absolutely necessary use pupil's name without interrupting the child reading.

Good, you handled the question about the stone very well and admitted you did not know, maybe you could go a step further and say, 'But I/we shall try to find out'?

11.25 *Cognitive Challenge and Relevance*

I should like you to consider the notion of cognitive challenge and the principle of Accommodation (Piaget). You are achieving this in some degree by asking questions which require inference, i.e. 'What is the meaning of the "Hammer of the Scots"?', and use of past knowledge in the current context. But so far by 11.25 the course of the lesson is:

Introduction and setting 5 mins Q/Ans

Stage 1	10 mins. Story telling some Q/Ans, i.e. information feeding
Stage 2	10 mins. Story reading – some of same information being told plus a few Q/Ans
Stage 3	Drawing of map/tracing of map, i.e. visual information, telling reinforced through drawing and writing
Stage 4	Completion of worksheets with questions about foregoing so that what has been done is reinforced.

What I think you might at first find unpalatable is that this could be seen as a memory training/rote learning activity, At least consider this for if it is so then if you apply this technique to another class when you are in a different school, in perhaps a less motivated setting, you may find the pupils see no relevance in this task – i.e. Why should this knowledge about old men in Scotland be of use or interest to them? Why should they bother to read about it when it is more interesting to talk about last night's aggro or create some by poking the pupils in front? Even more so, why on earth should they write it all down when it is already neatly written in the book?

11.32 After several minutes at the front with one boy you went back to the same boy twice. Good, now you are beginning to move around. Your remonstrance at the front for them all to be quiet, 'Noise level too high!' was effective, they are back again on the right level. There are other ways which you should consider to achieve the same effect when this does not work:

Consider during each lesson – try to move round and have a few words with every individual child about his/her work, try to be as supportive as you can and find things in *every pupil's work to praise.* For some children a whole day can go by without anyone saying a word to them except in anger or correction. The more difficult the pupils the more *absolutely essential* this is. It helps enhance self esteem and increases motivation on these tasks which pupils may perceive as not really relevant.

11.40 40 minutes into the lesson; they are getting a little tired. Good, you have stopped and given them a bit of a rest, i.e. an activity change – 'Stop, put pencils down' and very nicely made sure that they all did, this small detail is crucial and is contributing to your success with this group for even they would begin to misbehave a little if you did not quietly insist. *Very good technique.*

11.45 Some of them are getting quietly restless. Your tennis quip gave a few more the idea to watch too. From where they were sitting I don't think those boys could see the tennis through the curtain. In another class this could have caused an uproar of accusations and denials. Try to be accurate and very fair.

Going back to cognitive challenge:

A 1. The Scotland bit and the death of Alexander. Given the setting that they know about, you have choices.
    (a) to tell them what happened
Cognitive challenge:
    (b) to get them first to hypothesise what might happen in this situation. Then tell them what did.
2. Maid of Norway bit:
    (a) to tell them about her and what happened
Cognitive challenge:
    (b) to tell them about her and let them hypothesise what happened then tell them the story
3. Relevance: Are there comparable references you can make to similar situations today – parallels drawn etc.?

B The map work

11.46 Children like to copy and colour in maps; it makes them think they are learning something, it looks nice and it allows chat. But consider what they have really learned.

Cognitive challenge: Could they, before they look at the map, rough out what they think Scotland looks like and where they think these things happened? Fascinating results when they draw the original, they will have the incentive to observe in more detail the proximities and contours.

On the subject of contours and distance this kind of map drawing from the text book gives very little concept of space and place. Why were there places where there were, the battles fought there and not here? etc.

When you try to *make them hypothesise* and predict you are helping them bring their own prior knowledge and experience to the learning and then when they observe differences between their own knowledge and the information presented they will be able to adapt to this new information more readily and extend their knowledge hierarchies or schemata.

12.05 Good revision session at end.

12.10 The settling at end precarious indicating that some of the above will be applicable.

Summary

This was a good lesson, well-structured, prepared and presented.

You have a nice style, firm but kindly. You explained that you made efforts earlier in the term to make quite sure that they listened as a class even if initially you spent more time on this than on teaching. This proves to have been worthwhile and successful. Now you need to concentrate upon motivating them so that they want to learn because it is interesting and challenging. Consider for the future when you are not in such a sheltered environment:

1. Relevance perceived and felt – motivation to learn.
2. Cognitive challenge.
3. More use of non verbal control techniques will be needed.
4. More use of smiling and personal positive comment will be needed e.g. CBG, Catch them Being Good.

DANGER AREA. About 50–50 control and information questions used, only some positively praised or supported.

Summary from the two PGCE records

From these two early demonstration records it can be seen that the technique is still evolving. There is a large element of teaching in both in relation to PCI. In the first record the class is an older one and has within it a number of difficult pupils who would stretch most teacher's management skills. The student here has a particular disadvantage in that her voice, even under mild duress, becomes high pitched. She has great difficulty in controlling it. This is the first time we had met her but it was apparent instantly and the pupils tended to play on the fact. It was important to help her with voice control as in the notes at the end but without continually referring to it in the record.

The second lesson was to some extent a model lesson. Control skills were good. However, when the situation was probed below the superficial level, it was found that not enough was being learned by the student in such a well-controlled environment. The CBG levels were not high enough to ensure a positive classroom ethos and there was a lack of PCI. There was thus the danger that this student could be given a good pass in this situation only to find that in the next there were serious difficulties.

As each were training observations for the deputy heads it was important to raise all these questions in the one session. It was in the first session that the other observer developed 'role conflict' and wanted to sort out those difficult and cheeky girls instead of behaving as the 'fly on the wall'.

Two examples of primary school records

Miss M. (2 years' experience)   Nursery class in Infant School Approx. 30 children   2 nursery helpers, several parents

Good, the activities taking place were nicely varied:

1. 3 children drawing with crayons – one a house, one a 'lickel girl', one writes name and letters preparatory to drawing.
2. Jigsaw table large wooden pieces, 6 upwards, range of inserts for increasing sized cats, teddy, bus. Good, increasing in difficulty and different concepts. Nursery Assistant also engaged in questioning.
3. Matching cards to template – 6 pieces, four sets.
4. Number table – numbers in series 1–5; Nursery Assistant and 1 child – matching. 3 X shapes sets of jigsaws. 1–5 shapes. Could be helpful to reinforce number 'names' as placed on prongs rather than just shape words, e.g. NA may need guidance here.
5. Sticklebrick table – 3 boys doing construction work. Lorries and carts.
6. Simple 2 piece jigsaws – mixed number, 1 cow, 2 cats, 3 kangaroos.
7. Pastry table.
8. Paint table.
9. Floor/carpet wooden trucks and cars.

Story: Rosie the Hen

This was read by the new Nursery Assistant (her first day). She did well, good questioning, good use of voice and gesture. Children engrossed. Accepts their comments very well and uses them to keep their interest. Reinforces number work – how many . . . Reinforces the naming very well, encourages joining in. Is going to read another short story – children very pleased.

The children demonstrate well a number of interesting features about your teaching. They are socially skilled for their age, they do not shout each other or the adult down. They are sitting quietly and not interfering with each other in spiteful or disruptive ways. They have obviously already learned the classroom rules and roles ready for their move up into the reception class next term.

During the part of the session before the story the room was well laid out and there was a very busy working atmosphere. All the children were engaged in constructive activity except perhaps there was one with a tendency to wander although I did not have time to check this out.

A useful range of play apparatus outside. All well in use. I think I might have one more large box out for them to sit inside and perhaps occasionally a very low narrow balance apparatus. All the apparatus was being well used by both boys and girls except the trolleys, trikes/scooters – I think I should keep an eye on this for possible sex role reinforcement and positively encourage the girls to use them. It may just, on the other hand be a feature of this particular session.

One little girl in pink still on the rocket.

Do you sometimes engage in structured play over and around the apparatus or use the opportunity to engage in developmental work in relation to individual needs in terms of spatial/body concepts? Have you any children who are developmentally clumsy? It could be helpful if you keep records on this aspect, e.g. balance on one foot then other (for 5 sec). Climbing up steps alternating feet (central apparatus). Descending steps one by one (the wooden steps here). Height – some often seen to jump from heights with ease and good balance; balance on low rail.

10.28 One girl has now taken over a scooter and a boy is on the rocket giving it what for. Another girl has to hand over a trike. Interesting pattern – boys first, girls later when boys are fed up with these items. Another girl has taken over a scooter and another boy the rocket. At the slide you are now keeping an eye on them and making sure they go feet first and don't crowd on the steps. The slide always needs watching – well done.

Good, you are engaging in a little bit of language work here and at the centre of the apparatus.

Very little imaginative play going on around the apparatus – some in/on the box near the door – plus a territorial disagreement. You might encourage the imaginative play by suggesting one or two ideas when the occasion arises or join in if appropriate. Very good, you found the girl in pink on a trike and were very encouraging, she did seem to find it a bit tricky to get started but she is going very well now.

10.40 Out here the children are very talkative to each other. Some interesting imaginative play about being on the bus, over by the wooden steps and boxes. In the classroom they seem to be less so.

Good, you are doing some language work on the seat with the small group. They seem quite shy of a strange adult. Less talkative than one might expect. Is this typical of what you find and is it related to the area and home training?

What would you say was the emphasis of your college training?

Good, little bit of language work with the three boys at the water table. You have a nice manner with them, a pleasing style.

Although you felt very distressed by the difficulties and pressures of having new children, potential runaways etc. none of this was apparent in the calm of the lesson and the way in which the children behaved. They were a credit to you all.

Mrs D. (30 years' experience) Infant School
Class of 6–7-year-olds (Year 1) 26 children

1.40 Good, when we arrived there was a very nice steady working atmosphere.

1. A table flow painting
2. A number card table doing addition with a range of different levels of card
   e.g. 3 and _____ = 8 1 + 1 =
3. A weighing table with a large work card on an easel
4. A writing table
5. A flash card game on butterflies which you were winning.

1.52 Several of the groups – especially number and weighing – are becoming a bit noisy. You notice the change in noise level and speak to two different children by name across the room. As you pack up the flash card game 7 or 8 children come over for special help.

Prior to this a nice little teach-in with a girl J on 4 + 0 (sweets in hands). Good, changed to counters from the abstract to the concrete – immediately she was able to do it. Might be a strategy for her to use for a little while (i.e. separate hands). I worked through the first sum with her, e.g. collect 4 add 1 to them and count them all up. She could only do it while I 'programmed' her behaviour. As soon as I stopped she 'forgot' and came to you.

1.55 Quick threat to L – 'Do you want to be moved!' Another threat to a boy across room. You help with the weighing and get them going again.

2.00 Offer help to boy with writing. Then to girl, 'Oh Lisa, that's not a very long story. I am sure you can write a much longer one, a big girl like you.'

2.02 'Simon, are you doing your work?' Helping boy in grey write his sentence prompting. Now positively reinforce one pupil with 'Good'. V is having a bit of difficulty with the words he is copying. L sent round the corner to be quiet. 'Excuse me young man, I thought I told you to take your work . . .' 'I am tired of you running around!' Helping weighing table children again. Good, you are moving round. You say 'Ssssh, don't shout!' But this itself was rather loud.

2.05 'Boys! What are you doing? Will you get on please!' . . . Several just standing by the four girls with the sticklebricks. You are now sitting at a table helping with number work and look across, *monitoring*, to another table and say 'Ssssh', quietly. Well done – this was much more effective than previously.

Good, two positive comments in quick succession to two different pupils who have come to you. (Children now around you needing help.)

On the carpet beside you one of the boys has done a brilliantly imaginative construction (Barry). The Tate Gallery would pay money for something like that! I wonder what he has in mind – it's not buildings, it is abstract form. I think he is not too talkative. J who kicked it may have done so on purpose(?). Maybe because I commented on it to B in a positive way? I thought you handled the little scenario very well, making him apologise and assuming it was not a quick 'nasty'. Very good strategy.

Wall display. This is interesting and well mounted and very well set out. Not crowded. Do you put up their writing and number work too? e.g. writing when they first started or at the beginning of the term and then now (their latest best)? Can do this for a few at a time.

Now writing a whole word in a pupil's spelling book for writing story. Do you sometimes ask them to guess the first sound to start?

Nice little bit of questioning over the tulip and what was missed at the centre. Another bit of praise to child. Good, the effect of this ripples out over others. Very nice handling of L. Instead of a quick nag you helped him find the crayon and settle down again. Nice with Daniel, 'You weren't being silly, were you.' I liked your polite manner. 'Excuse me, A,' 'I am sorry I am in your way, darling.'

You are working very hard. Good, now questioning Helen about what she has made – her blue construction. Good bit of imaginative play with Tracy, e.g. sandwiches and tea without sugar.

Lisa – a lovely little session when you read her writing back to her. You have a lovely smile. You should use it more often, the children respond so well. You are just beginning to relax? Pleased with another child's work, keep working on the positives – CBG.

Nice session of imaginative play going on in the home corner with the telephones. They are a lively class, very forthcoming. Nice open manner with visitors.

2.30 Tidying up. Getting under way very slowly. L and J made to stand with noses to wall for being silly – but they have thereby avoided having to do any tidying up. L is addressing you in a very loud voice. You don't want to speak to him. You might try saying you will speak with him when he stops 'shouting' at you. Tidying up still going on, other children milling about. The sand timer is out, the five minute gong goes. You are still working hard. You very loudly say, 'Are we all quiet?'!

Nursery rhymes on the mat. Good idea just to hold the hand of Daniel to calm him down, 'You've been a silly boy. You can go and say you are sorry.'

'Are you ready? Is everyone lining up?' Again you don't sound as relaxed as you might be. You are still looking very worried. You could try the, 'Show me who's ready' routine.

Summary

Thank you for letting us observe this session. It was a very busy one, lots of different levels of cognitive activity were catered for as well as individual children's needs in other ways, e.g. emotional and supportive. You did well to provide for and teach on all these different fronts. I think that it was setting a high standard for yourself, e.g. six cognitive challenges to maintain is at the limit of our human span of attention. Be a little kinder to yourself and settle for four or five!!

I felt throughout the session as I said that you were under strain and having to assert control more strongly than I would expect in voice and manner. After talking with you I can see why this was. You had your class back after a term in which they had someone else who was inexperienced and not used to English primary method. They seemed to me (the class) as though this was your first week with them under your regime and I was puzzled that your control cues and calls were not well responded to but had to be demanded or emphasised. But of course it was in effect your first week with them. I should like to come again as we discussed and see them as you would have them. I am sorry that you were also feeling unwell with a headache, this obviously added to the pressure and made you look worried and sad some of the time.

When you *'caught them being good'* and when you smiled and praised and cheered them on even the naughty ones began to behave. So it was all there.

You have a lively class and more than one or two awkward characters but I enjoyed the session and all the children seemed to learn something and progress in the tasks set. I will try to find some materials for you that relate to the handwriting learning difficulties we also discussed in relation to the children's written work. I suggested that cursive writing might be looked at as a development in school policy to overcome a wide range of such needs.

Summary of the two primary school reports

These two reports were compiled in the initial phases of the funded research project while the researcher was being trained in the sampling frame method. It also took place during the period of 'Teacher Action' by agreement of the school staffs concerned.

Both reports were just one of a series in which the whole staff had agreed to participate in the project as part of inservice development and school development planning. They have been selected here because the records illustrate that there are aspects of the teaching which can be developed in the presence of satisfactory classroom control.

For example, in the first record there were two related issues. These were that there appeared to be a need for more development work and training to be done with the Nursery Assistants. Perhaps a more assertive role in leadership of the team from the teacher needed to be developed.

The question about the teacher's initial training was to flag a need for information gathering on the style of this. There was a clear policy in operation in the classroom on language development arising from the activities on which the children were engaged. There were some directed activities such as story, number and literacy in which all children were encouraged to participate but there seems to be a need to do more exploration of cognitive challenge across the full range of the curriculum and perhaps a more systematic approach to encouraging imaginative and fantasy play. This did not seem to come naturally to the children and perhaps reflected wider issues typical of the local area and parents' attitudes and experience.

In the second example we can see a highly experienced teacher finding herself under some duress, possibly unnecessarily, and perhaps an over strong response to this. The emphasis was therefore on describing the terms of the interactions and illustrating the positive effects on the pupils, even the 'awkward' ones, of much lower key interventions. Sometimes teachers are completely unaware of the very strong and positive effects of a smile and a mild word or two of praise. In this case the differences of the effects on the children were very marked indeed.

Two examples of pre- and post-intervention records from a Secondary School

---

Mrs D.   Newly Qualified Teacher
(3rd year/Year 9)   Longman's French   (Mixed class 30 pupils)
FIRST VISIT   November

(The CBG, 3Ms and PCI notes had been sent in advance of the visit.)

Good, you worked hard at the beginning to get them to concentrate and listen. Good, you've just got them completely quiet and switched on.

Well done, you achieved this by calling individuals by name. 3Ms strategy.

Extract on tape

Followed by questions. I liked the way when the girl gave her answer you said, 'Good, you have got the meaning.'

I wonder whether it would be a good idea to play the tape twice to really help them clue in before asking too many questions. I do not think they were well orientated. I had problems first thing on Monday getting into the French pronunciation. Good asides, e.g. 'Louise, your scarf.'

'Karen, are you ready?'

'Anthony . . .?'

Nice smile at 'Superman outfit' and you said 'I don't think so.'

'Just be quiet please', followed by naming, 'Louise', good technique. 'Will you *put your hand up.*' Do not say this unless you mean to observe the rule yourself. When a pupil puts his/her hand up you did respond but then you accepted called out answers.

'Look at your text again now please . . . Simon. Good.'

They have settled down to the written work and you are working very well moving round helping and involving them.

3Ms needed (Monitoring phase).

11.10. Good, by your detailed help you have managed to get them all to do some work. Keep your eyes lifting to monitor and settle those who are not. Settle them by gaze or gesture before you go to help them. Two boys to my right not doing anything.

11.13 Very good, they are nearly all except these two quite settled. Good you have arrived at them and now they have started – within 5 seconds of you turning your back they are not working again. Watch them more carefully – they respond to control by eye contact.

Good, you are working very well on an individual basis. I think I might intersperse the lesson with a little more contrast such as this:
e.g. Tactical planning
some listening/oral work
some writing
some more oral; work or Q/A
some more writing.

Some reflections – I hope not against policy!

I do not think I should be so quick to translate the French into English. When they are misbehaving or talking ask them a question about the work in hand. If they cannot answer move on and ask someone else.

You are working very hard but over their basic mumble noise. Our presence is probably preventing you from relaxing and taking some of this more slowly.

I do not feel you have explored the tape as much as you might have done. You might have found it more advantageous to read it yourself more slowly. I found it a bit quick – probably because I was writing at the same time as listening.

Might they have taken the parts of Yves M. Lagard or Danielle (p. 30 Longman's Stage A 3 Audio Visual French) – or is that for later?

In Summary

Despite all this you could at any time you really exerted your will obtain their attention. They were obliging and obviously were not resentful or alienated, showing you are capable of developing a good working relationship with them and it showed at intervals throughout.

I think the key factors were:

(a) getting the best tactical phasing of the lesson with activity change for them
    1. listening
    2. writing
    3. checking Q/A
    4. oral work
    5. writing
    6. reading out etc.

Then 'tuning' to extend sections that are going well and:

(b) concentrating more on the monitoring phase of 3Ms and making sure to use the 5 second check back to make eye contact or gesture to maintain the on-target behaviour.

You have a nice way with this group, just emphasise your own good points and with practice I think you will do very well.

Mrs D.   French
(4th Year/Year 10)
SECOND VISIT   February

9.30 Good, nice working atmosphere when we came in. Tape playing – good you stopped the tape to quietly tell several of them to put pens down and listen while following the pictures:

The questions, e.g. 'What are they doing first of all?'
                        'Shaving first of all?'
                        'Brushing their teeth?'

Good:
1. You ask questions and repeat their answers briefly.
2. You ask questions and say 'Right' when they give the correct answers.
3. Now also try to nod 'Yes' and *smile* when you accept an answer.
4. Try to say 'Good' more often – you do it just occasionally. It plus the smiles will enhance your interaction and the quality of it for the pupil.

9.40 Some good questioning. Have you tried using this as a control device? e.g. asking a pupil who is day-dreaming or not responding. There are a number sitting at the back.

Tape section lasted 10 minutes.

Good, you have introduced a different activity over 'mine and yours'. I think I might have acted the sequence and then got them to try to construct the response rather than telling them at the outset.

(Is it useful sometimes when talking about a word used, e.g. 'secours' to compare it with an English word which perhaps (?) comes from the same root? e.g. succour. It helps me remember such a word. It is an especially important word to remember; we may all need it.)

Good, you spent just about the right time on the practice of 'mine and yours' – should it have been written down on the board, there seemed to be about 50 per cent mishearings, e.g. 'bien'.

9.45 *Activity change*, good. They now have to write the grammar in their books. Good very clear board work, very well written and laid out.

9.50 Continuation with writing now to do an exercise.

Did you notice the disruption which can ensue at the activity change border? You handled it very well. I think if you used the 3Ms strategy it would go even more smoothly, e.g. 1. General remonstrance, then 2. Individuals by name.

When you do use a pupil's name, e.g. Andrea and she says 'Ay?' don't let her get away with this, she did it deliberately, rudely or provocatively, you could say something like – 'No, Andrea not "AY", in French you say "eh"' and smile at her. You can add 'Or even better you could say "Pardon".' Just judge how far you can push this to make your point.

10.00 '*Alan*, will you settle down please?' Good use of hard sound of name to draw attention and then quiet question.

Very good work now while you are going round helping. I think you need to go to those three boys at the back especially as they are talking loudly and for the second time you have had to call to Alan. Good, you are there now and already the noise has dropped. The others use their noise (that group) as a kind of barometer.

10.02 Good general finishing noise now and you have stopped them very well insisting quite quietly that they sit, pens down and listen. *Very well done.* This was excellent.

You did this again excellently after the Routiere dispute conversation. You surprise me by talking quite a lot in English and using the English version of their names. The odd 'Ecoutez' would help begin to build their vocabulary until perhaps a fair amount of instruction could be in French.

10.07 Quick outline of what is going on in the cartoon. Could any of them be persuaded to read the bits aloud?

10.08 Very good use of 3Ms, e.g. 'Er!' Attention gaining noise.
'Alan.' Quiet naming.
'Who is talking about . . . in the picture?'

Very good strategy, you deflected his attention to the exercise by asking a question about the work after getting his attention – and all the others became quiet. *Very well done.*

I think I might have followed this up by going to the back where they are and settling them down to write something. They are now sitting back again and yarning quietly about something else. You need to try to cut down their off target activity, they have got into bad habits. They need to build up an expectancy that after any instruction to write etc., you will follow up and check.

10.12 Good, you are there now doing this, try to close the gap between the *setting and the checking* with this group. Two of them have continued working, it is the boy in the middle who continuously distracts them – viz. Alan.

I wonder if since there was a a dispute in France over the lorries etc. that you should spend a few minutes with each class you meet on the news? A few pictures of lorries, vans and scenes from the newspapers and Sunday supplements might provoke some discussions in French at the level of their vocabulary/grammar. It might encourage a few to keep a folder of what goes on. Enrichment activity?

Much more confident approach to all the work. Class control strategies are developing well. Good preparation evident. Now concentrate on smiling as non verbal feedback and they will become more responsive and relaxed about their attempts.

I might, (a) put the key words on the board and get them to guess/hypothesise
             the meaning
        (b) establish general concept of what the tape is about.

Good you are waiting for quiet – got it again.

Do you think some or all of your simple questions should be in French? Is there a policy on language and/or comprehension?

10.17 'Read through quietly please.'

About 50 per cent of the pupils were not reading it through.

10.20 Writing vocabulary in vocabulary books. They are very responsive to you when you say, 'Listen please', they do – it takes a little time. You can afford to be more confident.

You have a very nice manner with them, one which does not set their backs up. Work away at this.

Good use of long 'gaze', i.e. use of eye contact to gain attention.

Vocabulary work. I think I might put the French on the board and get them to guess?analyse the meaning (PCI).

e.g. de bonne heure; douche; raser; -ment.

10.25 Good – you have dealt well with Jason, e.g.

1. 'Jason!' – he ignores you.
2. 'Jason!' – he looks at you.
3. 'Jason, turn round' – he moves round and looks at book.

Now while you dealt effectively with him you did not spend/waste time on him so the rest knew that your eye was upon them.

Good – use of gesture with Joanne, and then, 'Joanne turn *right* round.' Must follow with the second look to check to see if she has.

I think I should get them to list the verbs for themselves first then check (PCI). Good – 'Some people are being very rude and talking at the same time' – 'Shaun.' Long pause for looking round and ensuring they are quiet. Good. *Very well done.*

You lose it again on the questioning allowing the loudest to win.

Good, you ignored the loud cough (bark) noise – Anthony? Now he is attention seeking and banging the desk and turning round. He is very attention seeking, seems to have some personal problems. You could ask him a question and use it as a control device at times – gives him the attention he requires in the way *you* desire.

As the girl said, 'I can't be bothered to write the details.' They need to feel more motivated by being required to respond at a more adult level. It is a difficult balance to achieve but you are obviously making progress. We need to discuss this aspect further.

10.35 A little ragged in the activity change from finishing writing to sitting ready to go. Keep working at this.

Well done.

In Summary

3Ms: You have made great strides in your ability to control the class and so you now have a good opportunity to teach them something.

Tactical Planning: This was good you phased the lesson well with activity changes just at the right moment. You timed this well.

CBG: You engaged in a good amount of this and it helped motivate and interest them.

PCI: I think that this is the aspect which you can now afford to concentrate on.

1. Your questioning reflects this well with both closed and open questions in appropriate amounts on introduction to the lesson but,
2. I think you could work to get more from them arising from the practical work both in verbal and written form. You could expect much more from them in this respect.
3. Begin to extend your work, for mixed ability teaching the more able need greater intellectual stimulation as we discussed.

First comments recorded by Mrs D after the first French lesson

I was given a copy of the note a day or two before this lesson. I thought they looked helpful and I tried them out next day on my 4th year. I did CBG. I went round each one and if they had only scribbled half a sentence I took an interest in the idea and said something good about it. They were a bit surprised and looked at me strangely but they really did work hard. Their attitude was completely different it was a really good lesson. I really enjoyed it. I was using CBG again today when I was going round individually, it really does work. By the time I got round they were all quiet and working except those last two. I shall practise monitoring and check back next time as well.

Mrs D's comments and reflections after the second visit

In my first year of teaching it was with relief, but some trepidation, that I accepted the challenge of being observed in a lesson; relief because I had reached the point where I was grateful for anyone who could point me in the right direction, and trepidation, because someone would actually see how difficult I was finding it to control and teach a class of often hostile adolescents.

A couple of days before the observation I saw some notes which explained about the 3Ms – so much of this was immediately applicable, and in the light of recent experience made a lot of sense.

The debriefing was painful in many ways – having one's weaknesses exposed always is – but it was also a welcome experience because I understood many things that I had not previously realised, or that I had realised but had not been able to express coherently or identify.

The fact that the various aspects of the lesson were talked about and discussed in such a constructive and professional way made me feel much more objective, not just about that lesson, but also all the lessons subsequent to it. I started to practise the various techniques suggested, and made a conscious effort to be less 'apologetic' in the classroom, in my instructions to the pupils, and in my general manner and bearing. The comments made about the lesson were always made in such a way that one could only be encouraged by them.

Time had passed between the first session and the second, and had inevitably made my task somewhat easier – the pupils knew me, and I them, I was no longer an unknown quantity, and therefore a threat to them. The second observation was easier than the first; I knew what to expect and was eager to learn more about how to teach effectively. I was not disappointed, the debriefing session revealed parts of my teaching, my manner and reactions to the pupils, that had improved, and, as before, identified those areas which I could greatly improve upon.

Again, the comments made were either about things which I had not realised at all, or about things that I had not completely sorted out for myself, e.g. how to react in different situations that arise in the classroom. There were also the valuable professional and personal aspects to the observation, not only ideas about how to improve the content and method of my teaching but also how to make all of that more effective, e.g. by smiling or nodding at appropriate times, and generally how to relate better to the pupils.

The observations and debriefing sessions were not simply beneficial because of what happened on those days and the constructive and immensely practical nature of what was discussed, but also because they have put me in a frame of mind that is more objective and analytical – now I feel more able and better equipped, to stand back from a lesson and see just how much I am achieving through it, how much the pupils are actually learning and by what means or methods, and lastly how I can improve upon that.

Observation of the first debriefing session with Mrs D by the head of department

I was not, myself, present during the lesson. I was only able to attend the discussion session following.

It was apparent from the comments made that there were many positive indications of excellent preparation for the lesson done by Mrs D.

She had many of the natural attributes needed by a good classroom teacher and was learning rapidly to structure her lesson in such a way that allowed her to deal with a difficult class in an effective manner. A 'teacher's eye' was becoming evident.

Points to be careful about included:

1. Teaching over children's talking, mumbling and chatter must not happen.
2. 'Calling out' by children in response to questions must be dealt with effectively, immediately and consistently.
3. Getting quiet in a classroom must not involve the teacher 'pleading', it must be a direct request.
4. Worksheets provided a useful change of activity but careful monitoring is needed to ensure full use, by all the class, is made of them.
5. Getting a class to 'listen' *again* is very difficult – but was handled competently.

Apart from a general inclination to do too much work herself and not get the pupils to do it for themselves, the signs were very encouraging. Mrs D herself said she was beginning to gain confidence.

Comment: This was an unsolicited report of the feedback session and illustrates in several ways why Mrs D needed to be included in the project. She was certainly having difficulties but the feedback she was getting was of the 'points to correct' variety and so she did not know what to do to turn things round and was progressively sinking into despair and further difficulties.

Even so there is some attempt by the writer to begin with some positives before the list, perhaps given the nature of the project.

One of the major difficulties in this form of classroom observation is to produce a running record which is positive but which does describe the problem areas. The second major problem is to read the running record and to put in the suggestions and critical points in a positive and acceptable way.

In a recent training session for appraiser heads of department it was difficult for many to find a positive or neutral way of expressing problem points and for a few to insert question and analysis because they simply praised everything somewhat indiscriminately.

Mr C.   Science   (3rd Year/Year 9)   (12 pupils)
FIRST VISIT   November

Good, nice working attitude. Good use of quiet voice, it is keeping their noise down. One or two pupils on your right hand side seem to be getting more than their fair share of attention.

Good, you are looking at the two girls opposite for a response. One of them gives it to you but you have looked away. I think you could try distributing more of your questions to specific pupils – used as a means of control it is also effective.

The three girls opposite and the four boys are not joining in enough. Could try specifically asking them by name if you think they can respond and then work at getting the others to have the kindness to be quiet and listen while each of the others is talking – setting them slightly against each other to help you. They are tending to talk over you and each other, especially the boy with the loud voice to your right – the blonde one in particular.

They need to learn to have respect for each other's viewpoints and contributions – if they all talk at once only the loudest one has any chance of being heard. The boy opposite is responding quite well occasionally – you could support his responses more with a nod or smile or just saying 'good'.

Good. You have just done that and got a slight 'ripple' effect, i.e. the boy next to him also responded well the next time round and the one the other side began to concentrate.

I think that one of the things which is most interesting is that when you change the pitch of your voice occasionally or when you harden the tone, you gain their attention. Your continued use of soft voice tends to lose their concentration. Practise variation.

The blonde haired girl has given up and is obviously dozing – seeking your attention. She tried several times earlier in the lesson to give you answers and suggestions. On the whole, you accepted answers from other pupils and she gave up. Try to be more responsive in a small way by listening to her responses and saying' Yes' and 'Good' or 'What do you think?' Initially the attention needs to be quite subtle otherwise she will react against and perhaps be silly, but she definitely is trying to work for you.

Tactics

For this particular group who seem to have such poor self images from their comments at the beginning, i.e. 'We don't know any science.' 'We're no good at it.' 'It's no use listening to us' etc., specific tactics can help them become more confident and less disorganised . . . (See lesson plan tactics – no time to note them.)

Their responses are disorganised, and immature, and if you are not selective in relation to those you are listening to you encourage more unwanted responses. i.e. you tend to respond to those who shout loudest first. You also give a reply or comment to *every* statement, whether it is relevant to the task or not. Ignore some of the irrelevant asides and concentrate on the central issues.

Good, you hardened your voice and for a while they all concentrated. Thus it is still possible for you to bring them together to listen and work.

'If people will listen!' 'Julie!' 'You are the ones who said you wanted to go through it . . .' A pleading sound. This was not so effective in gaining attention, they responded better when you said: 'Listen! Look at Q6, Julia.' Thus it is better and more effective to deliver a short reprimand or reminder than long ones pleading or nagging.

'David, can you just try and be quiet for a minute? . . . round your head . . .'

Could not hear all this but constituted another desist response which was lengthy and negotiational, whereas short sharp instructions worked better. The 'round your head' bit seemed like an attempt to joke, best not to mix them.

Your relaxed style is good but it is acting against you – you pick up and respond to their asides when most often you should ignore them. I think you are also working too hard and doing *too much of the talking*. You seem to be doing almost all the talking and all the continuity lines as well. Your technique seems to be to catch them off target as well as CBG. Giving so much attention to their off target behaviours is making them engage in more and more off target attention seeking behaviour.

They need some help to learn to be less babyish. They are like five-year-olds with all their pointing and giggling and calling out. I think it would help them if you could decrease this. You seem by the way you respond to be not exactly encouraging it but at least maintaining the level. The effect in the end of all this is to inculcate them with the law of the jungle, 'might is right' and he who shouts loudest gets all the attention and interest.

To go back to tactics

I think your plan to go over the paper for the first ten minutes was a good one but in practice what happened was that it took 20 minutes till 12.15 p.m.

I think that it might have increased the pace of this part of the lesson if you had allowed them to read out their answer or say what the correct one was, gradually working round the group, so that every pupil had a chance to respond. While this is happening the other 'loud mouths' need to be told quite curtly to be quiet and listen to other people.

12.27 p.m. – 12 minutes looking at the pictures of the foetus, skin etc. and discussing them with considerable effort. I think you could have stood with the visual aids and ranged the pupils around a table with the table between you and them, they would have got a better view and you would be able to respond more formally to them. Sitting shoulder to shoulder with you encouraged their tendency to be over familiar . . . rather than just friendly and sociable. Their sexual innuendoes and blatant comments would then not so readily have reached you.

It is interesting that Vicki and the blonde haired boy both want to sit beside you. They actually want your support and approval but it might help you if you distance yourself from him in particular and from the group a little.

There have been some good patches but I do not think that you should have to fight against their noise all the time. It is very wearing for you and not helpful for them.

Tactical Planning

Your tactics:

11.55 – 12.15 Pupils listening, looking and answering about exam paper.
12.15 – 12.27 Pupils listening, looking and answering questions about picture.
12.27 – 12.35 Return to places and write something – maintaining their bodies.

e.g. *30 minutes mainly Q/A, 7 mins writing*

1. Could have speeded up the exam question section 11.55 – 12.05.
   (Good – very good use of voice, clear instructions, '3 minutes to write about Body Maintenance' – Then you said . . . 'You are not helping, X' – negative aside led you into difficulty. Again negotiated rather more than you needed. Glad you kept firm and insisted he moved. All would be lost if you made a threat you did not carry out.)
2. Discussion of the pictures interested them, seating needed to be different as indicated. Discussion and pictures seemed to be less integrated with the task which followed.
3. Writing activity. This was a good idea and went quite well, I think the clues you gave them could have been points which you worked out with them on the board then they would have a structure to write to.

You are reverting to Q/A mode again, where you are doing all the work and taking all the flak.

Lesson balance could have been:

1. 11.55 – 12.05 Examination Q/A.
2. 12.05 – 12.15 Pictures + board work for structure Q/A.
3. 12.15 – 12.30 Personal report writing with you going round and helping.
4. 12.30 – 12.35 Read out own work.

(When they shout out at you, get them to repeat it quietly and don't let others talk over them. This is probably the key and needs to be slowly achieved.)

Good, now you are standing, not responding to any of their calling out and it is diminishing. I don't think they know what you mean or how to 'Look through the book.' They also need to know why they should look through it. They see it as a pointless exercise which is undemanding.

'Do you think I can have your attention now?' less effective than, 'Chris, I want your attention now.'

Immediately you have a pause get in and give them some short verbal explanations to get them interested, e.g. 'Look at page _' etc.

PCI

You could get them to survey the book and make a list of topics/units to be covered. They need more structure to help them do things, and opportunities for responding in legitimate ways.

e.g. 'looking through book' a little too open ended for them and seemed trivial. Try: 'Look through and list the main units.'

'This is a survey skill which is useful for getting a quick structure and overall knowledge.'

They need you to explain these things and show them HOW to do it first. Again it would give them a structure for learning and orientate their thoughts. It also offers them a more obvious cognitive challenge.

In Summary

1. Try to discriminate more carefully among their responses and use CBG. Use it more evenly to all pupils.
2. Try to give them more structure for their responding and enable them to perceive the cognitive challenge.
3. Work on tactical lesson planning in relation to the pupil's task at each stage.

Mr C. Science (Making paper)
(4th year/Year 10 pupils)
SECOND VISIT

11.50 Good, you settled them down well at the outset – very well done. You moved David quietly and with no 'aggro'.

Good, you had an outline on the board to remind them of last time's work. Very good questioning going on now about this on short and long fibre. Good use of names quietly to control. Very good use of non verbal gestures to control individuals. Very good, e.g. 'Let us go back to David's point.' Makes them feel confident and that they have something significant to contribute.

Good use of smiles in response to some of their responses, nice especially when you did not put down the girl who had written 'white paper'.

Good also when you accepted 'grass' mishearing when the boy said 'rice' – I thought that was an excellent sequence. They just began to take advantage after that because they had enjoyed that and you very cleverly immediately asked them to write it down.

I like immensely the courtesy with which you treat them, e.g. 'Shall we write that down, Sir?' 'Yes please, David.'

While they are writing the outline from the board there is little noise, just the odd comment.

Very good barometer of control. You are giving out the copy worksheets and so all are organised for the next bit.

Very good work all the way up to this point. In fact *excellent*. Good, now you are going round settling them as individuals are writing and commenting on their progress.

12.00 Very good sequence in this first ten minutes, you have also kept a good distance from them when teaching the class group. This has given you more power and influence.

12.02 Now they are beginning to become a bit restless. Try to shorten the irrelevant bits of explanation, e.g. about the different books. They now want an activity change and are all set up to start the experiment.

I think I would have let them get straight on, e.g. this would have tested their ability to follow instructions or recipes. This accounts for their restlessness.

I think I would have wanted the challenge if I had been them – the scientific investigator approach. I might have resented being babied or read to at this point. I know some will probably have problems in reading but their partner can help them out. I think that two learning styles might emerge:

1. Those who will follow/check the instructions rigourously.
2. Those who will try to remember what you said and glance at the picture to remind them.

Very good idea to make notes on their scientific approach. This was obviously highly motivating. You could add, 'The task at the end is to see which pair can make the best paper to write on.'

I think that when one group is calling to another I might just turn and make eye contact to quieten them.

12.15 Nice busy working atmosphere. You could stand back a bit and look on now, let them get to it.

Good bit of positive verbal reinforcement to Chris(?). You could distribute a few more 'Goods' and 'yesses' around when questioning them, e.g. stand back as you did and nod, say 'yes' or 'good' very briefly as you direct the questioning.

Good, you made eye contact with one of the pupils who raised his voice – it immediately stopped him. *Very Good*, try to do more of this to keep the working noise at a gentle level.

(I found it amusing when you said earlier 'squash the pulp first' that at least three boys immediately responded by banging the table like five-year-olds in Piaget's preoperational stage might.)

Again a boy was loudly calling 'Graham', this time you ignored it and the noise level began to increase. Just try to remember the 3Ms *monitoring*.

12.20 Most of the groups have finished. What indeed are we going to do now? I think that I would now take away all the worksheets and ask them to write or draw their recipe with exact instructions. Then read out some to see if the stages have been missed or if their work is better than in the book. Good, you have set them to answer questions 5 and 6 and put away the apparatus. Are they going to stick the instructions in their books? If so my suggestion is unnecessary unless you want them to remember structure and sequence for later. Maybe a good idea sometimes as an alternative.

12.28 Most of them have settled down to writing. Two or three still pounding their cotton wool.

12.32 Answering qs 5 and 6 did seem a bit small a task for 12 minutes, most wrote one line on each.

I think that your decision to go over these answers resulted in the fact that some waited for this and wrote down what you said, the others did not seem to find this significantly challenging. I think I would have invented three more questions and given them 3 marks for each and gone round and marked them after setting the next exercise. Then I could have called in the marks at the end or taken them down later which would have concentrated their minds more on their own performance and accuracy levels.

I think you are doing well with the 3Ms now.

You have structured the lesson tactically to obtain activity changes at the right moments.

The practical work is an interesting and useful activity. The only thing which I now have some reserve about is the cognitive challenge. You seem to be responding to them as though they were a younger class expecting less from them than you might be able to get.

Extract from Mr C.'s reflections on the classroom observations

After the lessons – in the discussions after the lessons – it emerged that these points needed a good deal of attention on my part:

1. Organisation
   - planning use of board/books/apparatus
   - time spent on each part of the lesson
   - where I put myself
   - where I put the kids
   - class dynamics – what the kids were doing and with whom.

2. Control
    – setting careful limits on kids' behaviour
    – not getting too familiar
    – keeping interest up
    – using question/answer sessions effectively
    – different ways of getting kids to do what they need to do
    – the use of goals to maintain steady work from the kids.

3. Behaviour modification
    – the effect of ignoring behaviour
    – the effect of positive reinforcement
    – setting realistic goals
    – using different methods of changing behaviour.

Since the first discussion with D and A, when it was painfully obvious that these points needed attention, I have been doing just that, not only in lessons with the observed class, but others too. I think that these visits and discussions have been beneficial to me . . .

Evaluation of the 'Process Strategy' (Pre- and Post-lesson observation) from Miss A., Design and Technology Teacher (Year 10 and Year 9)

'My first visit from DM was in the summer term. The class to be visited had caused me some considerable problems with difficult noisy class disturbance, requiring a great deal of effort and struggle for control in all lessons. I agreed to the experiment, as I felt it would give me guidance, but more important the experience would help me sort out my teaching pattern and analyse the difficulties I was having.

'Although nervous at the prospect of being monitored, as a probationary teacher the days of tutors at the back of the class, rapidly scratching pen on paper, with raised eyebrows and knowing looks, had not been all that long ago so the situation would not be that unknown.

'However, what a different story it was. Diane appeared to blend into the background. Although I was conscious of visitors, there was no atmosphere of tension and being watched, it was just a lesson as normal. Of course there was a slight feeling of nervousness, but mine was more due to the fact that I felt this was a difficult class. My result? I was strained, lacking in confidence and asking the impossible! My class as aforementioned were highly strung and noise had been the main problem. What I had failed to realise was it was noise related to work! Due to these problems, I stood at the front of the class, never smiling, unrelaxed and blasting rather frequently with an overpowering voice.

'At the end of the lesson the debriefing was constructive and helpful. The lesson was written in depth and discussed in detail to each moment. It was amazing how you yourself can see where your high and low notes are and what can be done: 1. Concentrate on 3Ms. 2. Learn to relax. 3. Try not to shout, or rather control noise level. The second visit was in November, and by this time I had acquired a little more self confidence. I knew the pupils' names, etc. but was still a little unsure of how my teaching management would be.

'The group was a third year Art class, I was going to attempt a lesson on face construction, a topic I had never attempted to teach before, and in fact had never drawn before, but I thought it would be a good topic to cover.

'The group was of mixed ability as before, with some keen and enthusiastic pupils and a sprinkling of the highly strung. This time I was not at all nervous, but interested in the outcome. I had not consciously made any effort in changing my teaching, so what would be the outcome? The lesson went well, although the demonstration was rather long. The debriefing was interesting. I was slightly perturbed at my sense of humour brought into the class situation and probably curbed it more than usual. However, I discovered that this can be accepted and a useful tool in the right situation. The analysis still showed the need to concentrate on the monitoring and maintenancing of the pupils, which I am still working on improving.

'On the whole, I found the experience valuable, I found the information interesting and useful, and it helped me a great deal during the period of the first meeting and to the present time. Of course I still slip and 'screech' occasionally during lessons, or fail to respond to the 3Ms but the experience has taught me to analyse these lessons and to recognise where these weaknesses lie.'

This then was what Miss A. had to say. The final comments in the observation notes made on Miss A.'s lesson were:

In Summary

A good lesson. Objectives well achieved. Good PCI, good CBG, some maintenancing.

Concentrate on: 1. Activity change *monitoring*
2. Maintenancing – individual support.

It was such a vast advance upon the first session, you must have felt it too.

Congratulations and keep up the good work.

An example of a pre- and post-intervention from a Primary School

Mrs N.
(7-year-olds/Year 2)   (Mixed class, 19 pupils)

This classroom observation was the result of a special request for help and advice from a teacher who knew of the work of the project. The first visit took place in the last week of November and could not be followed by another after a three-week interval because of the Christmas preparations and the work schedule of the tutor. However, it was agreed that a fortnight later on the same day and at the same time the researcher would return alone and video record the session again and give the debriefing. The tutor would then view the video and send notes and suggestions which might be helpful.

Mrs N. had been working with older pupils for several years until this point. Because there were a number of pupils with problems in the class she had found it difficult to get them to come and sit down on the mat to listen to story or introductions to lessons although she really wanted to do this. She had been forced into the strategy of spreading the pupils around the large room and keeping them in their places but this was not an easy setting in which to teach and she wanted more intimate and informal sessions with the pupils close around her. The pupils, however, spent all their time on the mat annoying and interfering with each other and making a noise. The pupils were known to be drawn from a difficult local area with many deprivations.

As well as all this, there was pressure from the school to improve the situation but it was felt that nothing constructive had been done to help with this. This was the context in which the following record was made. The researcher arrived before the class assembled and set up the video to take in a wide-ranging view of the room and remained at the instrument to refocus if necessary. The register and so on were taken with the video present but not running so that the pupils would become used to the visitor and the recording.

Subject: History – Royal Family (Children all sitting at their desks)

9.29 Good, when I came in the children were listening very quietly. They were responding well to your questions. Good, you asked them by name to answer questions.

9.32 Their concentration is going and they are all talking to each other about what is going on. You have written a lot on the board; I wonder if they find this difficult as you switch your attention from them to it. As the board becomes fuller they may be finding it progressively more confusing, hence lack of attention.

9.33 Your first 'good' is followed by 'yes, well done'. This created a listening effect in the rest of the class. When one or two of them shout to each other, try asking the noisiest one a question. It helps them concentrate – can also just frown and ask someone who is quiet a question and explain why.

9.35 Sharpened your voice and said, 'Now, listen, I am going to give you some pictures to look at . . .' Very good, you ask Alan and Katy to fetch the pictures for their table. Good, you have enough for each table.

9.37 Having given them out you are moving round the tables. Have become stuck at the back talking to the girl who came in late (you dealt very kindly and well with her – well done) while boy at front table is calling, 'Look, look everyone!' I think when you hear this you should look and frown and do one of the monitoring strategies. As you move quickly round each group try to settle them; start by keeping them talking only to their group. You are back at the front and have missed the two front groups. The children are now moving to the different groups to look at the other pictures and talk – their decision.

9.40 A number of them start to follow you, this is a good sign that they want to talk to you but not helpful in your organisation. They need some very gentle soothing and calming. I think this is one thing which you might like to work on.

9.41 Some of them are still looking interested but . . . 'Now, class 7 will you go back to your places. Sarah, put your chair leg down. Now I want somebody from each group to say which picture you have seen. A spokesman for each group . . .'

This is a good idea. I think you needed to give an inkling of this before they started looking at the pictures so that you could direct or focus their attention, e.g. 'Look through you pictures and choose one. Then I am going to ask each one of you (as there are not too many of them) to tell us about one picture.' They must do it without looking at the picture. (The rest of the children on the table might also have to guess which one they are talking about.) This was a good try at language experience work.

9.46 Sharp voice, 'Now, put your pictures in a nice tidy pile on your table.' Follow this up by saying such things as, 'Show me who's ready,' or 'Very good, Lisa's table are ready, look at them; so quiet and smart.' Give them models to follow.

Monitor gives out the books quite nicely – you could make sure he knows you are pleased with him. These children need a lot of support for good behaviour so they know what is acceptable.

Copying the notes from the board on the Royal Family will keep them quietish and it practises handwriting. What you need to consider is to what extent it 'engages their brains'. Why not follow the line you first started? Good, you use the copy writing quickly to stop the attention seeking behaviour.

Tactical Lesson Plan

Be brave! Try:

- Talking about the Royal Family with group (class).
- Looking at pictures individually.
- Short 20-second talks on one picture of choice. Use a timer – they like this kind of challenge, each stand up and speak to the group. The very shyest need not be made to but allowed to when they become confident. Lots of praise and encouragement to the rest even if they do not complete the presentation and fill the time, praise for good ideas, funny talk, good vocabulary, fluent speech etc.
- Asking pupils to write down what they said about their picture and stick the picture in their books, e.g. they could pretend to be a TV broadcaster describing the snapshot to the viewers. If you do something like this next year you could in the meantime tape an extract from the radio and show how they conjure up the scene in words for the audience. This type of work could be repeated with different ideas and the pictures can be passed round for them to decide if the description is a good one. They can also project what will happen next in the sequence.

(10.00 Children busy copying from the board, it certainly keeps them quiet.)

- Those pupils who cannot write from inside their own heads can tell you what they want to say and you can write it for them, leaving key gaps so that they have to think to try to fill them in (e.g. study skill – deletion exercise).

10.04 Good, those who have finished copying are now filling in the family tree of the Royal Family. On questioning you will find that they fill it in by using the initial letter cues, not knowledge or understanding, e.g. Pr . . . C . . . unmistakable. They then look for these letters in the work they have copied and copy them from their history books onto the paper without necessarily understanding the construction and nature of the family tree. They are not necessarily using initial sounds to get the words either. It is a good idea but I think you are assuming too much prior knowledge – they mainly use an infill strategy without understanding. One or two of the more able ones might understand. Good, I noted you change to this because the children were restless and had to be given something to do.

- If you really wanted to check their understanding, as a game ask them to draw their own family (or the Royal Family) tree as a test. If they cannot do this then you need to consider how you would teach it. One way might be to start with your own family tree and show parents, siblings and children. Let them try and write theirs. One way which is easier than a family tree is the family circle, e.g. this leaves out sibs but enables you to draw the tree from it and extend it to put in the relevant information.

I know that you may need to be careful about their missing bits of tree but there are ways of getting round this – inventing an absentee in your own tree – saying that such things do not matter, just leave a space . . . or let pairs work on the task for one of them, or you could let them choose a family from EastEnders etc. for a tree.

10.16 Clearing up. Why not have a lively one from each table tidy up rather than Lee, this will keep four or five of them occupied. Again, the 'show me who's ready' style will work. You did try a bit of it – 'Who's sitting up ready?' but you did not follow it up by saying, 'Good, look at . . .' 'Well done . . .' 'Perfect' etc. Try more praise for a task and on-target social behaviours to show them how you want them to behave. If you say 'don't' and 'stop' they do not know what to do next. You are very easily able to control them and also call them to attention, what you forget to do is to follow up and reinforce this, e.g. the monitoring and CBG.

Summary

Try to introduce more CBG for social as well as task objectives.

Remember to do monitoring from the 3Ms. You are good on 'management' and 'maintenance'.

> Try to introduce more PCI and engage brain tasks.
>
> You actually have a lot more control than you think you have, this will become apparent as you begin to follow the suggestions: particularly the Tactical Lesson Plan plus cognitive engage brain strategies. I will send you a draft of some typical Lesson Plans based on a revision of today's session and the various ways in which it might be followed up.

Mrs N. brief description of what was seen on the videotape two weeks later

The children are seen at their desks waiting silently. Mrs N. asks them very quietly to come and join her. They are to sit quietly on the mat. They do so except one and he is asked very quietly to 'Come and sit down by me'; he does so. The children wait expectantly all eyes on Mrs N. and she begins the introduction to the lesson about Christmas cards and how they might explain the meaning of Christmas to someone who did not know about it, citing the example of a pupil from Korea of several years ago. Good control strategies were in use, e.g. lots of CBG, calming gestures, questions asked instead of nagging, quiet naming, choosing one who is restless to do a task etc.

After the discussion the pupils are sent back to their places to do their writing. Key words are put on the board and Mrs N. goes round helping individuals to get started. The lesson proceeds throughout in an orderly fashion. The pupils are very quiet and calm. They quickly became absorbed in their writing which they were going to read out later and were looking forward to the Christmas cards they were going to make.

The scene has been totally transformed. Mrs N.'s crisis in confidence is over. She is in full control and lessons are no longer a battle. The difficult children are still there but all of them are getting more attention and praise and so are working for this.

If pupils can feel they are learning this also contributes to their confidence and esteem and helps them concentrate on learning. More attention to the work enables them to progress. Mrs N. kindly agrees for the videotapes to be used on the project training courses and books to help other teachers.

After the second video session the researcher interviewed Mrs N. She was asked: 'How have things been since we visited you the first time?' Her reply was: 'I think there has been an improvement. I've relaxed and I feel much better. I needed to have someone from outside whose opinion I trust to tell me I was coping so I can believe it. I heard Diane lecture several years ago, and I've heard her speak since, so I really value the effort and the interest. I had a wonderful letter from her, full of marvellous ideas, which I will use. They will make some super lessons. I'm really grateful.' In this record, it can be seen that time was spent on noting events as they happened in a factual way, especially the difficult episodes and interventions and then suggesting positive strategies which might be used instead. In addition where the strategies used were effective these were detailed to show that Mrs N. had all of them in her repertoire and when she used them systematically they worked. The good relationship she had with the pupils was emphasised, they wanted to work for her. If she could structure the learning experience in a tactical fashion she could get a better match to their needs. The result was she raised her praise, lowered her voice, engaged in tactical lesson planning and achieved the match. The pupils 'engaged brains' and together they created the busy hum of a learning environment.

A case example school

This particular school had operated an appraisal system as part of its school development plans. However, it was situated in a challenging catchment area and with an urgent need to raise standards across the board, and the strategies being used were not proving effective enough. It was decided to introduce the formative classroom observation strategy into the performance management system alongside the summative assessments which had to be made for threshold standards and surviving the next OFSTED inspection 18 months hence.

First the senior staff and middle managers were given training in the system to help enhance their observation and feedback skills. Then a few months later all the staff in the school received the same training so that they understood the system and were encouraged to team up and begin a programme of peer observation and feedback. This was followed by further training with senior staff on case work observations and feedback sessions. A whole range of teachers experienced this and shared in the feedback sessions. Some teachers needing extra support were included in this as were one or two in severe difficulties. As a result, one new teacher was encouraged to find a different profession and another on a temporary contract had this discontinued. It would have been possible to help these people, but it would have taken a considerable amount of time and expense. Much excellent teaching was seen and was affirmed and other performances were improved. The OFSTED inspection went very well and the school was complimented on its staff development scheme. This continues and a cycle of case work coaching has been established, with annual training inputs for new staff to keep up the momentum.

Summary and conclusions

These records have been selected from the development period of the Learning Difficulties Research Project (LDRP), Programme Four – The Evaluation and Enhancement of Teaching Performance. This is to protect the teachers from being identified. As can be inferred they are drawn from the period before the introduction of the NC. The records selected were from those in distinct difficulties or where some concerns had been raised. The improvements in each case were measurable after a period when there had been no improvement before the project interventions began. As can be seen it is difficult in field work to arrange for two observers, one of them a deputy head, to be at a school for a specific lesson and then repeat this with the same class a month or more later. In the main research study with the randomly assigned subjects this was only made possible by the recruitment of a research assistant.

These findings were also backed by studies with a range of satisfactory and good teachers in both primary and secondary schools with whom similar findings were obtained. There were improvements in general teaching performance in all of those who were not functioning at the highest level.

Those teachers who were already excellent found the process also extremely useful. First it affirmed in a constructive way that they were good teachers. It then explained to them why and how they were good, which none of them seemed to know.

It gave them a language about teaching and a set of analytic skills which they could share with colleagues and so help in their development. It is this common language which seems to have been lacking over several decades.

Norma Hadfield and Nerys James, researchers with the programme, went on to undertake posts with advisory responsibility for appraisal and staff development and are still using the methods detailed here.

With the advent of renewed interest in classroom observation and staff development, in these last three years a series of appraisals have been undertaken in primary and secondary schools for demonstration, school development and retrieval purposes. The method does still work and in the same ways for the same reasons.

It is interesting to note in reviewing all the records that it is the junior schools which are the most closed and unresponsive to new initiatives such as this. Not one junior school volunteered to join the project whereas many infant and nursery and secondary schools did. The method does work in junior schools too of course. This was verified with students on ITT courses over a number of years.

Despite its effectiveness, it is surprising that the method has not been widely adopted. Some of the reasons for this perhaps lie in the criticism once made of it that it seemed to be too 'feminine' a method for many males to adopt, i.e. because it was positive and constructive about another colleague's performance. The second reason is, no doubt, the problem of the investment of time. It takes at a minimum one and a half to two hours, depending on lesson length, for the observation and the feedback session. A review interview need only take about an hour, although the average has been found to be 30 minutes. This method requires the utmost concentration by the observer and very rapid writing at an average speed, where possible, of 40 words per minute. The observer needs training in coaching skills and needs to have a good grasp of the underlying theory and practice so that the suggestions made are constructive and have the power to work. However, the renewed interest and use of the method in this new phase within performance management has caused it to be accepted and adopted by male and female heads and staff of both secondary and primary schools with good effects.

Following on from the method of positive classroom observation, it seems that the crucial elements needed to support this is an analysis of relevant theory and practice of teaching and learning, especially in relation to PCI. In the next two chapters some consideration will be given to these topics under the headings of Effective Learning and Effective Teaching.

CHAPTER FOUR
Effective Learning

Introduction

The study of learning has had an intense and detailed history of theory and research, especially during the twentieth century. Yet it is only in the last two decades that the evidence from the various traditions and schools of psychology has been brought together to provide a more coherent account of what constitutes human learning, how it is acquired and what is needed to facilitate it. Despite this long history, theories of learning took little account of what went on in classrooms and had little impact upon the practice of teachers (Ausubel and Robinson 1969; Eisner 1983; Desforges 1998).

School learning has been based much more upon custom and practice in association with the needs of mass education (Resnick 1987) rather than upon the theory and practice of learning. Thus different traditions have grown which have not necessarily integrated theory and practice. Dichotomies in education, learning and teaching abound such as – progressive versus traditionalist teaching methods, formal versus informal methods, discovery learning versus directive teaching, behaviourism versus constructivism in learning and so on. In the specific area of teaching reading a long-standing dichotomy was meaning emphasis or 'look and say' versus code emphasis or phonics methods, when what was required was a judicious mix of both at appropriate stages plus other methods to support these basic strategies (Montgomery 1997a and b).

The theory and practice of learning and teaching have proved to be such complex areas that they have been difficult to integrate. In comparison, learning about a subject in order to prepare to teach it is relatively simple. Subject contents can be ordered, structured and defined for imparting to pupils as in the NC. The process by which we actually teach learners to learn is much more complex. It hinges upon many intangibles and depends upon the complexities of social contexts, social control, motivation and human interaction in changing environments where there are no longer the same sanctions and overt controls as in the past. Jackson's surveys of classrooms (1968) showed that teachers take part in

200–300 exchanges every hour of their working day. Many of these were about the control of behaviour and events rather than about teaching interactions (Southgate-Booth 1986). Bloom (1976) described it as teachers spending most of their time managing learners rather than managing learning. This was also noted in our case studies in classroom observation and is the reason for 3Ms and CBG being important parts of the sampling frame.

Learning is said to be any relatively permanent change in behaviour not due to drugs or fatigue (Hilgard and Bower 1981). This simple statement conceals how complex learning is. It is both a product, the memories, and the processes by which we commit things to memory. In contemporary studies of learning the most common approach is *schema theory and practice.* The schema is now used as the unit of analysis rather than simple stimuli and response connections. It is the mental representation of a person's organised experience and is specific to a setting or context. At the age of five years when children enter school they will have vast stores of schema representing all their experiences and knowledge up to that point. Learning in this context thus becomes a matter of growing or extending and modifying these schema.

To find if learning has taken place in schools it is traditional to use teacher assessments and attainment tests in reading and number. Now we also have national assessments called SATs (Standard Attainment Tasks) in mathematics, science and English at ages 7, 11 and 14 and of course public examinations such as GCSEs, GNVQs and A levels. It was envisaged that ten curriculum subjects would be assessed at each key stage but this burden of assessment proved too much and has been modified.

SATs and public examinations not only provide feedback for teachers to plan the curriculum but they also enable pupils, classes and schools to be compared. There are also hypothesised 'standards' against which these comparisons can be made. Standards are what pupils of a particular age and experience may be expected to attain. However, there are no absolutes or even research to show us what a distinct standard is – only historical and comparative profiles showing what some have achieved. What is not controlled are the methods by which these results have been obtained and what might have been obtained by other methods. In addition, what is set as a standard by comparison with other cultures and education systems is not necessarily what ought to be one.

Teachers need to assess pupils' work in an ongoing process so that they know how the work is going and whether it is of an appropriate standard so that it feeds back and feeds forward to both teachers and learners for the next part of the curriculum. What Savage and Desforges (1995) found, however, was that in busy classrooms teachers' capacity to assess work was limited and their assessments were often inadequate for work design.

Classroom observation shows that teachers move round the room monitoring pupils' work and spending time with difficult pupils or pupils with difficulties, ignoring the rest. They have not done the systematic and detailed PCI so they do not have a clear grasp of what the pupils are achieving. Even when the books come in for marking the distinction between class work and homework may not be clear and the marking may be cursory. The results of Bennett and Desforges (1984) can be seen often repeated throughout education – that 50 per cent of work set to high achievers in primary school was too easy and 50 per cent of the work set to low achievers was too difficult. The problem solving tasks set often failed to achieve their desired result because the pupils were already familiar with the concepts and the teachers failed to notice this.

When PCI is engaged in systematically during class time and is followed by detailed attention to marking and assessment of ongoing work, these issues can be identified and this illustrates why PCI does work and belongs in the sampling frame. It acts as both a reminder to check pupils' work and as a strategy for doing so.

Teachers themselves have been the subject of formal assessment over recent years through OFSTED inspections. These inspections which seek to determine the effectiveness of schools have, according to the NAHT (1999) survey, proved to be generally fairly conducted but because of the focus that they have on failure they failed to make any contribution to school improvement. It would be far more beneficial to have a system which focused upon strengths and motivated teachers to fulfil their professional duties rather than seeking to catch them out. To counteract such pressures, schools do need to have their own supportive professional system of appraisal and performance management. We learn more from having our strengths identified and we then know how to proceed. If our weaknesses are focused upon we only know what not to do and not how to put them right.

Assessment of school learning

Good examination results are used as a prime indicator in the evaluation of schools. However, these do not necessarily mark successful learning or teaching. The intake of some schools is such that if they do little or nothing in the way of promoting learning the pupils will still achieve good results. It is for this reason that the notion of 'value added' has been introduced to try to determine which schools are making a difference. This will still, however, be defined by what tests can measure rather than by what ought to be measured. It was more than 15 years, for example, before the real value of the Headstart Programme became apparent (Hohmann *et al.* 1979). The differences did not show in annual tests of basic skills and curriculum attainments but in success in life and careers after school.

In the year when there was a prolonged teacher dispute and strike, the pupils' national GCSE results in England and Wales continued an upward trend of improvement. Few people questioned whether the teachers were necessary or how the results had been achieved.

We need to question whether it really is reasonable to assess the success or otherwise of learning by a system of tests and examinations of school subject attainments. Indeed should the results of these tests permit access to higher education and training in the absence of other considerations such as independence and autonomy in learning abilities, study capabilities, communication, creative and cognitive abilities? Entwistle (1998) found a predictive correlation of 0.38 (14.44%) in pure sciences and 0.25 (6.25%) in social science between A level and final degree results using regression analysis. Personality was related to both study methods and degree performance. Motivation and study methods showed the highest correlation with degree performance. It was therefore concluded that variables that described behaviour and attitude within the academic curriculum context were likely to be better predictors of achievement. Could this also be true of pupils' performance in schools?

The achievements or results of school learning of our pupils is traditionally found to lag behind that of pupils in Germany and Japan and more recently behind that of other European and Far Eastern countries (Reynolds and Farrell 1996; Osborn 1997). These achievements are of course defined in terms of school curriculum subject content and skills. The researchers concluded that the 'successful' countries shared common characteristics. They valued education which is shown in the greater respect for and the status of the teacher. There was greater involvement and commitment from the pupils and the education and training system was not just for an elite. There was a greater stake in education and the workplace by the people and greater equality in literacy, skills and incomes in these countries than in the UK.

At face value this analysis seems to make sense. However, it is unlikely that there is such a direct and transparent explanation for these differences for there are other contextual differences and traditions which might equally explain what is being observed. In Germany, for example, there appears to be highly coercive system of didactics in operation which is punitively assessment driven and in the Far East the system of rote learning bodies of knowledge is much favoured. Content learning is the primary objective in these countries whereas in the UK the superordinate goal has been that pupils should be able to apply what they have learned to other situations and use the knowledge in some subjects to solve problems. These differences did in fact emerge in the third TIMSS study (TIMSS 1997). The results of 19 countries were compared and showed that English pupils had done relatively well in written science tests at 9 and 13. They were, however, below the international average in maths. In the TIMSS survey (1997) it was found that English pupils had done much better in applied maths and science. English pupils were among the best in the world at 13 in applying their maths and science to real world problems and were second overall only to Singapore. Edge and Stokes (1997) found that much of the poorer performance could be accounted for by the smaller amounts of time devoted by our pupils to their subjects and the fact that our pupils learn a broader curriculum within these subject disciplines. In other words, our pupils were not subject to a 'fair test' in scientific terms and the results were not correctly reported by the media. Yet our education system may well be changed on the basis of the misreporting of these results. The fact that there is pressure to change must result from either an incomplete analysis of the situation or a deliberate attempt to promote a particular philosophy of education despite the facts.

The NAPH (1999) undertook a survey and had SATs scores re-marked for Key Stage 2 in a large number of schools across the country. They have demonstrated that there have been systematic inaccuracies among the front line markers in English and Science and maintain that these League Tables should not be published as they reflect markers' incompetencies and not pupils' attainments.

Successful school learning

High school achievement is not necessarily the mark of a good education according to Rutter (1989). His extensive researches showed that in the pathways from childhood to adult life it is not high school achievement that makes the difference, but the positive experiences of a kind that are pleasurable and rewarding and which help children develop a sense of self worth together with the confidence that they can cope with life's challenges and can control what happens to them.

Earlier studies with which he was associated found that when there was an overemphasis upon academic goals and a neglect of the personal needs, more children seem disposed to fail and become 'problem children' in the schools' eyes (Rutter *et al.* 1979)). These differences could not be attributed to the catchment areas that the schools served (Hargreaves 1984). The number of pupils regarded as having special needs on the basis of their difficult behaviour depended more on the school they happened to attend rather than on the pupils themselves or their families (Galloway and Goodwin 1987).

'Those pupils whom their teachers regarded as more successful tended to be given greater attention than others. The teachers interacted with them more frequently, paid close attention to their activities and they subtly structured and directed their efforts in ways which were noticeably different from the relationships with pupils less favourably categorised' (Sharpe and Green 1975: 115). This can still be observed in classrooms today.

Academic pressures, coercive and didactic environments and negative teacher attitudes and behaviours can seriously dampen the will and motivation to learn in schools (Mongon and Hart 1989). Intrinsic motivation is fostered by a consistent, positive, supportive climate and positive constructive feedback (Deci 1988). In controlled studies it was found to be destroyed under pressure to reach and maintain standards and that pupils lost autonomy and self regulation in response to extrinsic motivation (Ryan *et al.* 1985).

Despite these research findings we have those responsible for education insisting on moving schools in the opposite direction. They are demanding a content approach to learning, more formal teaching, even in the earliest years in school (and now in preschool it is threatened), more assessment of curriculum content learned and stronger discipline and stricter class control. It is important therefore that teachers learn to review the nature of teaching and learning so that they can evaluate these demands and balance them and so regain some control over their professional life and its concerns.

Education

Education is the system, structure and organisation of learning as well as the processes and contents of that learning. Our system of education is thus the way we organise our children's experiences for learning as well as the curriculum and pedagogical methods used to achieve it. Although there might be many ways of approaching the same learning outcomes by different systems and educational processes, we have adopted a compulsory system of primary and secondary education organised on an age cohort basis. Summerhill, a private school based upon a different system, of elective attendance and learning by interest and commitment rather than age preparedness, fought closure over a number of years against the State monolith. Education Otherwise or at Home is now the main alternative to the 'system', private and public, but it is mainly only available to children of parents with considerable capital. The fact that the UK in common with many other countries has adopted a particular system does not mean that it is the best one. It probably means that it is seen as economically efficient for mass education while something better is always available to look after a country's 'elite', usually the privileged. But any system should be able to be made flexible to enable best practice to be developed or be adopted.

However, at the turning of the century was what was at issue in the UK was that this flexibility was not permitted and that teachers were beginning to feel deskilled as they received more and more prescriptions and policies which they must follow. As will be seen, many of these prescriptions arise from tradition and fly in the face of what research shows to be a 'good education' and one fit for the people of a new millennium.

Learner needs in this new millennium

What then is an appropriate education for the new millennium? It has traditionally been held that education should be the transmission of knowledge and skills considered worthwhile in a particular culture to the young. For the young people education should enable them to develop their potential to the full. Potential, however, is indefinable and children in any case have an enormous capacity to learn which no amount of schooling might fulfil. In addition to this in the twentieth century, knowledge and skills vastly increased so that even an expert cannot now know all there is to know in one subject, much less across several as was the case in earlier centuries. It is thus that education for the young has to be a matter of selection of appropriate and relevant content and it becomes crucial who is permitted to select this content. Teachers in LEAs by common consent and custom and practice used to select curriculum content backed by training institutions and inservice programmes. Government appointees from business, commerce, the media and university subject departments excluding education formed into Quangos (quasi governmental organisations) led by the DfES (civil servants) now do so.

In the face of this we have government ministers, and leaders of commerce and industry, proclaiming that it is essential for all pupils in school to learn for being workers in the twenty-first century:

- Good communication skills.
- Problem solving skills.
- Creative thinking.
- Flexibility.
- Good listening skills.
- Ability to learn from experience.
- Ability to learn from others.

The subject content approach specified does not automatically transfer these skills to learners. They have to be specifically taught, preferably in the context of school subjects but with direct examples and practice connected to real world learning.

In the past it was enough for the few to learn Latin, Greek and Hebrew to enable them to enter the Church. In the Merchant Schools mathematics was taught so that this would help boys with trade and navigation. Now it is not enough for them to learn just to read and write, calculate simple sums and be able to quote extensively from the Bible and poetry, the curriculum of the elementary schools at the turn of the century. Today the school curriculum is mandatory and broad based. It purports to transmit in large measure what our society considers to be relevant bodies of knowledge and skills. It is presented as the NC sectioned into ten subjects. This division is despite the fact that when subjects are approached from interdisciplinary perspectives the pupils' understanding reaches higher levels and enables them to apply their knowledge better in different situations.

The core subjects are English, mathematics and science. Each subject has a vast field from which the school curriculum has been selected by a panel who determined what it was the young should know. Characteristically, each of the ten panels drew up a subject curriculum which could equally have taken up all the children's time in school if they were truly to learn it. The panels did not contain experts in teacher education or child education and very few classroom teachers. Even though the NC has been trimmed (Dearing 1994) and there are elements which may be selected, the teachers are now beset by an overriding concern to 'cover the syllabus'. This used to be a phenomenon only observed in the later stages of secondary schools but now it is rife throughout schooling.

Despite this concern to impart subjects, when we look back on our own education it is seldom the subject content that remains with us. Instead it is the skills we learned, the people who taught us, our peers and the things we did that we tend to recall. We may remember some of those poems and items that we were obliged to learn by heart but this does not mean that rote learning should be the primary vehicle for learning. Even the Koreans are rejecting this their favoured system as it has been found to handicap their society and limit its workforce's creativity and problem solving ability.

Donald Kennedy, a college principal in the USA, drafted the following letter in 1987 on behalf of 36 college principals which was sent to all the rest. It was a warning of a national emergency for schools and the country and ran as follows:

It simply will not do for our schools to produce a small elite to power our scientific establishment and a larger cadre of workers with basic skills to do routine work. Millions of people around the world now have these same basic skills and are willing to work twice as long for as little as one tenth our basic wages. To maintain and enhance our quality of life, we must develop a leading edge economy based on workers who can think for a living . . . If skills are equal, in the long run wages will be so too. This means we have to educate a vast mass of people capable of thinking critically, creatively and imaginatively.

The implications of such worldwide economics were already recognised in the UK, and the Department for Employment commissioned a number of research projects to find ways of changing education and training for work. It emphasised the need for employees at every level to be workers, learners and managers. 'Business success depends upon the ability of educators to develop learners' self management, transfer and 'learn to learn' skills' (p. 1, Foreword by Ann Widdecombe, Parliamentary Under Secretary of State for the DE, 1993, in Blagg *et al.* 1993).

The CBI had the same perspective when they drew up the document *Towards a Skills Revolution* (CBI 1990) in which it was stated: 'All education and training provision should be structured and designed to develop self reliance, flexibility and broad competence as well as specific skills' (p. 1).

This message also seems to have reached our competitors in the Pacific rim and Eastern Europe for at international conferences over the last three years specific references to such needs have been made and examples given of ways in which their educational practices are being transformed. In the UK the school ethos and method have regressed since the introduction of the NC to subject specific learning of a large body of content.

What we do know is that such an overfilled content curriculum is not the best vehicle for developing the thinking capabilities of the large majority of learners. Nor is it motivating the lower attainers (Montgomery 1998a). In case studies in schools the pressure to cover the syllabus is beginning to show in increased alienation of pupils and resultant behaviour difficulties (Blum 1999). To counteract this, more attention will need to be paid to curriculum theory and practice by education planners.

The problem was clearly illustrated by Paul (1990) who developed an analysis of knowledge, learning and literacy which distinguished between nineteenth-century learning and twenty-first-century learning. The former concerns a process of education which he refers to as Didactic Theory and the latter as Critical Theory. He describes a Didactic Education as one in which the fundamental needs of the students are to be taught more or less WHAT to think, not how to think. In Critical Theory the students are taught HOW, not what, to think. In Chapter 5 on Effective Teaching, Paul's analysis will be presented in more detail.

Learning

We know that the nervous system at birth is 'wired' to respond to certain external stimuli through reflex responses and there are a few innate behaviours such as the ability to respond to human facial patterns such as smiles from a very early stage. These are called ethograms and need little input to establish them. The rest of what we know is learned in contact with our environment. The famous 'Kitten carousel' experiment (Hebb 1958) showed that the kitten that walked round in the carousel was able to see normally while the one which was carried round and was not in contact with the outside world appeared on release to act as though blind.

Human babies have a long developmental period when it would appear that they are laying down the fundamental patterns and neural connections upon which all the rest will be built. According to Kelly (1955) we are born as investigative problem solving organisms and operate on our environment like scientific investigators. Babies push, pull and suck things in their immediate environment and observe the results. As their capabilities become more complex with both maturation and learning so their ability to investigate and react becomes more and more complex.

Thus by the time most children arrive at school having had a typical infancy they are already repositories of a vast base of knowledge and skills and hopefully are ready for the new challenges of school learning.

At this stage they are essentially 'good learners'. They are keen, motivated, curious and full of zest for life and learning. They have already internalised vast complexes of learning schemas. They will have schemas and scripts for eating and drinking and hopefully for putting on shoes and coats as well as holding pencils and drawing. They may have already developed schemas about reading and writing and certainly for talking and listening and playing with toys. Some schemas may already have built-in errors. Other schemas are about self concepts, both positive or negative, which have been built up over time and experience.

If we develop a poor self image and a set of failure to learn schemas in the first weeks in school this can have profound effects for the rest of school life. Most of those who develop learning failure in school may only return to education if they really have to in order to develop their career prospects rather than as an end in itself. It is significant that there are a large number of pupils leaving school who never want to have contact with education again, despite the current commitment of Governments to lifelong learning.

What then is it that we learn? Gagné (1975) identified five major categories of learned capabilities. These were verbal information, intellectual skills, cognitive strategies, attitudes and motor skills.

Verbal information consists of facts, names, principles and generalisations. It consists of the organised bodies of information such as in the NC and the learning of meanings (concepts). *Concepts* are the building blocks of learning (Anderson 1980).

The interaction with the environment from the early years enables us to build up mental representations of the external world which are termed 'concepts'. Concrete concepts refer to objects and events in the real world which can be seen and touched such as tables and chairs. A category concept can be derived from these perceptual referents using various key attributes of the group. Thus chairs, tables and settees make up a group, category or class which is termed 'furniture'.

Event concepts or *scripts* can also be linked together and give concepts such as to 'chair a meeting', implying a whole set of related procedural concrete activities associated with the chairing. A range of concrete concepts and schemas can be linked together to form a constellation or abstract concept such as 'love', 'learning', 'justice' and 'education'. Individuals contribute their own idiosyncratic patterns of experiences to concept formation. Sets of concepts and hierarchies of abstract concepts are referred to as *constructs*. Hierarchies of constructs are referred to as *attitudes* or conceptual hierarchies within which emotions and feelings may also be bound. Thus it is that learning is often intimately bound up with feelings of anxiety or pleasure and can provoke intense feelings. It is often only the emotional content that causes things to be remembered.

When engaging in thinking at the simpler levels new concepts may be being constructed, and this is the process of *concept, script and schema development*. This is particularly evident when learning new subject contents and skills. Programmes overloaded with content may occupy all of student learning time in the area of concept development so that on entering employment there is little competency and capability to do the work for which the students are employed. They have too few applications schema and scripts.

Concepts themselves are not simple units: they are little complexes of relationships or schemas. For example, the verbal label chair connects to its various images of chairs we have known and sat on, its spelling feel and its writing feel. It links to notions of backs and seats and legs and crossbars, nails and glue and so on. The more experiences of 'chair' we have the bigger and more complex its schema structure. This is why the notion of schema theory has developed, concepts are themselves schematic representations. It has its origins in the works of Piaget (1927, 1952) in constructivist theory and the processes of *accommodation* in which the schemata are modified and extended to encompass new learning.

Organised bodies of knowledge – learning as a noun – are believed to provide the vehicle for thought. In problem solving a person thinks of many things and searches the stores of schema knowledge, information and concepts. It is thus easy for curriculum planners to fill students' time with content learning for concept development and omit thinking about their needs to learn to use this knowledge. Thus they have insufficient *application schema* and cognitive processes to make any sense of what they have learned or use it in real world problem solving.

Learning as a verb can be thought of as the process or processes of schema and script modification. Norman (1977) described three processes of schema modification as follows: *accretion, tuning* and *restructuring*. During learning there is the interaction of experience with the already stored schema.

Accretion, according to Norman, is the acquisition of new responses. The child may know the names of a number of fruits and recognise they can and have been eaten. Acquiring the name of a new one such as 'strawberry' means that they may also acquire the category concept 'fruit' which puts all of them into a new and even more complex relationship.

Tuning is the process by which the use of a schema such as writing, problem solving, word processing, eating or riding a bicycle becomes more routine or automatic. The routine is run more efficiently and there may be short cuts found, all of which free up the attention to learn new things. In tuning no new input is involved.

Restructuring involves the creation of new insights. We may give the thinking time and thus reorganise our knowledge or see it in a new and different way. All three of these processes of schema modification may and frequently do occur together during learning. However, this change in the schema really only occurs satisfactorily if we are engaged in *'deep'* learning and nothing much at all will happen unless the pupils actually *attend* to what is to be learned. Over the years in schools pupils frequently develop habits of inattention and non attending so that at the outset of all parts of a lesson the pupils' attention must be captured and maintained.

First there must come the teacher's attention gaining tactics as in the 3Ms, closely followed by interest, novelty, activity, personal involvement and whenever possible an open ended problem to solve. Teachers can get into the habit of repeating everything three times before they expect pupils to listen. This sort of cycle needs to be broken. Pupils need to see the consequences of listening and not listening and this can be done by engaging in the occasional 'warm up' exercise to practise listening skills (Rawlings 1996).

Using the same format and procedures for lessons can give rise to habituation so that pupils' attention flags and they only begin to listen when the appropriate cues occur such as – 'Now this is what you are going to do.' They then 'do' but as they missed the explanation leading in to it their efforts may be of a trial and error nature and what they learn if anything is disconnected and remains unconnected with previous learning.

Deep and surface learning

This notion of learning was first developed by Marton and Saljo (1976). It seems to be a more easily understandable version of Piaget's (1952) accommodation and assimilation. In accommodation new learning is incorporated into the old by modifying and adapting the existing schemata to take account of the new information. In assimilation the new may be adapted to fit in with the old learning or may be held in a sort of limbo capsule unintegrated. In accommodating we integrate the information into our existing concepts and schemes and in the process fully understand it, or understand it in our own particular fashion. This is also characteristic of deep learning and means we can use the knowledge in a variety of ways and different applications and we can use it to construct new knowledge. Surface learning remains essentially superficial, probably repeatable but not capable of transformation or enlightening. It tends to be the sort of learning without understanding which arises from rote or parrot learning. It may be the only level of knowledge achieved in revision sessions where strategies have concentrated too much on memorising as opposed to understanding.

According to Gibbs (1990), Biggs (1987) and Marton and Saljo (1976) there are a number of characteristics which result in superficial learning and these are:

- a heavy workload;
- relatively high class contact hours;
- an excessive amount of course material;
- a lack of opportunity to pursue subjects in depth;
- a lack of choice over subjects;
- a lack of choice over methods of study;
- a threatening and anxiety-provoking assessment system.

These as can be seen are typical of teacher education programmes and the NC in schools. If all these things lead to superficial learning of the school curriculum the consequences for teachers and learners are dire. The system is then set to favour the pupils who have very good memories and those who are more verbally skilled. This usually includes the more able and those pupils brought up in linguistically advantaged environments by the 'chattering classes'.

The oral language of pupils from other cultures and lower socio-economic groups in this country is more distant from that of the school and so does not map easily on to its structures. These pupils' language is frequently abbreviated and content bound. For example, a pupil looking at a series of stimulus pictures sees first a boy and girl playing football and then a broken window. The third picture shows an angry adult gesticulating at them. When asked to explain what the story is about, the pupils with distant language usage might say: 'They broke it 'n' 'e's angry.' There is nothing wrong with the comprehension but the form does not help them with school work: it is too closely dependent on having the pictures present. Lack of practice in listening to and using extended oral language gives them little opportunity to understand the language schemas that teachers and textbooks use, discover and then implicitly make use of them in their writing.

If we can teach lower attainers what other pupils pick up from their ordinary listening and reading and apply them in their writing then this could be a significant support to them. A grammar of listening and writing schemas can then be taught to pupils (Montgomery 1998a).

Good writers and successful pupils in school learn about the internal organisation of texts spontaneously from reading; others do not. These others tend to be the slower learners, the learning disabled such as dyslexics and those with subtle language difficulties with verbal CATs scores being 15 points lower than non verbal scores (Mellanby *et al.* 1996). Brown and Palinscar (1984) attributed these differences to a difference in learning style and Torgeson (1982) suggested that it was because they were inactive learners. The inactivity was attributed to a problem in *metacognition*.

The deficits in metacognition were a lack of awareness and use of organisational strategies. This lack of awareness prevented them from using the schemata for writing. Hence dyslexia teachers find that with very much older pupils they are still having to remind them to use the basic story schema – beginnings, middles and ends – whereas very much younger good readers will already have absorbed this.

It could be argued in the case of all these pupils with learning difficulties and lower attainments that they are so effortfully preoccupied with the mechanics of reading they fail to grasp the overview of the organisation of what they read. This then has implications for their writing and they are doubly handicapped for they are then struggling with the mechanics of spelling and handwriting as well as content so that they have little cognitive time and space for higher order aspects of processing.

Culturally different pupils frequently lack the standard text knowledge of the school. The closer the match of the language of the home to the formal language of the school then the closer will be the match to school texts, making it easier for this group of pupils to acquire writing grammars.

Making these implicit understandings explicit or directly teaching pupils to use and respond to them can enable them to move from superficial to deeper learning for they are not so dependent on rote memory but can use the schemas to aid both retention and recall. This is one aspect of teaching for metacognition and can make learning more efficient.

To foster a deep learning approach we need the reverse conditions from surface learning – relatively low class contact hours; an intrinsic interest in the subject; freedom in learning in content and method; scope for intellectual independence; and experience of 'good' teaching. These conditions are easy to state but rather more complex to create, for example 'intrinsic motivation'. In this the pupils should want to learn what they do rather than what they wish and this learning is self motivated. Creating the environment for making pupils want to learn is one of the key roles of the teacher and will be more fully explored in the next chapter. Regrettably pupils in our education system do not always come with an enormous desire to learn anything the teacher cares to teach whereas it is still the case in many developing countries that pupils *do want to learn*. In these places, class sizes may be 55 or more, there are few textbooks and the sessions are didactic, relying on extensive rote memorising. In Arab countries this form of education is highly valued.

Making explicit and teaching listening and writing schema to pupils is one of a range of learning strategies which can be imparted to help all learners become more effective. Regrettably learning strategies are often confused with memorisation strategies which tend to be far more tedious as they do not have power for generalisation nor the power of 'chunking' and relating information to existing frameworks.

Intellectual versus cognitive skills and schemas

Intellectual skills are about 'knowing that' and 'knowing how'. They include converting printed words into meaning, fractions into decimals, knowing about classes, groups and categories, the laws of genetics, how to form sentences, adverbs and adjectives and so on. Concepts are the substance of intellectual operations from which we derive rules and principles and higher order rules. The general aspects of these skills are tested in intelligence tests. Thus these tests have a major component of 'that which has been learned' or acquired in contact with a particular cultural and schooling environment.

Cognitive strategies are internally organised capabilities (Gagné 1975: 64) which the learner makes use of in guiding his or her attending, learning and remembering. These capabilities make possible the executive control processes that activate other learning processes. He thus distinguishes between cognitive skills and intellectual skills in that intellectual skills enable us to deal with the numbers, words and symbols of the world 'out there'. Cognitive strategies are directed to internal operations. The learner uses cognitive strategies in attending to what is being learned or read; in thinking about what has been learned we use cognitive strategies (Gagné 1975: 66).

Sophisticated thinking involves the manipulation of various levels of schema by what we call *cognitive processes*. These may involve searching through concepts and constructs in sequential order, ranging through hierarchies of concepts for critical features, probing deeply into a construct, focusing on 'key' concepts with similar tags of reference, re-ordering and reconstructing to develop new constructs, scanning data and schemas, listing key attributes and using personal or idiosyncratic attributes. It may also include retrieving old well-tried schemas and strategies to solve a new problem or using part of an old strategy to help in the process. On appropriate occasions analogies may be used to solve old problems in an entirely different context in an imaginative and new way. Broad reading and broadening experiences can facilitate creative modelling and analogous thinking but only where there is flexibility in thinking and time for reflection. Many processes occurring simultaneously, drawing on many conceptual hierarchies, is typical of this kind of multilogical thinking. An overfilled curriculum and pressure to cover the syllabus is thus a handicap to thinking and problem solving. This then damages the student's ability to gain competency and capability in real world problem solving.

A thinking skills agenda?

The Gifted and Talented Advisory group was established by the Government in late 1998 to advise on the curriculum and provision for the more able pupils in schools for whom the NC had not proved sufficiently challenging. None of the advice given by this group drawn from experts in the field appeared to have been heeded (Stopper 2000; Montgomery 2000). However, the DfEE did commission a report of research on thinking skills (McGuinness 1999) and have heralded a new initiative for schools on developing thinking skills approaches. We are at least back on track where we were before the NC was introduced in 1988 and probably several billion pounds worse off.

Remembering

Different learning inputs have been found to be more effective than others in single presentations. For example, in the *passive reception* mode we remember 10 per cent of what we read; 20 per cent of what we hear; 30 per cent of what we see; and 50 per cent of what we see and hear at the same time (*AVA News* 1985). This only of course applies in schools if the pupils are literate – can understand what they read with the same facility as what they understand when something is read to them, which is not always the case. However, the teachers' talk, direct instruction, supported by visual and other material is crucial for maximum learning possible before repetition is entered into. When pupils are *actively engaged* in constructing the message themselves then they of course remember much more. We remember 80 per cent of what we say and 90 per cent of what we say and do at the same time. Thus it is that teachers are often the ones who are learning the most and feeling the most satisfied. They also find it hard to give up this active role to facilitate the learning of their pupils. If they are not talking and explaining they think they are not teaching.

In undergraduate learning the amount remembered is cited in Race (1992) as follows: from the lecture 5 per cent; books 10 per cent; audio visual presentation 20 per cent; dramatic lecture with audio-visual presentation 30 per cent; discussing 50 per cent; explaining 75 per cent; teaching 90 per cent; assessing 95 per cent. This further reinforces the points already made about active and constructive learning and was supported in our studies with teacher education undergraduates (Montgomery 1993, 1995, 1998b). When we changed our programme to enable them to learn by the active methods which we were advocating they used with the pupils (Cognitive process methods – see Chapter 5) their final exam grades rose exponentially while the tutor input was dramatically reduced. By the end of the programme the students had almost entirely taken over the regulation and conduct of their own learning and had enjoyed the experience.

Intrinsic motivation, as already indicated, is fostered by a consistent, positive and supportive climate and positive constructive feedback. It is destroyed under pressure to reach and maintain standards. Pupils and their teachers lose autonomy and self regulation in response to extrinsic motivation – the 'carrot and stick' methods. In cognitive process pedagogies and PCI, positive and constructive feedback are essential input in maintaining motivation and keep it running intrinsically.

Real world learning and learning in classrooms

In any analysis of learning in school it is necessary to distinguish between 'real world learning' and that which takes place in classrooms. The former is normally self initiated, self regulated and the learner is actively engaged in solving problems posed by life situations. In the latter the learner is essentially passive and the learning is mediated verbally by the teacher. It is also mainly teacher directed and organised. It is not surprising therefore that real world learning tends to be intrinsically interesting and motivating and lasts lifelong whereas much of school learning is extrinsically motivated and temporary.

Educators concerned with effective learning in classrooms are thus not infrequently seeking to change the processes of school learning from passivity to activity and to cause it to be more regulated and directed by pupils so that they can become more motivated particularly intrinsically so. Because school learning is very much concerned with the transmission of knowledge stored in books and on disk in verbal and pictorial forms, real world scenarios are often difficult to construct from it in classrooms. In the real world the knowledge and skills we learn are essential and have to be put to use as soon as possible. An example of this might be the fast learning curve in knowledge, skills, vocabulary, stories, histories and maritime geography that one needs to know and suddenly acquire when estuary sailing a boat for five hours. This is in contrast to what might be learned in the same time in a schoolroom. The closest we might get is in the virtual classroom or simulator but five hours of that would still need to be accompanied by real world experience.

Desforges (1998) expresses this problem as follows:

> More fundamentally pupils are expected to learn to use and apply their knowledge and skills in situations outside schools, in their domestic and professional lives, for example. These different learning outcomes require very different learning processes which in turn would be promoted through different teaching processes as might be expected. (p. 12)

Because knowledge has been traditionally stored in books teachers have resorted to presenting it in the form of abstracts and verbal summaries or illustrated lecturettes. These verbal transmission methods are supported by question-and-answer sessions to check on pupil recall followed by paper-and-pencil exercises to represent learner activity and help the material be assimilated. These techniques enable the material to be repeated in three different ways so that the majority of the pupils absorb it. Later they may be required to revise it and repeat it in written form in an exam. This is then the evidence used to award certificates for the amount remembered and applications learned or derived. The better the pupils' memories, the more efficient the teacher analysis of questions and drill; the more efficient the revision strategies, the higher the grades obtained. This all applies of course as long as the pupil can spell adequately and can write quickly and legibly to get enough of the ingested material down and is motivated to learn in this way.

There have been a number of long-term research studies which have looked at how best children may be educated and the most effective ways in which they learn. One of the most important and well documented is the Perry Preschool Project, now called the Highscope Project. David Weikart established it in 1968 as a Cognitively Orientated Preschool Curriculum in Ypsilanti, Michigan. It was a response to finding in 1962 that 50 per cent of pupils in one 'working-class' school were retained in grade by the fourth grade while only 8 per cent in a 'middle-class' school had been retained. The majority of so-called mentally retarded students, discipline cases and referrals to outside agencies were from the lower socio-economic population, both black and southern white.

The purpose was to reduce alienation and juvenile delinquency by offering preschool education. However, the theory and practice of early education and research on its effectiveness were not then available and so the team engaged with teachers, parents and pupils in a programme of continuous development (Hohmann *et al.* 1979).

The later studies compared the progress of former students at intervals in academic and social terms. Three types of preschool curriculum learning experiences were evaluated. It was found that those who had experienced a form of free play education based upon the 'cognitive curriculum' developed into well adjusted adults with positive attitudes to their education and lifelong learning. In this free play setting the adults encouraged the use of student language expression and thought. This was compared with children in the DISTAR method classrooms (Direct Instructional Systems in Teaching and Remediation – highly structured sequences of learning derived from task analytic approaches, Carnine and Englemann 1982) and the traditional group who received the more formal teaching in teacher-directed groups as found in many nursery and Reception classes today.

The pupils at the outset of the experiment were from disadvantaged backgrounds and the groups overall had low measured IQs. The typical student product of these other classrooms at 35 years was one with a career in social deviance, a dislike of what had been experienced at school and an aversion to education. However, it was demonstrated (Weikart 1998) that only the cognitively orientated free play was the form of schooling which protected them from their disadvantaging environments and enabled them to develop into well-adjusted stable and achieving adults. They also grew in cognitive capabilities, took on work responsibilities and engaged in further college training.

Similar results are available from an English study into nurture groups (Bannathan and Boxall 1998). The nurture groups were small classes set up in primary schools with about one dozen pupils, one teacher and three assistants in each during the 1970s and early 1980s. The pupils engaged in self directed free play while the adults modelled and made explicit pro-social behaviours in their own and the pupils' interactions. Head teachers in the London schools which set up these nurture groups were convinced that they had a remarkable effect. The majority of the pupils referred to the nurture groups because of their disordered behaviour were able to be reintegrated into the normal classroom after a year. The rest of the classes from which they were drawn were able to function properly again when the disturbed individuals had been removed.

The data showed that 20 years later 82 per cent of those children who had been in nurture groups had maintained their place in mainstream school and had not acquired a police record or resorted to crime. This was in contrast to only 29 per cent of children who had been selected for the nurture groups but had not been permitted to go because most of these special classes had been closed down with the demise of ILEA and the GLC as well as the prevailing views of those in command of the education service at the time, notably male and secondary orientated.

This is of course data on disadvantaged and disturbed children from disadvantaging environments. However, Roberts (1986) reported similar findings about her studies of normal nursery and Reception class children. The four-year-olds put into formal Reception classrooms as 'rising fives' showed many distress behaviours in the formal work and they were frightened of the 'big' children (the five-year-olds!) and bullied by them. When asked what they had learned, they were preoccupied with things like knowing what was in the teachers' head, and 'you mustn't cry, or, tell lies like Samantha'.

They presented a sad little spectacle when compared with their Norwegian peers who do not experience formal schooling until they are seven and who within two years quickly out-perform our pupils who have been at school learning to read and write since five. Silva (1998) is currently engaged in a long-term international study of comparative preschool education which is already showing signs of the value of free play and the cognitively orientated curriculum.

If we can establish this special form of free play preschool education then reception classes too will need to become more flexible and permit greater autonomy for pupils as they demand greater independence of thought and action within the more formal framework. This then follows throughout the school. What has recently been proposed is that now the NC should reach down into nursery schools and preschool education providing a foundation of basic skills.

A senior teacher in a secondary school before the introduction of the NC in a disadvantaged inner city area, persuaded a team of teachers to work together with the whole Year 7 intake as mixed ability groups on interdisciplinary projects. This lasted the whole year and was based on a primary classroom model. The pupils were very comfortable with it and the staff saw big improvements in literacy and study skills, social and behavioural skills in comparison with previous years. The project was discontinued mainly because the staff receiving them in Year 8 complained that they were always asking questions and were unmanageable, moving about the rooms just as they pleased. A little autonomy too far! It is frequently found that pupils lose motivation as they go through Year 7 (Alexander 1998, James 1984/1989). They continually move from room to room and teacher to teacher, hardly known by anyone unless they misbehave. It is not surprising that their interest declines as teachers fail to take an interest in them. This transfer year into secondary school is a crucial one – as important as Reception class – and in both class sizes of 15 would be more appropriate to counteract the alienating effects of mass education.

Effective learning

The nature of learning and learners' needs of which teaching methods have to take account based on De Corte's (1995) analysis of research in instructional psychology is as follows:

- Fundamentally *learning is constructive*. This means that pupils are not passive recipients of information. In order to learn they have to participate in the construction of their own knowledge and skills. This he contrasts with the implicit view current in teaching practice that learning is the transmission and passive absorption of knowledge gained and institutionalised by past generations.

- *Learning is cumulative* and it is on the basis of what they already know that pupils construct new knowledge and derive new meanings and skills.
- *Learning is best when self organised.* This is related to the metacognitive nature of effective learning especially the managing and monitoring of learning activities – self regulation.
- *Learning is generally goal oriented* although a small amount of learning is incidental. An explicit awareness of and orientation towards a goal facilitates effective and meaningful learning especially when the learners can choose the goal and define their own objectives.
- *Learning is situated.* This means that learning essentially takes place in interaction with the social and cultural environment. It follows from this that learning which is collaborative is more effective because the interactions can induce and mobilise reflection and thus foster the development of metacognitive knowledge and skills.
- Finally, *learning is individually different.* Individual differences in ability, skills, needs, interests and learning style etc. mean that we each construct our learning of the same experience in different ways. Learning styles such as whether a deep approach or a surface approach (Marton and Salgo 1976) is adopted can mean very different learning outcomes.

When *learning is collaborative* many of the above principles are realised. Interaction and cooperation induce reflection and so foster the development of metacognitive skills and constructive learning.

Teaching methods which have bound into them an automatic recognition and fostering of the principles of human learning will be far more effective than didactics and will provide greater opportunities for differentiation at all levels of ability. These are methods of *teaching for learning*.

According to Jones (1998: 39) there is a wealth of evidence to indicate that participation for democracy in education and training is linked with enhanced learning and efficiency. She linked enhanced performance in schools to the development of democratic skills displayed in whole class teaching. In the UK apparently we have hierarchical systems of organisations in business and schools. This acts against the exercise of the democratic skills seen in team building and teamwork. She lists broad team skills as discussion, communication, problem solving, decision-making, self and team development. Functional skills were defined as initiating, consulting, informing, presenting, supporting, requesting, seeking information and advice, receiving critical questioning and feedback, evaluating, revising, linking, suggesting, expressing, describing, clarifying, planning, inferring, delegating, producing, promoting etc.

She argued that the student-centred approach to learning creates 'deep' enquiry-based learning which is characterised by:

- life/work – ties theory to relevant practical examples;
- hands on – simulated/real practical activity;
- collaborative – coaching, mentoring role of teachers.

She identified collaborative interpersonal skills which are essential for team work such as – listening, openness, non abrasiveness, non judgemental tolerance, genuineness, consistency, objective rationality, self reflection. The core of these are collaborative interpersonal attitudes of – respect, trust, honesty, humility, fairness, justice, empathy, liking of people etc. Genuine teamwork is characterised by reciprocal or collaborative relationships (Jones 1998: 29). Without the core attitudes we cannot involve others as equals and engage in the broad skills. Other labels have been used for these core skills such as critical thinking skills, people skills and life skills.

'In males a lack of respect for others, arrogance and lack of humility, an inability to listen acts as a major factor in undermining performance in classrooms; democratic skills such as described are downgraded as "soft" or feminine and further lack of respect' (Jones 1998: 23). Her argument is that traditional hierarchical teacher/learner, manager/employee relationships undermine democracy and are anti learning, blocking it so that the focus is on individual gain at the expense of others. She criticises the general failure to tackle the authoritarian hierarchical relationships between teachers and pupils for preventing the move towards *student-centred learning*. Small group work restricts communication and cooperation between individual pupils and the rest of the children, according to Jones, and encourages them to do their own thing. She favours the horseshoe and the circle setting of chairs and worktops. There are some important points presented in this view and it would seem important that there should be a place for student-centred learning experiences of the kind she outlines in all classrooms. She comes to this from an industrial training perspective and it is typical of management and business training programmes to engage in student-centred learning.

The differences between this and school learning is that often in the training setting there is a problem to identify, data to collect and issues to resolve whereas in much of school learning there is a specified curriculum and no overt problems to resolve.

This does not mean that we should not at times create these learning situations within the NC. It might even make a valuable experiment to turn over the curriculum learning to this method and find if at the end of a year groups learning differently have made the requisite progress. It would not work well, however, if the student-centred learning had to fit into the lesson timetable of the ordinary school. Such learning does not suddenly end when the bell rings.

Ruddock (1995) summarised the ways in which we can make a significant difference to pupils' learning. She stated that it is necessary to have respect for pupils as individuals; to be fair to them irrespective of gender, ethnicity, ability and class; to give them autonomy and responsibility; to offer intellectual challenge with learning presented as a dynamic and empowering activity; to provide social support for academic and emotional concerns; to ensure there is a lack of threat to self esteem; and that there is security in the physical and interpersonal setting of the school. How precisely can we do these things in a busy classroom?

Capability

After a successful launch of 'Education for Capability' in 1978, little seemed to happen as a result in schools and thus attention was turned to higher education to try to get the movement for change under way by influencing the planners and leaders of the future.

'Education for Capability' believes that capability is best promoted and motivation enhanced if learners exercise responsibility, take initiatives, are creative and cooperate within learning programmes. Real experience of these activities, and of exploring and accounting for the relevance of their learning to themselves and to the society of which they are part, can build learner's confidence: in their ability to take effective action; in their worth as individuals and members of groups; and in their capability to learn (Stephenson and Weil 1988). These will help develop abilities to:

- acquire and apply knowledge;
- communicate ideas and information;
- listen to and collaborate with others in mutually planned activities;
- set achievable and relevant goals;
- assess the effectiveness of their actions;
- be critical of and creative in their thinking and actions;
- see both success and failure as opportunities for learning;
- take account of their feelings and intuition;
- show respect and concern for others;
- reflect on their values.

It is possible to distinguish between general capabilities, knowledge and skills which are transferable across fields such as problem solving, social and communication skills and specific capabilities. Specific capabilities are those aspects of knowledge and skills which are specific to a discipline or a type of work. This might be how to plan a lesson for teaching, knowledge of disease symptoms in medicine, how to prepare wood and make joints in carpentry and so on.

In school learning with the curriculum divided into separate subjects, each teacher spends the time developing specific knowledge and skills, only sometimes with reference to general capabilities. English and drama teachers often do work to promote some aspects of general capability. However, a review of the cognitive curriculum and its application in capability will show that this learning is very patchy and sometimes negligible. Schools are not yet equipping pupils for the world of work or for a future of non work.

Learning style

Hemispheral differences in learning and cognitive style

The different hemispheres of the brain are set up to engage in different forms of data processing. The sequential ordering processes are thought to be typical of the left or language orientated hemisphere. Imaginative, inductive and appositional thought processes (Gazzaniga 1967, Bogen and Bogen 1969) are found to be characteristic of right hemisphere activities. The most creative of our scientists and artists appear to have had great facility in the use of both hemispheres. Regrettably Western education has been accused of only valuing and educating the left hemisphere linguistic functions (Ornstein 1982). This tends to permeate attitudes to all the subjects in the school curriculum, e.g. the so-called 'academic' versus the 'non academic' subjects.

Some cognitive abilities tests by Gagné's definition consist mainly of tests of right and left hemisphere intellectual skills and some of only one hemisphere. Teachers of science, maths and technology frequently claim to be developing problem solving abilities but now it would appear that this may not be so, and they are posing problems to be solved mainly using intellectual skills. Examples they give might be to to plan a party menu for four people with £10 to spend, and design a bridge from straws and paper to carry the weight of a can of coke.

Cognitive style

Personal style describes the way in which a person habitually approaches or responds to the learning task. It has two aspects: *cognitive style* which reflects the way the person thinks and *learning strategies*, the processes used by the learner to respond to the learning task. Cognitive style according to Riding and Raynor (1998) appears to be present at birth or fixed soon after. They argue on the basis of a meta-analysis of research that style has a physical basis and can control the way individuals respond to the events and ideas they experience.

They identified two orthogonally related dimensions of style. The *wholist-analytic* and the *verbal-imagery* dimensions. The former represents whether an individual tends to organise information into wholes or parts; the latter whether during thinking the individual tends to represent information verbally or in mental pictures. These styles also relate to preferences for attending to and analysing information in the preferred mode. Thus some subjects will say they cannot understand information in figures such as graphs as well as they might if the information was in words. (This is after problems in dealing with graphs are controlled.)

The wholist-partist style is often reflected in people's approaches to problem solving such as how to assemble a model from a kit, complete a jigsaw and so on. The Partist will lay out all the parts, read the instructions and follow them as in a recipe in the prescribed sequence. The Wholist (holist) will take out the parts and immediately begin the assembly without doing more than look at the picture. Only if this strategy begins to fail will the holist get out the instructions and begin to follow them. In these examples one can see the elements of the different hemispheral processing preferences.

Learning style

Learning style or learning mode refers to the way most people tend to approach a task, with a preference for one or other cognitive strategy but in the end we may use a mixed method as appropriate. Anxiety, learning experiences and minimal cerebral dysfunction may make people adopt an extreme reliance on one or another style as a compensatory mechanism. On the whole we should be educating people to be able to select the most appropriate strategy and dimension to gain the particular learning outcome most efficiently. Flexibly switching styles between holistic and sequential processing styles and verbal and iconic imagery should be an important part of the learning process. It is this flexibility that highly creative individuals appear to enjoy.

Because of the importance of style preferences for some learners it is necessary for teachers to make sure they make their materials accessible to learners by supporting verbal input with visual and iconic representations and by allowing pupils some choice and determination of methods of learning and recording.

Multiple intelligences (MI) and cognitive codes

Howard Gardner's (1993) notions of multiple intelligences, although not necessarily valid, do encourage teachers in MI schools to broaden the scope of their teaching and learning strategies to take account of the different ways in which we learn. Thus a pupil who excels in science may not excel in maths or English but will gain recognition and affirmation for success and achievement in science. The interest and motivation thus generated is then used and developed in other areas.

More important perhaps than the notions of MI could be the range of codes in which we encode information. Bruner (1960/1977) first outlined symbolic (verbal), iconic (imager) and enactive (motor) codes by which we learn to process and use information. This was used as a developmental model in which the baby first encodes enactively then iconically and finally symbolically. All three forms of coding are available once acquired. Munro (1996) developed this notion of cognitive encoding and decoding during learning patterned upon the curriculum subjects reminiscent of the MI approach. Ideas during learning need to be represented in the 'sites' in forms that allow learners to think about them. Whenever we think about an idea we need to link it with other ideas, using what we already know. Our existing knowledge gives us these ways of thinking or 'thinking codes'. These codes represent what we already know about how ideas can be related or linked. Ideas can be encoded or represented in different ways.

Munro proposed that students have access to several different codes in which they can learn:

- verbal-linguistic;
- scientific mathematical;

- episodic/spatial or visual-imagery;
- body/kinaesthetic;
- rhythmic;
- affective/mood;
- interpersonal.

He explains that learners need to learn how to move between codes, to switch ideas from one code to another by a recoding process and to learn to manipulate ideas within codes. They can do this by analysing them into constituent parts (analysis) and linking them or integrating (synthesis or holistic strategies) them with other ideas. Learning to use both analytic and holistic strategies is important for all learners. However, children with learning disabilities may be obliged to depend upon one more than the other. For example, dyslexics may have to adopt holistic learning strategies and visuo-spatial coding to compensate for their verbal processing difficulties. It is thus important that they are permitted to use other codes and these are given similar value and affirmation.

In management studies literature it is common to find four learning styles devised by Honey and Mumford (1986) designed on the basis of Kolb's (1984) hypothesised stages in the learning cycle. The proposed styles were:

- Activists involve themselves fully and without bias in new experiences (Kolb's concrete experience).
- Reflectors like to stand back and ponder experiences and observe them from many different perspectives (reflective observation).
- Theorists adapt and integrate observations into complex but logically sound theories (abstract conceptualisation).
- Pragmatists are keen on trying out ideas, theories and techniques to see if they work in practice (active experimentation).

Using their style questionnaire it is common to find low style preferences which suggests that the concept of style in this form is incorrect for there are flexible learners with no dominant style. This would be worth much further study. In addition questionnaires are subject to many design flaws and this may also be part of the problem here.

Transfer of learning

The results of five DE projects were summarised by Blagg *et al.* (1993). One of the key issues arising was that of transfer. They found that all too often learning was highly specific and did not transfer to new circumstances and situations. The DfEE argues that the NC is a prescription for offering a broad and balanced curriculum for every child. However, in application, in the way it is 'delivered' it does not result in the appropriate learning outcome of transferability. Thus it is that a broad and balanced curriculum does not necessarily lead to a broad and balanced education.

Transfer means to learn something in one context and be able to apply it to another. In expansion experiments in science the pupils lower a ball through a ring, then heat the ball and find it will not go through until it cools down again. Transfer questions are later posed such as why are there gaps in railway lines, why the lid is taken off a tin of beans before cooking and why telegraph wires are put up slackly in summer. Large numbers of pupils find it hard to transfer the principle of expansion to these simple examples. Even when they do solve one problem they may not solve the others or relate them to other similar problems they might meet in daily life.

Three models of transfer were identified by Blagg *et al.*, as follows:

- The Bo-peep theory – this is that transfer will take care of itself. However, their research showed that this was not the case – learners too often failed to deploy or adapt their intellectual resources in unfamiliar circumstances.
- The Lost Sheep theory – transfer rarely occurs so most new problems are likely to require additional training.
- The Good Shepherd theory – transfer does occur if it is shepherded, nurtured and mediated. Their researches showed that there were certain kinds of learning and teaching activities that are likely to foster the ability to transfer. In a wide range of industrial and training contexts they found the following were needed for transfer:
  – Thinking and problem solving skills need to be made explicit.
  – Holistic tasks should be used.
  – Occupationally relevant simulations should be used.
  – Attention needed to be given to the key aspects of training and delivery.

'Increasingly it is recognised that learning about and gaining control over one's thought processes is fundamental to improving the ability to learn and transfer' (Blagg *et al.* 1993: 5).

Learning and transfer using problem solving techniques

In terms of school learning Blagg *et al.*'s work (1993) as well as that of Swartz and Parks (1994) indicates that thinking and problem solving skills must be made explicit as well as situations set up so that they may be applied.

The simulations need to be set in the subject context. Thus in history, the Battle of Hastings can provide a ground plan of the troops and the problem to decide how to use them to predict who should win. This can be followed by reading accounts of what was reported to have happened and follow-up discussions. Comparisons can then be made with the same setting, the same problem and modern warfare weapons. Pupils should be allowed to share their ideas with each other in pairs before contributing to class discussion. There are several reasons for this:

- It allows them to identify what they know, for often we do not know what we think until we try and explain it to someone else.
- It enables them to work over the material making sure they have covered or included all the points.

- It helps develop their communication skills for they will need to question each other and use extended language.
- They will each engage in a small element of teaching their peer which ensures learning takes place at deeper levels.
- They will learn to link what they are working on to their previous frameworks of understanding and this helps to make the learning secure.
- They will engage in problem solving and thinking and not just waiting for other pupils to tell the rest the answers to the teacher's questions.
- They will practise some social and negotiation skills.

As can be seen, the original problem is 'fuzzy' and its resolution also has to be part of the problem. At the end of any such session, it is therefore important for the teacher to make explicit what were the best problem solving protocols in this case, using the pupils' examples. These can then become part of the repertoire too for later problem solving.

Surface learning strategies

These are usually defined as post-study activities. The pupil reads the material or listens to the teacher's exposition and then at a later date, even though practice exercises have been undertaken, a number of post-study activities have been designed to help reinforce the strength of the learning and aid later recall. Examples are: rereading, note taking, diagramming, charting, concept mapping, mnemonics, and SQ3R (*Survey* the information, raise *Questions* about each part, then *Read, Recite and Review* – 3R). Each of these when first introduced can be interesting to the learner but as time wears on, interest wanes. Creating a mnemonic such as SQ3R or its counterpart 'Richard Of York Gave Battles In Vain' to remember the colours of the rainbow is a device known as clustering. The sentence is mildly more memorable than the separate colours, a semi-cognitive activity but the end product involves rote learning and of course is wrong as there are only six colours in the rainbow (red, orange, yellow, green, blue, violet). ('Scientists' of the day were much influenced by magical notions associated with the number seven and its universality.)

The typical content of study skills programmes is illustrated by Pascal (1998) in his one-day courses for NASEN. The programme covers *Active Classroom Revision*; *Examination Skills* such as question analysis, answer planning and proof reading; *Specific Skills* – organisation of notes and study time, note taking, note making, essay planning; and finally *Learning Techniques*. These activities are directed to organising memory for better recall and are useful end strategies.

Most revision strategies involve rote learning activities after the event whereas if the initial learning task was involving and constructive, directed to some real purpose the learner wanted to achieve then there would be little chance of forgetting. It would be better if we did not start from there. If we can make the original learning more effective, detailed and extensive revision would not be required. Revision is required in inverse proportion to the effectiveness of the original learning.

Deep learning and transfer strategies

Learning strategies are often called study skills or even DARTs (Directed Activities Related to Texts). They may also be referred to as higher order reading or learning strategies. The important aspect is the process in which the learner is engaged which causes him or her to engage with the material at deep cognitive levels so that what is already known is linked to the new or is changed by it. The learner in the process learns the relevance of the content and how it may be applied, perhaps in a modified form, to another situation. In the 'Information Age', when information is so readily available that key words can summon it up from disk and no search skills are necessary, what is becoming increasingly important is to know how and where to find information when it is needed and then how to understand, manage, organise, use and communicate it effectively to meet specific purposes such as in decision-making and problem solving.

Study skills are a form of self directed learning and are used whenever material is read or viewed in order to be used in a communication. In the Schools Council Project (1980) to promote literacy in the secondary school, reading was defined in two ways – *receptive reading*, a running read such as we use when reading a novel, and *reflective reading*, a more complex activity in which we use study skills to glean information and ideas from the text. In fact it is equally possible to apply the same terms – *receptive* or *reflective viewing* of video and screen data or real life events. One of the major concerns of the Project was that pupils did not distinguish between the two forms and tended to apply the same strategy – receptive reading – to all their study tasks. In their Reading to Learn Project, Thomas and Harri-Augstein (1975) found similar results. First year students on degree programmes who were ineffective readers engaged in several rapid read-throughs of text. They were later unable to summarise what they had read or complete satisfactorily a short answer factual recall test on it. Successful readers engaged in reading through the text but rolled forwards and backwards in order to check up on points and also paused for thinking and reflection time as well as to organise their notes. Partially effective readers engaged in slow runs through the text, stopping to make notes as they did so. These students were only successful on the objective test and not on the summary. This is typical of the strategy which students use to collect information for an essay. They do not do a survey read to get an overview but just do a note taking run, expecting by this means to understand what is written. The result is that the essay looks like a neatly written version of the original note taking exercise and is not organised to answer the question or written in a coherent form.

DARTs were devised in order to encourage pupils to slow down and engage with the text in more reflective reading. The activities illustrated different ways in which pupils could be obliged to give detailed attention to text and the results could be discussed with them to show the value of adopting different study strategies. Reflection helps them gain metacognitive control over their mental processes of which they may initially be unaware but which they can promote and control better in subsequent activities. Watson (1996) showed the value of such reflection to her groups who had moderate learning difficulties.

Different types and levels of study skills are needed for different tasks, from simple note taking to writing a report or doing research. The first thing which should be done is to *survey* the information by *scanning* the title, subtitles, looking at the pictures, reading the summaries, flipping through each page, using the index to locate specific information.

Most pupils are unaware of these skills and such skills need to be specifically taught. They may even feel they are cheating if they do not start at the beginning and read through. In addition to scanning a text, Anderson (1979) found that there were other activities going on. He found that nearly all his students were trying to answer three additional 'how' questions. These were:

1. How much do I already know about this topic and text? If anything is already known it can act as *advance organisers* (Ausubel *et al.* 1978) to make later acquisition more effective.
2. How interested am I in it?
3. How difficult or time consuming will it be for me to learn what I need to know from it?

If by scanning they could not answer all these questions they went on to read sections in more detail or the surveying would break down and they turned to another book or another activity.

Some cognitive activities used in studying

In reading for information surveying, locational and reference skills may be used. In reading for the main idea or to understand the logic of a piece, interpretative skills are needed to understand structure and sequence, to find meaning and to understand tables, graphs, illustrations and ideas. If it is necessary to understand the overall structure of something then information has to be organised, summarised, outlined and perhaps labelled. Critical comprehension will involve the use of thinking strategies at literal, interpretative, critical and creative levels. In the process we may reflect on ideas presented, tap into the writer's organisational plan and relate new ideas to old using mental imagery. All of these activities are potentially at work together and, as can be seen, it is essentially a constructive learning activity. This means that it is constructive in the sense of the learner or reader being actively engaged in *making meaning*.

Study skills and the curriculum

Even though pupils might know how to survey text, there was no guarantee that they would use the skills and save themselves time (Neville and Pugh 1977). They needed systematic teaching in primary and then again in secondary school. There was also little correlation between reading ability and the ability to use effectively a range of study skills.

Because of the Information Revolution and more particularly because of a concern to ensure that students at all levels really *learn how to learn* and can become *self organised learners*, the conception of study skills has been significantly developed beyond a consideration of the narrow confines of information skills (Weinstein *et al.* 1988).

The teacher organises the pupils' learning, setting them to learn how to learn by organising the material and the tasks in various ways. For example, instead of taking a poem or a piece of prose and asking the pupils to read it silently in sections and then questioning them about the content, trying to get at their factual and inferential comprehension, the teacher might ask them to read it and then in pairs identify the MAIN POINT or main idea. The strategy is READ – THINK – PAIR – SHARE. After their deliberations, they then can present their main ideas to the rest of the class and can be evaluated by all. The rest of the structure can be explored in like fashion: pictures can be examined and ideas about them discussed using this procedure. Identifying main and subordinate ideas can lead on to producing flow charts and chronologies or time lines, whatever method of recording and representing might be appropriate. The pairing and sharing ensures that all the pupils have an opportunity to express their own ideas in complete sentences – not just one word responses to the teacher. There is also the opportunity for pupils to question each other and where necessary engage in teaching the other how they have arrived at their main ideas.

Concept mapping comparisons

Concept mapping is related to the notion of identifying main points. Now the mapping links them and also includes related ideas in the net attached to each main idea. The essence of the map is that it represents one's own ideas about a subject and by representing these on paper they can be inspected, compared with those of others and discussed. As new knowledge is accumulated it can be incorporated into the map and a new map may need to be drawn, showing a complete change in the whole structure so that developments in learning can be seen.

It is a useful strategy for finding out what pupils bring to a topic and getting this recorded. Subjects might be: castles, settlements, rivers, weather, flowers, fish, food, tools – any subject in the school curriculum and can be begun with a 'brainstorm'.

After several teaching inputs, readings and so on the pupils can be asked to draw another concept map to show their current thinking. From this the teacher can see conceptual developments without having to read large volumes of notes which may or may not reflect knowledge or understanding. To help the pupils reflect upon what they know and have learned, ten differences between the pre- and post-teaching maps may be asked for, together with their reflections upon these. Again pairs work can help focus the attention as each discusses the work with the other and tries to explain it.

The rationale behind all this is that we so often do not know what we think until we try to explain it to someone else. Brainstorming and drawing the concept maps enables the pupils to bring to the forefront of the mind their previous knowledge and experience and inspect it to try to establish connecting links. By creating a heightened awareness in this way, there is a better chance that the information in the new learning will be integrated into the past structures.

Concept completion

Cloze procedure is used in comprehension tests. Gaps are introduced, for example, every seven words and the pupil must complete the sentence. In concept completion the gaps are not at regular intervals but are defined by the concepts the teacher wishes the pupils to focus upon.

In pairs the pupils read the text and discuss it to try to fill in the gaps to reconstruct the author's meaning. On completion they can be asked for reasons why they have produced their particular words.

An example of a concept completion activity for pairs of pupils might be to read the poem by Stephen Spender and try to reconstruct the author's original intention:

Ultima Ratio Regum (first verse only here)
The guns spell money's ultimate reason
In letters of _____ **on the Spring hillside.**
But the boy lying _____ **under the olive trees**
Was too young and too __ _____
To have been notable to their important eye.
He was a better target for a ____ _____.

Assessment

If learners take on an assessment role then their learning of the material is likely to be as high as 95 per cent (Race 1992) and is able to reach deep levels so that it is available for transforming and using in various creative ways. ITT students were asked to evaluate one of the tests of reading set out in a workshop and to use the criteria set out in a lecture on 'What makes a good test'. Inservice students on a distance programme were asked to write a short answer paper on Dyslexia worth 100 marks. It had to consist of True or False, multiple choice and sentence completion items. The main bulk of the questions had to be based upon three recent research papers and their own knowledge of the subject.

In general science and biology teaching pupils were asked to work in small groups to produce an end-of-year exam paper. They then had to draw up answer plans and assign marks to model answers to each question. Younger pupils did similar activities but in relation to two questions. They were all given previous exam papers to base their ideas upon and all their textbooks and notebooks.

Editing and marking

Pupils' writing from previous years can be used as edit material. Good and poor examples can be used for comparison to discuss what makes quality writing. The subject can be a story or a narrative such as about the Wars of the Roses. The original can be used as a *scaffold* for producing a good account and pupils can learn from assigning grades based upon subject criteria. They can use these scaffolds to build their own accounts for homework, for example.

Older pupils working for public exams can be given the task in pairs to mark an exam essay using a criterion referenced grading system given. They then have to justify the mark they have given and write some positive points of guidance on how the writer could have improved the essay. Again content is learned incidentally in this process as well as exam technique.

Summarising

There are many summarising strategies which can be used as part of study skills to enhance learning. Most study material contains information of various kinds such as facts, opinions, methods, steps, ideas and so on. A quick assessment by the teacher can enable the following type of task to be set:

Identify the five (ten etc.) *main points* in the chapter, e.g. the role of the church/monarchy/peasantry. Extra marks and special praise can always be given for finding more points. Write the points in *order of importance* from most to least important.

Ask the pupils to write a summary of a book/chapter they have just read, in exactly 50 words: a *mini-saga*. This really causes them to focus on the essentials of the text and to consider each word of their sentences carefully.

A book or a section of work can be recorded as a *summary*. Pupils often do not know how to summarise something and so the introductory techniques of stating how many main points there might be or how many words they are to use can be helpful training exercises. They have to stop copying out sections verbatim and think over the sections of the content. Discussing how they approached their task will give helpful clues on how to develop their techniques further. Many careers such as police investigation work, travel agency, travel guiding, advertising, teaching, research, journalism, medical practice and so on require summarising skills. The value of the technique should be emphasised.

Writing summaries for different *audiences* can help pupils understand the deeper structure of learning contents. For example, a section of historical information might be written up in the style of a modern day newspaper such as the *Sun*. Pupils can have a lot of fun with this a well as secure their knowledge of a historical topic.

They might be encouraged to put all their work together as a historical newspaper, or present it as a version of the 'Today' Programme on radio or a news broadcast on TV. The NC is still so full that much of the development work on such projects would be need to be done independently outside lessons but the enthusiasm which can be generated is usually sufficient for this to happen. Writing the same information for different audiences can also help it to be learned in a pleasurable way rather than by rote. The audiences may be real, imaginary or historical, and presented in different registers or for different cultures and sub cultures.

Critical reviews of topics will include a brief description of the key aspects with some appropriate evaluation. Examples of the structure of such reviews can be used as models for the pupils to follow. They have to gain more than a knowledge of the content in order to do any summarising task such as this. It is also important to identify the overall structure of the ideas and their relations to each other.

Different review perspectives can also be adopted such as in relation to gender, ethnicity and class, not only in English classes but also in technology, science, art, geography, mathematics and history.

Comparing and contrasting information is another approach to identifying main points and summarising the key issues in many subjects. Sometimes it can be helpful to *tabulate* such data. At other times the differences can be represented *diagrammatically*.

Organising, tabulating, classifying, ordering, diagramming and categorising are all strategies for reducing information into smaller manageable and more meaningful chunks. The process of doing so is also very useful for assisting learning at deeper levels to take place, especially where the learners have done the work for themselves.

Time lines, lists, critical incident analyses and chronologies are in their own ways summaries which can be useful processes to aid learning.

Teaching. In order to help pupils to learn it is sometimes helpful and interesting to provide them with learning materials and set them to design a short teaching session on some aspect. This can be prepared in small groups and then the mini-teaching session can be given to the group. Some might be encouraged to give their presentation to the class. Nothing concentrates the mind more on getting down to the essentials of a subject than when it has to be taught to someone else as every teacher knows. After assessment it is one of the best methods for ensuring something is learned. Teaching sessions need careful structuring so that the same material is not repeated and the class do not have to listen for long periods to topics which the teacher could present better. This is where group work is an important substage and all presentations must have a time limit. An alternative may be for the presentations on what they have learned to be offered at parents' evenings as a change from wall displays and neat books. Both parents and pupils gain an enormous amount from these teaching sessions.

Exhibitions and posters also summarise achievements and can be accompanied by pupils giving mini presentations on their work and what they were trying to achieve. Even the youngest of pupils can do this.

Other types of summary might be to *make two overhead transparencies* to illustrate the main points of a topic. Only seven words to a line are permitted and only ten lines are to be used so that it is large enough for all the class to see easily and compare summaries. They can learn from this that the best method is to put little on the overhead transparency and then the presenter uses these key points to elaborate upon. On another occasion they might be asked to produce their summary notes as an A5 *four page leaflet* for visitors or as a *cartoon sequence*. Pin men drawing needs to be taught for those who would rather not exercise or exhibit their artistic repertoire. Personal computers can be used to support this, if pupils prefer.

Sequencing

Pupils can read a research paper/story/chapter or piece of poetry or prose to identify its main and subordinate points, separate these out and then put them in an order which reflects the meaning of the text. They can then be asked to make this into a flow chart. Alternatively the teacher can take a *flow chart* designed by another class, empty it of its contents and give it to the new class to puzzle out what goes in the empty boxes. In each case a puzzle or problem is given for the pupils to resolve. In the process they will have to give the content their most detailed attention and they learn it very well without any apparent effort, enjoying themselves in the process, especially if they are allowed to work in pairs and are not made to feel it is some kind of test.

Any process or procedure in a subject area can be made into a sequencing activity. For example, there is a *set sequence or procedure* to lighting a Bunsen burner in science or following a routine or recipe in technology, geography and maths.

Once the procedure has been demonstrated and practised it can be useful to say, instead of 'Now write down that procedure', 'Now look at this worksheet with your partner and you will see that someone does not know how to do it at all. Write down the number of the sentences showing the order in which they should be.' This means that the poorer writers are not handicapped and can focus on the real issues. Scissors can be provided if they need to cut the text up and move it about physically. If there is a fear that scissors would be too big a distraction then prepared cut slips can be given out in envelopes which adds to the little bit of mystery.

The same technique can be applied to paragraphs or short stories. What sometimes results is that the pupils may produce a better order than the original author. Very young pupils enjoy being given puzzle envelopes in which the lines of a nursery rhyme have been cut up and jumbled. In pairs they can then practice their reading skills while they try to reconstruct the nursery rhyme correctly. Self correction can be built into the task by having a picture on the reverse of the card which is only complete when all the lines are in the correct order. A self checking device.

Cooperative learning strategies

Dansereau (1988) gave student dyads scientific content to master. He broke the cooperative learning strategy down into six stages which he found facilitated cooperation and learning and labelled them *MURDER*, i.e. establishing the positive *Mood* for studying; *Understanding* while studying; *Recall* – summarising what is read; *Detecting* errors and omissions; *Elaborate* to facilitate learning; and *Review*.

The THINK – PAIR – SHARE collaborative strategy is a much less formal procedure than Dansereau's but none the less valuable for younger learners.

The main problem in classrooms at present is that the desks are often arranged in groups but that pupils are engaged in individual work while at them. Their talk then tends to be social chat (Bennett 1986), not problem solving or collaborative talk. It is therefore the teacher's responsibility to set the task in such a way that the pupils do share their knowledge and that they do this in a purposeful manner which has an appropriate outcome. Teachers need to legitimise the talk which goes on in classrooms by defining it as purposeful activity leading to more productive solutions and learning outcomes. It is these sorts of experiences that can prepare pupils for teamwork in their careers.

Thinkback

This is an extension of collaborative pairs work developed by Lockhead (2001) based on his earlier work with Arthur Whimbey. Lockhead's book is written for college and high school teachers in the USA but could usefully be used in UK classrooms at junior and secondary levels. It is written for those who want their students to become more intelligent. This claim is based on his work with thousands of students over more than 20 years. Although intelligence is thought to be relatively stable, it is not fixed and the Thinkback strategy appears to be extending students' repertoire of learning and organising skills in a transferable way. The Thinkback strategy spans the gap between unstructured constructivist teaching and reception learning and rote memorisation drills. It connects process and product approaches by placing the learners in central control. Thus using Thinkback can convert a teacher-centred rote mastery lesson into an intellectually challenging student-centred exploration, while maintaining specific content mastery objectives.

It is a modification of a talking aloud strategy (Whimbey 1975). It can be used across all subjects at both simple and complex levels, with concrete and abstract concepts. It can be used to promote creative problem solving and with the study skills materials (DARTs) outlined in this chapter.

Lockhead gives examples of three months training in TAPPS (Thinking Aloud Pairs Problem Solving) followed by maths training leading to up to four grade levels of gain on the Iowa Tests of Basic Skills. At Xavier University only a handful of their mainly black students gained entry to medical school. In 1993, using TAPPS 49 students gained access, followed by 55 in 1994, and 96 in 1998, with over 100 in 1999 and still rising. The results are more widely beneficial too: students' reading grades rise by an average of three levels and their IQ scores increase by 20 points. Updates on this summer programme called SOAR (Stress ON Analytical Reasoning) may be found at www.xula.edu

All of this has fostered an atmosphere of achievement which many pupils in our schools could benefit from. There is too much teacher talk in classrooms still and not enough cognitive challenge, even in questioning. This was first revealed by Flanders (1970) and has been confirmed each year since 1991 by my MA students researching their own classrooms using Flanders' sampling frame (Montgomery 2001).

The basic thesis underlying Thinkback is that humans learn much by the process of social imitation. However, thinking is not an observable event and so it is impossible to learn by imitation. Thinkback uses the notion of the video playback in sports training. The person doing the thinking – the problem solver – is paired with a listener and thinks aloud. Together they work over the problem, making the thinking about it explicit. It is a slow and noisy process, easy to observe and question.

For example, the problem solver reads the question aloud twice and then might say – 'If the circle is larger than the square and the cross is shorter than the square, I'll put my finger on the circle then I'll read the problem again.' At this point the listener might say, 'Why did you put your finger on the circle?' This is to identify a hidden thought process or 'stealth thought'. Feuerstein (1995) uses a version of this when he demonstrates his 'mediated learning' techniques. Here the essential difference is that another learner takes over the listening and questioning role and as they become more experienced they often switch roles or share them. The problems may not only be verbal but also visual, and graphic organisers such as tables, diagrams and flow charts can be used in support as 'scaffolds'.

Scaffolding thinking according to Beyer (1997) '. . . consists of supporting student application of a cognitive operation by structuring the execution of that operation with verbal and/or visual prompts. They . . . benefit immensely from having their initial attempts to practice a procedure scaffolded until they have internalised the procedure and can execute it on their own' (p. 171).

Thinkback can have a wide application to learning at all levels and in all stages of education. Even children in infant school could be helped to learn by this strategy. They would of course need explicit teaching and modelling of the technique by the teacher.

Summary and conclusions

An outline has been given of the nature of learning and current learning or schema theory. There are many different learning processes and each learner on entry to school has a vast repertoire of knowledge and learning skills at their disposal.

In order for learning to occur, pupils must attend to what has to be learned and then by the processes of accretion, tuning and restructuring the schemata may be modified to encompass the new information and skills. A distinction was made between deep and surface learning, linking them to particular teaching methods. It is deep learning which results in schemata development and change.

Motivation, particularly intrinsic motivation, is essential for learning to occur and suggestions were made as to what encourages and discourages this. Pressure to achieve standards and extrinsic motivation leads to a decline in learning potential.

The conditions for effective learning were identified and linked to teaching and learning strategies. In the penultimate section details of particular learning strategies which foster surface and deep levels of learning were exemplified.

CHAPTER FIVE

Effective Teaching

Introduction

In 1995 Jim Rose the Director of Inspections at OFSTED reported on teaching problems found at Key Stage 2 in the following manner. The 'below the line lessons', lessons of unsatisfactory standard, demonstrated factors that stood in the way of pupils making better progress and reaching higher standards. Of these three factors were more prevalent in these lessons than in others. First the pupils in some lessons received little direct teaching because the teachers were preoccupied with controlling too many group activities at once. In others teachers pursued a programme of individual work that was self defeating because teaching time available to each pupil was insufficient. In these cases the high teacher work rate was in direct contrast to pupil work rate. Similar circumstances and results were found in the teaching of reading by Southgate-Booth *et al.* 1982; Southgate-Booth 1986. Pupils might expect to receive only about 30 seconds' actual reading time per day and even then the teacher's attention might be shared out on controlling pupil behaviour. She advocated teachers should work less hard and engage in individual, group and whole-class reading teaching. These are strategies which have been incorporated into the National Literacy Strategy (NLS) (DfEE 1998) in the daily literacy hour.

The second problem in unsatisfactory teaching sessions found in the OFSTED reports was that the assessment of pupils' capabilities left much to be desired. The pupils rarely received the critical and supportive feedback and 'feed forward' or developmental advice that they needed and were left unsure of what they had to do to improve their work.

The third problem observed was that the teacher's subject knowledge was insufficient to match the developing abilities of their pupils. In a sense this is not surprising especially in the junior school stage for although there is some subject specialisation by teachers many still have to spread their knowledge across more than a dozen subject areas with at least six of them being the content areas of the NC. The former Chief Inspector for Schools Chris Woodhead (1998) annually presented his report and made similar points, arguing for more direct teaching or more formal methods as a result.

However, the results obtained may lead us to different conclusions and strategies for there may be many more ways to improve teaching than the modes advocated in the official reports. The causal connections made in them do not appear to be established in or supported by research.

The impact of these OFSTED inspections and reports over the years has been to drive teachers to rely more and more on verbal transmission modes which, as can be seen, could be creating problems for a wide range of learners (Montgomery 1998a).

Already the demotivation of the grading system is being felt by teachers. A teacher who is generally working at a very good level on the days of the inspection may only be seen to teach for the second half of two sessions when the interactivity with the class is not in operation. The resultant grade will be good/satisfactory, the same as that of someone who has performed at a marginally competent level who is not then a failure but known to be underperforming during the rest of the year.

Teachers are currently graded on a seven-point scale but the feedback is in three categories: excellent/very good; good/satisfactory; fail. If the teacher is not seen engaging in interactive teaching, the grade cannot be more than satisfactory, even though the pupils demonstrate that they have learned and are following up the work in a highly motivated manner. The message is that 'real teaching' is interactive and direct, and anything else is not of significance. Thus it is that when teachers organise group work because this is an appropriate method for enabling the pupils to learn a particular part of a topic, they do not feel they are teaching and do not value the pupils learning in the same way as if they had done most of the talking themselves. This is despite the fact that we know that the more we as teachers talk the less the pupils tend to learn.

The overfilled curriculum also creates pressures on teachers to cover the syllabus by engaging in more and more direct teaching at the expense of the learners' learning. There is no time to take account of local phenomena such as floods and gales or death of the hamster: the syllabus must be covered.

This content curriculum is required to be assessed at frequent intervals. Such a system leads, according to the researches of Feller (1994), to a lowering not a raising of standards. This is in direct contrast to what we are continually told by the quasi governmental agencies (quangos). The system of didactics also has to be bolstered by spoon-feeding of critical information as well as a regular regime of testing and reinforcement of the information. The tests act as external or extrinsic motivators to keep the pupils' attention on the tasks, however irrelevant they might perceive them to be. Achieving good test results can become an end in itself.

Thus we have seen results year on year at GCSE and SATs at the Key Stages have been improving except at Key Stage 2 – junior school level. This may not be the improvement in pupils' learning but more about the teachers' abilities to teach to the tests and so appear to gain general improvements as the tests bed in.

In Asian cultures where memorising and rote learning have dominated there is now a move in many of them to seek to enable their learners to begin to think and problem solve and learn how to be more creative. English education, however, is being measured by their content standards and has been driven towards their methods. Such rote forms of education are more in the mode of brainwashing and make the learners vulnerable to the irrationalities of emotion and social pressures. It can release fundamentalism.

What will be recommended in this chapter is a move towards more 'brain engage' strategies and methods of learning and teaching throughout schooling and across all subjects. We can call this developing intellectual and cognitive capabilities.

Advice to Government from the Gifted and Talented Advisory Group over three years has consistently been directed to ask for the increase on emphasis for the development of cognitive abilities in schools across the curriculum so that all children can benefit. We have at last seen a movement in this direction with the publication of research on thinking skills in schools (McGuinness 1999) commissioned by DfEE.

Teaching

But what is teaching? According to Curzon (1992) it is 'a system of activities intended to induce learning, comprising the deliberate and methodological creative control of those conditions in which learning does occur' (p. 18). The critical points here are the activities inducing learning.

Despite what is continually presented as the accepted wisdom we do not teach subjects, we teach pupils *how to learn* subjects. Thus instead of the dichotomy continuously being proposed that we must get teachers to become better and better subject teachers and stop them, particularly primary teachers, from all that child minding we should be focusing upon a *learner-centred curriculum* and *teaching for learning*.

Let it be proposed that effective teaching is occurring where the majority, preferably all the pupils, learn most of what the teacher intended. Good teaching is occurring where the pupils want to learn and do not have to be made to. It is seen when the pupils want and do continue with the study long after the lesson ends. They are to be seen animatedly talking about the subject during and long after the session ends. All the pupils complete their assignments and may do extra studies and investigations with enthusiasm and creativity. The classroom ethos is a hive of energy and activity and is presided over by a positive and supportive teacher playing many different roles. These roles may be teacher, follower, leader, facilitator, coordinator, manager and so on, not auto didact as we are frequently told by those who do not teach and have never trained a teacher.

School effectiveness is seen to be, in large measure, a direct result of the learning and teaching taking place in classrooms (Reynolds 1992). The success or failure of the teacher–student relationship has been identified as a critical factor in setting standards of learning performance, as well as greatly influencing positive or negative individual behaviour (Riding and Rayner 1998: 167).

Work presented by the teacher which is too difficult or irrelevant may create learning difficulties and problem behaviour. Mortimore *et al.* (1988) also found that the pedagogy and curriculum process played a significant role in generating and preventing EBD. The markers they found associated with effective schools included: consistency among teachers; structured well-planned lessons; intellectually challenging teaching; a work-centred focus in lessons; an easy dialogue between teachers and pupils; good record keeping (personal, social and academic); and a positive attitude.

The ethos of a classroom and a school, the quality of staff–student relationships, a structured and purposeful learning situation with adaptive flexibility within which individual contribution is encouraged and acknowledged are arguably prime factors in the successful classroom. Their absence will make for difficulties, troublesome behaviours and learning failure. Such conditions may also produce EBD or, at the very least, reinforce such behaviours and result in learning failure (Riding and Rayner 1998).

For Eisner (1983) teaching is both a skill and an art. The teacher must perform with skill and grace; must exercise qualitative judgements in achieving qualitative ends regarding tempo, time and pace; it involves a tension between automaticity and inventiveness, and as a result many ends are emergent, not preconceived. However, for others it has been considered as either a skill or an art. Depending upon in which frame the research is set, the results obtained will be likely to confirm the hypothesis. This thus demonstrates that teaching is both and more than each individual part.

Another method used by researchers to demonstrate effectiveness or otherwise of the teaching activity is to measure the amount of time that pupils spend on task, the amount of time spent attending or looking at the task, and/or the amount of the material taught which has been learned. What is seldom taken into account is also what has also been learned that was not directly or specifically taught. There is a tendency to concentrate only upon the curriculum content and skills when assessing learning as a result of teaching. Pupils may also be learning a wide range of social and communication skills, ethics and values, attitudes and intents and cognitive strategies. Factors which cannot be easily defined and quantified seldom find a place in educational research for instead of undertaking observational research to determine patterns and develop hypotheses, the general practice is to approach the classroom with a number of predetermined hypotheses based on literature research to test out. Thus previously worn out theories and research are revisited rather than new or different ones being developed.

Effective teaching practices for inclusive education are suitable for teaching all students, according to Knight (1999). Effective teaching as outlined in the National Competency for Beginning Teaching (Commonwealth of Australia 1997) includes:

- being sensitive to students' academic and emotional needs;
- negotiating goal and expectations with students;
- making explicit the intent of activities to students;
- selecting, adapting and sequencing learning content to suit individual students;

- using a wide range of teaching approaches and pacing to meet students needs;
- actively teaching strategies to students;
- setting appropriately challenging tasks;
- modifying materials and assessments to suit students needs;
- adapting instruction to appeal to different learning styles, and
- continually monitoring teaching programmes and student learning.

When we compare this list to the everyday practices in classrooms where didactics reigns and the teacher controls all aspects of interaction and task work and students are all undertaking the same tasks in the same way from the standard text or worksheet we can see a mismatch between expectation and reality if this was to be promoted as effective teaching in the UK.

Explicit teaching for inclusion is also important. Students with special needs do not develop skills incidentally, these have to be explicitly taught so that they can later be applied in new situations. The teacher is working with the pupil within each students' 'zone of proximal development' – ZPD (Vygotsky 1978). Knight describes the process of working with students within their instructional level and ZPD as *guided internality* (Knight 1999). It encourages students to be active learners in control of their own progress.

A guided internality teaching process is generated by:

- the teacher modelling and making thought processes overt;
- the teacher in collaboration with individual students setting realistic goals;
- promoting students' active role in the learning process in decision-making and risk taking;
- giving students sufficient practice to ensure the mastery of skills; and
- teaching strategies which match students' cognitive abilities so that the task is first analysed to check that the students have the requisite skills.

(Knight et al. 1998 cited in Knight 1999: 6)

What is absent from all these lists of effectiveness research is the 'how' to be effective detail. For example, how can pacing be taught and challenge introduced if it is not already present when teachers know it should be. Presumably they think it is. Thus in relation to the above lists we need a further set of descriptors to convert them into advice for practice. Researchers seldom have the teaching expertise to do this or even realise that this is necessary.

Teacher education

All these recommendations and attributes are far removed from class teaching procedures which may be generally observed. Not that it is the fault of the teachers. How is it possible for undergraduates trained to teach their subject to adapt what they do to teach pupils how to learn it? Even after many years of experience, teachers may be using the same practices and repertoire of skills which they used in their first year of teaching and find it hard to adapt them to suit new situations. Changes of school can promote development in teaching but a career in the same school may not. The single training day and short course are not effective in promoting changes in practice (Montgomery 1998b, Barker 1998). Long courses of systematic inservice training with systematic assignments in classrooms linking theory and practice can induce development and change in teacher thinking and practices (Montgomery 1993, 1994, 1998b).

The 'good' graduate with a PGCE has had a course of training to teach lasting nine months, two thirds of which is spent in a school where experience and training can range from 'sitting by Nellie', a weak form of the apprenticeship approach, to prescriptions from personal practice. The twelve weeks' teacher education training, marginally longer than the time it takes to put a policeman on the beat, has to equip them for the most complex job anyone can ever do. They have to be taught the contents of and how to teach the NC a curriculum remote from their degree programmes and which occupies most of the 18 hours per week contact time which they might be required to undertake. This requires hard effort after their more relaxed low contact hour degree programmes where attendance was mainly optional.

Theory and practice of education which is used to underpin teaching programmes in most countries has been mainly expunged from the programmes in the UK. In the decade following the introduction of the NC, theory was regarded as irrelevant to learning to teach and institutions were gradually obliged to remove it from their programmes, leaving method to be taught by the subject tutors. Thus it is that a decade of teachers has nothing rational in the way of theory and research upon which their teaching is based. Only recently a teacher student on a Masters programme asked what Piaget levels were, having never heard of him.

This anti-intellectualism in initial teacher education and training has resulted in the expansion of the reflective practitioner movement in the inservice field to attempt to compensate. In PGCE programmes, students from a wide variety of institutions have complained that they are not taught to teach and that a single lecture on classroom management and a few on special needs are not sufficient (Hadfield 1990, Tufnell 2001). Thus in school-based work the ITT students must spend time attached to the SENCO to compensate for this, but is 'sitting by Nellie' appropriate?

The primary PGCE students' task is even more broad ranging and complex than that of the secondary subject teacher and so it is not surprising that their skills are found wanting. It is of great credit to them that they make such huge efforts to catch up. In other countries a two-year specialisation in teacher education after an undergraduate programme is considered essential. Even the four-year BEd, now the BA QTS, has been converted to a subject degree programme on the PGCE model interspersed with concurrent practice for it was found that teacher supply could be switched off and on more effectively (and economically) in this 'three plus one' training model.

Teachers who have no grounding in relevant professional theory become vulnerable to fashions and fads for they cannot bring an appropriate critique to what they are told. The proposed contractual obligation to engage in regular professional updating (DfEE 1999a) seen in this light is essential but it is also proposed to control this centrally, so we can expect more problems for both learners and teachers.

We have seen the introduction of the National Literacy Strategy (DfEE 1998) which specifies how and what teachers will teach and then the National Numeracy Strategy (DfEE 1999). The Literacy hour training and materials have been very helpful to many young teachers, according to Moriarty (1999). It demonstrated that they have simply not been properly trained in the first place and that it is also a case of 'Back to the Future' for primary teachers taught 'Basic Skills' for two hours each morning before the NC was introduced ten years ago. Even despite the prescriptions in the NLS of what and how to teach this has been necessary but not sufficient for now we find that the DfEE's own research through OFSTED has shown that children's spelling and writing skills have remained below standard. There are of course two aspects of this not explored. First spelling and writing are more complex recall tasks and will always lag behind reading which is only a recognition skill. Second the whole of the NLS is geared to teaching reading and largely subsumes writing instead of giving it the significance it requires and using distinct and often different strategies to develop it from the outset of learning (Montgomery 1997a, 2001).

In the HMI document *Teaching Quality* (DES 1983) we were told:

Teaching and educational quality go together. It is the teachers who have to shoulder most of the task of giving the children and young people in our schools the education which attempts to measure up to the nation's aspirations. They are performing that task with professionalism and skill. But still further progress is needed.

(para. 93)

Two years later we learn in *Better Schools* (DES 1985a) that teachers are suddenly not up to scratch at all. 'The Government view, in the light of reports by HMI is that a significant number of teachers are performing at a standard below that required to achieve the objectives now proposed for our schools' (para. 138). These quotations illustrate what can be done with the same data. The first presents the positive supportive view directing teachers towards self improvement. The second shows a complete change of attitude towards the negative and punitive. It is this climate which has pervaded ever since and in which teachers as learners themselves find it difficult to remain positive and, like pupils, find such a regime stressful and leading all to easily to bullying and scapegoating. What is needed is a supportive and constructive ethos to promote teacher development, for we grow best from our strengths.

Mentoring in ITT

Since 1992 British legislation has given schools the prime responsibility for teacher training practice. Schools can now develop their own teacher training programmes with HE or independently and once they obtain accreditation they can carry them out on their own. There has always been a tension between schools supervising the teaching practice of ITT students and able to spend considerable time with them in the classroom and the HE institution sending out the supervisor for the weekly visit. Some supervision schedules might only permit funding of one or two visits per practice. Subject specialists were very often ill equipped to supervise primary teaching practices or even their own subject areas in secondary schools if they were not engaged in research on teaching and learning in their subject areas.

The role of the mentor was seen as overcoming many of these perceived deficiencies. Mentoring is based on the idea of supplanting the imperious visitation by a transfer of responsibility to on-the-job, in-house personnel in daily contact with children and the curriculum. It should offer the novice teacher full and free daily access to relevant, real and practical advice, criticism and guidance (Batteson 1998). However, the administrative burden upon teachers in schools is such that observation of teaching and mentoring duties frequently become lower order priorities.

Batteson (1998) describes mentoring as the Faustian embrace:

> . . . within this shift from the ivory tower to the classroom there are inherent tensions. Pre-eminent amongst these is celebration of the role and power of 'real' teachers in reproducing the nation's teaching workforce whilst a fairly remorseless moral panic has clustered around convictions that schools and teachers have contributed to declining standards of literacy, numeracy and behaviour. It is odd that schools which politicians and the media allege, have contributed to a levelling or lowering of standards can increasingly take on the task of training new, improved teachers (and can apparently avoid – to paraphrase the 1992 Three Wise Men report – recycling their inadequacies).
>
> (p. 29)

There have been a number of reviews of the partnerships arising in this new purchaser–provider framework and they also do not give cause for optimism that mentoring and the school-based training model have solved any of the former problems and may indeed have introduced new ones.

It was found by Edwards and Collison (1997) that:

- Schools were treating the training as 'projects' and had not developed an overall rationale to give it a status in everyday school life. Mentors felt unable to link the responsibility to pupils with their responsibility to students.
- Teachers valued theory but said they could not provide it and would not risk discussions which went beyond task setting and performance. For secondary teachers, theory meant subject not educational theory.
- Teachers were providing model lessons but did not expose their practice to further scrutiny and discussion. They did not explore problematic events or engage in co-enquiry.
- The tutors acted primarily as trouble shooters and did not take part in any development activities.

- The mentors had not developed any identity as mentors.
- The relationship was one of 'colonisation' of the college by the school.

Furlong (1996) found that in 45 courses genuine partnerships were rare. They were very much constrained by the economics of the system in that the costs of teacher and tutor time militated against the scheme. It appears to be a less economically efficient system than the old one. Even the claims of the course leaders to follow the reflective practitioner model were seen as problematic for in practice the move from disciplinary theory was supporting a very superficial level of personal reflection.

Good teaching

The teaching techniques used by teachers carry ideological beliefs and are thus more than just classroom behaviours (Fenstermacher 1986; Jackson 1968). The dominant view of teaching is that effective teachers have a broad repertoire of skills and techniques which they use in skilful ways to meet the changing needs of classroom demands (Glaser 1977, Gagné *et al.* 1988). However, these optimistic views are not borne out by the research.

Goodlad (1984) observed 1,000 classrooms and Cuban (1984), 7,000. They concluded that teaching was mostly a teacher-centred activity. The teachers lecture and the students practise. Student-centred teaching made up only a small per cent of of the observations. The methods changed slightly with mathematics or social sciences contents (Stodolsky 1984). In maths there was more recitation, teacher control and skill organisation; in social studies the work was more varied and included group work, student reports and a variety of cognitive levels were identified.

Joyce and Weil (1986) identified four families or models as follows: information processing; personal; social; and behavioural – in which the theory guided the style. Joyce and Shower (1988) found that the more effective teachers:

- taught the class as a whole;
- gave an animated presentation;
- were task orientated;
- gave non evaluative relaxed instruction;
- had high expectations of the more able and for them the pace was faster and created alertness;
- related comfortably to pupils and so got fewer problems.

Scheerens and Barnes (1991) looking at effective schools in an international analysis found that effective teachers:

- made clear what had to be learned;
- managed learning units in a considered sequence;
- gave much exercise material for pupils which involved use of hunches and prompts;
- gave regular tests with immediate feedback.

The data from each of these investigations shows a bias towards the notion of the reproducibility of knowledge. It also indicates a conception and construction by the researchers of effective teaching as what effective teachers do. In fact what teachers do, even successfully, is not necessarily what they should be doing. This is well illustrated by Paul (1990) in his summary of didactic versus critical thinking theory and its influence on the educative process. In the following sections three of his seventeen categories are summarised to illustrate these differences.

The Fundamental Needs of Students in didactic theory are to be told *what* to think: they are given details, definitions, explanations, rules, guidelines and reasons to learn. In critical theory the fundamental needs of students are to be encouraged *how*, not what, to think. They learn that it is important to focus on significant content and it is accompanied by live issues that stimulate students to gather, analyse and assess that content.

In the Nature of Knowledge in didactics the students learn that knowledge is independent of the thinking that generates, organises and applies it. Students are said to know when they can repeat what has been covered. They are given the products of someone else's thoughts. In Critical Theory classrooms students learn that all knowledge of content is generated, organised, applied and analysed, synthesised and assessed by thinking; that gaining knowledge is unintelligible without such thought. Students are given opportunities to puzzle their way through to knowledge and explore its justification as part of the process of learning.

In his Model of the Educated Person Paul identifies those from didactic education as literate people who are fundamentally repositories of content analogous to an encyclopaedia or a data bank, directly comparing situations in the world with facts in storage. This is a true believer. Texts, assessments, lectures, discussions are content dense and detail orientated.

An educated literate person from a critical theory background is fundamentally a repository of strategies, principles, concepts and insights embedded in processes of thought. Much of what is known is constructed as needed, not prefabricated. This person is a seeker after truth and a questioner rather than a believer. In such a system teachers model insightful consideration of questions and problems, and facilitate fruitful discussions.

It can be inferred that in the world of the twenty-first century and the Internet where all the data in the world is available online it is of very little sense having an education which has as its main preoccupation the stuffing of children's heads with facts. The Gradgrind era of 'What we want is facts' has passed. What we want is knowledge and understanding and the ability to apply what we know in appropriate situations. We also need to be able to construct new applications and solutions and apply them creatively. It is difficult to see how the current State system of education in the UK is going to meet the needs of this new millennium. Perhaps the process of development in education and learning has only been temporarily set back. However, within a few years more it will need to be set in motion again if the UK is to maintain its current position in the world, much less improve it.

Teaching methods

Over time during the twentieth century two different teaching and learning traditions were seen to evolve. Subject teachers, mainly those in secondary schools, adopted methods which involved the verbal transmission of material to be learned in the didactic subject-centred form using a watered-down method such as might have been experienced by the teachers in their university education. The primary school movement favoured a more child-centred learning organisation with much more practical and self directed learning activities by the pupils. This was rooted in theories of child development and education based upon the work of early childhood educators such as Friedrick Froebel, Lilian de Lissa, Margaret and Rachel Macmillan, Maria Montessori and so on. It did in fact have a substantial base in theory and practice whereas secondary education did not.

Secondary education grew by extension of education into the later years of adolescence and an extension of the number of curriculum subjects to fill this time. After the 1944 Education Act when the tripartite system was established the secondary modern schools tended to adopt a mixture of the two approaches to fit better the learning needs of their pupils as they saw them and the grammar schools offered more in the way of didactics. Of course within these general trends there were individual variations as teachers and schools experimented with both curriculum and method. They had more time for this up as far as Year 9 when pupils might begin formal study for the public examinations such as O and A levels. In subsequent years a number of significant attempts were made to influence these traditional teaching methods and heated arguments reigned with the battle lines drawn between keeping up traditional standards and not succumbing to the progressive ideologies of the 'great unwashed'. This were the terms used to disparage the suggestions of a new generation of teachers and lecturers who might wear jeans and have long hair (especially of the men).

In the 1960s and 1970s, three new models of teaching and learning emerged. These were the Behaviour Control methods of Skinner (1958) underpinning task analysis and programmed learning, the Discovery Learning method of Bruner (1960/1977) and the Cognitive Orientated curriculum of Weikart (1967) which did not emerge in the UK until much later. In the UK we had the Logical Constructive theory of teaching proposed by the philosopher Hirst (1968). Hirst's papers and lectures set me thinking and working on a psychological model by which to express his general principles and then to convert these into practical applications for my students in teacher education. This was the basis of the 'modern model of teaching' which follows in a later section. Skinner's ideas and principles underpinned the work on CBG and 3Ms, especially in relation to positive behaviour management in schools.

Discovery learning

Bruner undertook a considerable amount of practical work in classrooms and established some principles which many constructivists have incorporated into their own themes and theories and practices. He coined the term 'Discovery Learning' and it is worth looking at some of the issues he raised in more detail.

According to Bruner (1960/1977) the class teacher has the responsibility of ensuring the methods of teaching and learning are realistic in that they allow discovery activity. He states that purely expository teaching on its own is of little value for it does not help a student acquire the capacity to think creatively and critically.

Discovery learning is an inquiry training so that pupils gain the most fundamental understanding of the underlying principles that give structure to a subject. The pupil in discovering the meaning of the principles learns in the process the concepts and relationships. This can be compared with what Bloom (1956) describes in the process of Analysis in his Taxonomy of Educational Objectives. The fact that Bruner is suggesting that very young children can engage in this form of activity as well as teenagers should in their curriculum subjects, was bound to upset a lot of people! Even though he may have been right.

He found that when pupils worked in these ways there was:

- growth in intellectual potency;
- intrinsic motivation;
- mastery of principles which enabled them to apply the learning;
- gains in memory as a result of the organisation of their own knowledge.

Bruner also insisted that pupils needed training in the plausibility of guesses. If teachers or parents suppress guessing they are inhibiting a process inherent in discovery or, as Kelly (1955) might suggest, we would be preventing them being scientists and hypothesisers, our natural selves. Parents in particular tend to stop their children guessing, seeing it as wrong and correcting them with the truth or facts.

Bruner maintained that if there was a de-emphasis on extrinsic motivators then the learners needed steady feedback on performance, giving them accurate knowledge of their progress. This can be seen as a fundamental reason for PCI: it feeds intrinsic motivation and that is why it is important to construct it in a positive format or to use it to raise questions for the learner.

One of the important programmes which was developed by Bruner and his co-workers was the curriculum project – Man: A Course of Study (MACOS) – which became very popular in the 1980s with tutors in ITT and Humanities students. In the process he also introduced the modified notion of 'Guided Discovery Learning' to counteract the major criticism that no one lived long enough to rediscover for themselves the first principles of all the subjects they needed to study.

Taba (1963) identified four steps in discovery learning, which can also be used as a teaching/learning protocol as follows:

- the problem creates bafflement;
- the learner(s) explore the problem;

- the learners are prompted to generalise and use prior knowledge to understand a new problem or pattern;
- there need to be opportunities to apply the principles learned to new situations.

Another significant researcher and thinker in the teaching field at that time was Ausubel (1968). He criticised Bruner's notions of discovery learning, claiming that not all discovery was or could be made meaningful. In his view beginning learners learn more effectively by 'Reception'. This involved presenting the entire content of what is to be learned in its final form. The learning is meaningful if it allows reproduction with understanding at a future date. He rejected the idea that discovery learning engendered intrinsic motivation. *Reception method* is common throughout the education system. It places a great emphasis on the teachers' skill in structuring the subject content to be learned. The NC could be seen as an important contribution to underpinning Reception teaching by teachers. It is a variant of expository teaching and didactics.

Ausubel also coined the term *Advance organisers*. These consist of a short arrangement of the whole material introduced before the lesson begins. It might consist of a list of the main points or the main topics or side headings to be covered, showing the structure of the lesson or lecture. It is required by OFSTED inspections at the moment to state the 'learning outcomes' or targets of programmes and lessons. These organising principles form a Gestalt which both aids learning and later helps recall. The advance organisers for the classroom observation method are given as CBG, 3Ms and PCI.

Progressive differentiation is a system recommended by Ausubel for teaching the most generally relevant concepts first followed by second order concepts and so on. This process gives stable hooks for the learning to be attached. He rejects the notion that the learner might have some autonomy in selecting what might be learned. For Ausubel it is the teacher's role to determine the subject of teaching.

It can be seen that there is room for both Reception teaching and Discovery Learning as part of the teachers' repertoire of skills. At present pupils are suffering from too much reception method and not enough eclecticism.

Teacher reflection

The development of effective teachers is the primary goal of teacher education programmes and Smyth (1989) described the emergence of reflectivity as a conceptual thrust in teacher education. There is currently a general consensus that reflectivity leads to professional growth (Van Manen 1991) and according to Wildman *et al.* (1990) professional growth is unlikely without it. Reflective teaching is currently viewed as a paramount vehicle for enhancing the development of effective teachers (Allen and Casbergus 1995: 741). However, in the miniscule amount of time initial teacher education students have to devote to reflection on their activities, it is inservice education in England and Wales where this has had a better opportunity to be fostered.

Systematic reflection allows the teacher to be self directed, it facilitates the growth from novice to expert. It enables the teacher to view teaching from a more interpretative and critical perspective. Reflective teaching is the process of assessing the origins, purposes and consequences of one's teaching at a variety of levels. These Van Manen (1991) identified as follows:

Level one: technical rationality, efficient and effective application of pedagogical knowledge.

Level two: practical action learning concerned with explicating and clarifying the assumptions and predispositions underlying competing pedagogical goals and assessing the educational consequences of a teaching action.

Level three: critical reflection, moral and ethical criteria, such as whether important human needs and purposes are being met, are incorporated into the discourse about practical action.

Once again it has to be pointed out that teachers' practices are not always the best sources for reflective analysis. What a teacher may be doing may not be what they ought to be doing which can lead to problems for extrapolation and for mentoring and so on.

Teaching approaches to text

Zahorik (1990) studying reading teaching and social studies teaching identified three different teaching approaches which were described as follows:

Text coverage: In the reading lesson there was an introduction of new vocabulary and pupils were briefly told the content of the story. The story was then read by the pupils, next they took turns in oral reading. There was then a discussion of the story focusing on the recall of events. The pupils then did word attack or comprehension practice in their work books or on worksheets.

Text extension: In this method there was text content teaching with an acquisition focus at a level mostly beyond the knowledge level and it was indirectly related to learning activities that extended the textbook content as well as activities directly related to the text. The skills of story writing drawing on listening to records, additional reading and genuine discussion were developed.

Text thinking: In this method the text content plus other content was used with a development of thinking focus at Bloom's (1956) analytic, synthetic and evaluation levels. These were used both directly and indirectly related to the learning activities. Thinking critically and creatively were encouraged and independent thinking was fostered and rewarded. Open questions were used and children were encouraged to give opinions and support them with evidence.

This last method is presumably another version of interactive teaching with more challenging questions favoured by Government inspectors.

A set of teaching methodologies was described by Curzon (1992) writing for teachers in further education (FE). However, there is less on method and more on organisation of settings and presentations. For example:

- the formal lesson – a teaching/learning sequence based on mastery of intellectual skills;
- the skills lesson – motor skills teaching to a required standard requiring demonstration and practice;
- the lecture – a one way communication;
- the discussion group – a small number of students discuss a problem set by the tutor;
- the seminar – a class member presents a thesis or topic for scrutiny;
- team teaching – a group of teachers collaborate and teach a topic together;
- tutoring – learners and tutor discuss problems presented by the tutor;
- audio visual instruction – used as parts of an instructional sequence;
- programmed instruction – self administered programme on the basis of stimulus response connections presented in small steps;
- computer-based instruction.

(Curzon 1992: 237)

There are of course many variations on these themes; there can be demonstration lessons and seminars in which all the students are set to read a paper and then produce the main ideas, issues and sequence without reference to their notes. This is more challenging than having one or two students reading their prepared notes, ending up as a very poor version of the formal lecture. Tutorials may be with individual student and tutor and discuss problems raised by the pupil as well as the tutor, or the student may read an essay and discuss the points in it which the tutor may raise.

There has been a move in FE to introduce more methods based on 'good primary practice' (FEU 1987) so that there is more action learning. Gibbs (1990) introduced the concepts and techniques of experiential learning (Kolb 1984) and linked these with methods necessary for 'deep learning' encouraging them to be applied in both further and higher education (Gibbs 1994, 1995). These methods have much in common with the Education for Capability movement (Stephenson and Weil 1988, Yorke 1995).

Britzman (1991) in her study of teacher education programmes and how students learn in them showed that the foundations and sources of theory lie in teachers' practice. She claimed that 'educational theorising is situated within the lives of teachers, in values, beliefs and deep convictions enacted in practice, in the social context that encloses such practice, and in the social relationships that enliven the teaching and learning encounter' (p. 50). The field is the direct site of theorising and it is the irrelevancy of much academic theory to field settings which has led to so much hostility in practitioners.

However, irrelevant theory was not promulgated in all teacher education courses (Montgomery 1993, 1998c). There is a coherent theory and practice of teaching to be found now. During the previous 25 years it has been in development. Education tutors in that period were employed because of their teaching expertise to complement the subject expertise of other staff. Much of the theory and practice of teaching framework is to be found in constructivist and instructional psychology with which these practitioners were not usually conversant. They were seldom engaged in research in the problem areas of pupil's learning. Without research on learning and teaching and especially grounded research to test theory and practice, many programmes lacked application and relevance.

> A grounded theory is one that is inductively derived from the study of the phenomenon it represents. That is it is discovered, developed, and provisionally verified through systematic data collection, analysis. Practice and theory stand in reciprocal relationship with each other. One does not begin with a theory, then prove it. Rather, one begins with an area of study and what is relevant to that area is allowed to emerge.
>
> (Strauss and Corbin 1990: 23)

This is indeed the process and methodology by which the theory and practice of teaching in this book have been constructed.

Later in this chapter some examples of teaching methods promoting enhanced learning outcomes are given. These are based upon grounded research in classrooms across the country and in the international field.

Curriculum

The curriculum is all those planned experiences of the school (Neagley and Evans 1967) and consists of programmes of activities to enable pupils to attain, as far as possible, educational ends and objectives (Hirst 1968).

The NC purports to be broad and balanced. However, this must be questioned as it is only one aspect of the curriculum of schools, an important one of course. It should consist of all that information and skills that the culture thinks important to transmit to its young people bound up in the ten subject syllabi.

Despite the NC being cut by 20 per cent by the efforts of Sir Ron Dearing (1994), teachers complain that there is still too much content to be able to teach classes of pupils effectively. Interactive teaching only allows them to 'cover' this content. In terms of providing an education for the nation's future, the NC can be regarded as a narrow vehicle for transmitting the culture to the young. In 1998 after ten years it has been discovered that the English curriculum is not the best vehicle in primary schools for transmitting literacy, thus the Literacy hour (DfEE 1998) and then the Numeracy hour (DfEE 1999) were reintroduced. Prior to the introduction of the NC in 1989 primary teachers had always devoted mornings to such Basic Skills teaching.

There are at least seven different curricula which the pupil might be learning and aspects of all of them at once although these may not be being directly taught.

These seven curricula are as follows:

- *The National Curriculum:* English, Mathematics, Science, RE, Geography, Technology and IT, History, Music, Art and PE.
- *The basic skills curriculum:* reading, spelling, handwriting and number skills. These underpin the other subjects and may be the main vehicles for reinforcement and learning.
- *The extra curriculum.* These are all the out-of-school activities such as orchestra and chess clubs which the school provides and also those extras which parents and the local community may provide.
- *The hidden curriculum.* This is the system of attitudes and values transmitted by the ways in which pupils, teachers and staff in general are treated and treat each other. Remedial tutorials in scruffy corridors and rooms with broken furniture transmit a hidden agenda.

Despite the kindliest intention of teachers, fear is the central debilitating characteristic of many pupils' school lives (Mongon and Hart 1989). They found that the effect of the hidden curriculum was to exert a destruction of dignity which was so massive and pervasive that few pupils subsequently recovered. The sad thing was that it was never intended by the teachers to be thus. Its effect is a legitimate criticism of the schooling process. When we add to this that the majority of girls come through the process with a diminished sense of esteem and self worth while boys overestimate their abilities and yet underachieve by comparison in co-ed institutions because they feel they must preserve a macho image and not be seen to try, we can see the schooling process as less than facilitative. There is also widespread bullying and denigration of any pupils who have learning difficulties or differences so that their sense of self worth is even further diminished.

- *The personal and social skills curriculum.* After the NC had been designed it was then realised that several important areas of learning had been omitted. They were reintroduced as cross curricular issues in the context of PSE. Other aspects such as equal opportunities and meeting the needs of the more able were bundled into cross curricular themes. Civics was looking for a place, as was education for parenthood, and have emerged as a curriculum for citizenship.
- *The moral and ethical curriculum.* Having specified a Euro-centric Christian approach to RE despite the range of religions followed by pupils in schools there was little opportunity to consider moral development in general and wider ethical issues.
- *The cognitive curriculum.* The most neglected of all has been the cognitive curriculum. Children's cognitive development has generally been regarded as incidental to learning the school curriculum. Teachers in the past learned about cognitive development but seldom was this integrated with what they might teach and how they should foster cognitive development. It is not surprising therefore that two-thirds of the population may not achieve the intellectual independence of abstract thinking. It was this that Donald Kennedy was concerned about in writing to all college principals in 1987. It is the same issue raised by Paul in 1990 and by

many educational thinkers before and since. In the final section of this chapter an attempt will be made to tackle these issues. It will deal with the problems of differentiation, cognitive challenge and the nature of a cognitive curriculum.

Teaching the cognitive curriculum would mean that every teacher would be expected to be developing thinking skills and study skills in the medium of their own subject. This would offer the cognitive stretch that all pupils need. It enables them to work independently and alongside peers in a variety of different ways. It offers all pupils more flexibility in learning giving them greater autonomy to learn more and to learn at deeper and more secure levels. This has been shown to be beneficial to all learners (Montgomery 1998a).

It was Bloom (1956) who first established what he called a taxonomy of educational objectives in the intellectual domain. These were cross curricular and have begun to play an important part in the development and design of learning methods and teaching materials (Montgomery 1995, 1996).

Differentiation

This is the term reserved for individualising the curriculum task so that individual needs and difficulties are catered for. There are a number of strategies which may be used and they can be grouped under two main headings. There are those methods which are structural and which are generally applied across the school for grouping pupils for teaching. Examples of this technique are streaming by ability, now commonly replaced by 'setting' or streaming for ability in a limited number of curriculum subjects such as English and mathematics. Acceleration involves moving highly able students up a year or two, known as 'grade skipping' in the USA. Although teachers worry about the social implications of this strategy, individual pupils may cope remarkably well with this situation. The choice should be left to the pupil rather than the teachers, a case of pupils know best as they directly experience the advantages and disadvantages and know how with support to balance them.

Differentiation is concerned with the delivery of the curriculum and its assessment. In practice. Figure 5.1 shows diagrammatically the two categories. In integral approaches it is the basic curriculum which is individualised and forms in the best examples a whole lifestyle approach. The structural approach deals mainly with groups and it is less certain in that system that the same basic curriculum is available to all.

Structural methods all involve accelerating or de-accelerating the learner through curriculum contents in various ways and include methods such as 'grade skipping'; which was mentioned above. Even some enrichment materials merely teach what the learner could expect to learn in another phase of education. For example, primary pupils might be given sections of the secondary school or even university curriculum in the periods allocated to 'enrichment'. This form of provision is 'bolted on' to the normal classroom activities whereas a more sophisticated form which is integral to the normal curriculum is what is required.

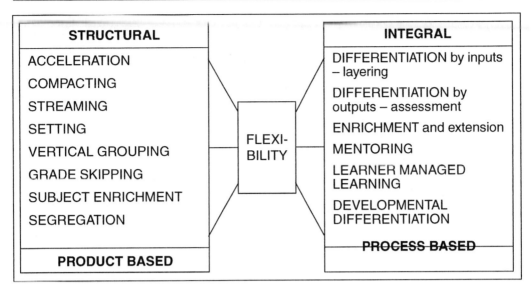

Figure 5.1 A model of methods of differentiation

Content enrichment is really not enrichment at all but content acceleration. This is what happened in many of the Summer Schools arising from the Government's *Excellence in Cities* Initiative (DfEE 1999d).

If differentiation is integral or built in to the mainstream work *all children* can have an opportunity to profit from the enrichment. Most structural approaches tend to be product or content based whereas integral approaches have to be concerned with process, in particular cognitive processes in which there is both content *and* method.

The integral approach has the enrichment or the differentiated work built into the daily curriculum and thus is *inclusive education*. There is, however, a serious problem in that not all differentiation is inclusive. It actually segregates pupils from others, giving them a separate and different curriculum, usually in the same classroom, and this was found to be a feature of the earlier integration policies in schools.

Three models of Integral Curriculum Differentiation

By inputs – the setting of different tasks at different levels of difficulty suitable for different levels of achievement (layering).

By outputs – the setting of common tasks that can be responded to in a positive way by all students (assessment).

Developmental – the setting of common tasks to which all students can contribute their own inputs and so progress from surface to deep learning and thus be enabled to achieve more advanced learning outcomes.

The first two offer little more than the formal or didactic methods of teaching to the middle with their inbuilt disadvantages of which teachers need to be aware. These two forms of differentiation are no more than a within-class selective education system.

However, they may be the first signs of teacher's efforts to develop differentiated approaches and be aware of pupil needs, but they are not fully inclusive strategies.

The form of differentiation by which higher cognitive abilities and skills have been achieved (Montgomery 1990, 1996) has been termed *developmental differentiation* and it was cognitive process methods which enabled an inclusive education to be offered to all the class in a form which could be enriching for all. It is termed developmental differentiation because pupils gain access to the curriculum at a level suited to their linguistic, cognitive and other developmental levels. Through their studies the activities enable them to progress towards higher levels of skills, both in the cognitive and subject curriculum and in general developmental terms.

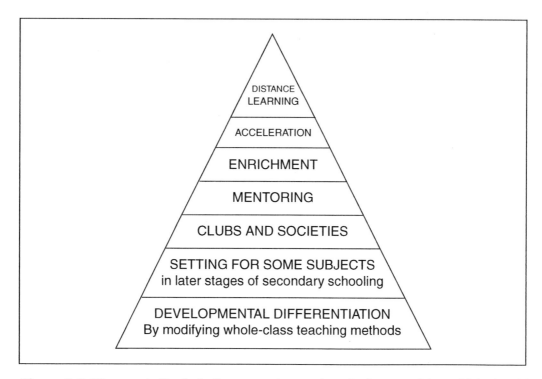

Figure 5.2 Diagram to illustrate the seven types of curriculum provision which should be on offer in every school

The basic plan should be that every teacher would use a range of teaching methods which offer developmental differentiation. This would mean a modest change at times in their teaching methods so that they taught both the NC but at the same time the cognitive curriculum.

Critical thinking theory as a background to cognitive process teaching methods

Critical thinking is the art of thinking about your thinking so as to make it more precise, accurate and relevant, consistent and fair (Paul 1990). This had been expressed as metacognition by Flavell in 1979. He argued that thinking about how we are thinking and learning while we are doing so contributes in a major way to intelligence.

Teaching the cognitive curriculum would mean that every teacher would be expected to be *developing thinking skills and study skills* in the medium of their own subject. This would offer the cognitive stretch that all pupils need. It enables them to work independently and alongside peers in a variety of different ways. It offers more flexibility in learning, giving them greater autonomy to learn more and to learn at deeper and more secure levels. This has also been shown to be beneficial to all learners. It is also possible, given the right sort of preparation, to get five- and six-year-olds to function in abstract thinking modes. This is not to deny Piaget's (1952) work on stages of intellectual development but to suggest that intellectual development can be promoted by encouraging more reflective teaching and learning.

Intellectual skills are about 'knowing that' and 'knowing how'. They include converting printed words into meaning, fractions into decimals, knowing about classes, properties, groups and categories, laws of, for example, genetics, how to form sentences and so on. Intellectual skills enable us to deal with the world 'out there'. These refer to the contents and skills of the subjects of the NC.

Cognitive skills are internally organised capabilities and are directed to internal processes such as thinking, planning, organising, problem solving, creativity, self regulation, reflecting upon and monitoring one's own learning. Their development is at present incidental to most school learning but needs to be made explicit and the subject of systematic development if we are to enhance the capabilities of our future workforce for the challenges of the new millennium.

Research by Wang and Lindvall (1984) showed that self monitoring and self regulatory activities not only contributed to improved acquisition of subject content but also to improved generalisation and transfer of knowledge and skills. They also gave students a sense of personal agency, a feeling of being in control of their own learning. Self regulatory activities were defined by Brown and Palinscar (1984) as including planning, predicting outcomes and scheduling time and resources. Monitoring included testing, revising and rescheduling with checking to evaluate outcomes using criteria developed by the individual and also those which were externally defined. There was, however, a failure to develop these higher order cognitive or thinking skills in schools and colleges, according to Resnick (1989).

Schools had historically been most conservative, uncritically passing down from generation to generation outmoded didactic, lecture and drill-based models of instruction. The result was that students, on the whole, did not learn how to work by, or think for, themselves. They did not learn how to gather, analyse, synthesise and assess information. They did not learn to enter sympathetically into the thinking of others nor how to deal rationally with conflicting points of view. They did not learn to become critical readers, writers, speakers or listeners and so did not become literate in the proper sense of the word. They did not critically analyse their own experience and would find it difficult to explain the basis of their own beliefs and so did not gain much genuine knowledge. They therefore lacked the traits of mind of a genuinely educated person, such as, intellectual humility, courage, integrity, perseverance and faith in reason (Paul 1990). Fortunately Paul identified a means of overcoming these problems which he called the application of Critical Theory. He emphasised the fact that normal individuals do not naturally think critically nor are inspired by rationality. They do not engage in reflective thinking automatically. They have to be encouraged and helped to do so at all levels of education. It is thus applicable to *how* people learn with teachers as models of the investigator after truth and fairness, the reflective questioner, the opener of minds. Unfortunately, minds are apparently happy to adopt biases, prejudices, stereotypes and short cuts to thinking and will state these authoritatively, quite genuinely believing them to be truths.

In a previous decade Flavell (1979) had established that *metacognition* was a highly important contribution to higher order learning. Metacognition was defined as the process by which we think about our cognitive machinery and processing mechanisms (Flavell 1979). These metacognitive activities underpinned the development of the self regulatory and self management skills already referred to, as well as the sense of personal agency. Failure to develop learning conversations inside the head, or metacognitions, left the learner in 'robot mode', according to Thomas (1976). This was a state of learned helplessness where the response to problems was to use old well-worn strategies even if they had little hope of success and to profit little from experience. He estimated that some 80 per cent of the population might be in robot mode.

Failure to develop higher order cognitive skills in schools and colleges was, according to Resnick (1989), not surprising for it had never been the goal of mass education to do more than develop basic skills of literacy and numeracy and core subject knowledge.

Paul maintained that as societies become less isolated and more complex, lack of rationality at both global and local level becomes increasingly dangerous for the maintenance of human existence. To combat these dangers of didactic education which brings with it its own kind of ignorance and prejudice, education worldwide needed to change.

If teachers work together on a whole-school basis it is possible to achieve the goals of critical thinking, usually with a small amount of extra time and frequently with no additional time. It could be equivalent to each curriculum area offering one cognitively orientated training session per term. The orchestration of this would be an important task in developing the cognitive curriculum and could be the remit of year group leaders and planning teams.

The cognitive curriculum

There are six main aspects to developing the cognitive curriculum in the context of *developmental differentiation*. This is the setting of common tasks to which all students can contribute their own inputs and so progress from surface to deep learning and thus be enabled to achieve more advanced learning outcomes. Through their studies the activities enable them to progress towards higher levels of skills both in the cognitive and subject curriculum and in general developmental terms (Montgomery 1982). This was expanded upon in Chapter 4.

Positive cognitive intervention (PCI)

This is the information which the teacher gives to the pupils when on task, explaining how the work in progress is going, how good it is and what steps might be taken to make it even better. This was given more detailed treatment in Chapter 2.

Cognitively challenging questioning

Questions are capable of being roughly divided into two main groups. These are closed and open questions. Closed questions usually demand one word factual responses such as, When was the Battle of Hastings? Who were the leaders of the battle? Where did the battle take place? and, What did . . .? etc. It is only when we get to the Why? questions that we begin to ask pupils to give reasons and causes and these require more extended answers. These are termed *open questions* and can elicit thinking. Sometimes asking for a personal response will cause the pupils to reflect and connect their own experience to the new. Even the when, where and what questions can be converted to more open ended versions when we add, When do you think . . .? Who do you think . . .?

Some examples of causal reasoning – thinking carefully about causes follow:

Q. Who if anyone was responsible for the death of Romeo and Juliet?
   a. Feuding parents?
   b. The Prince?
   c. Friar Lawrence?
   d. The lovers?

Propose an argument which holds each one in turn responsible for the deaths.

Select the 'best' argument and draw the causal chain you describe.

Q. On what basis do we hold people responsible for their actions and the things that happen?

Q. Are there analogies between the play and real life today?

Q. Are there any similar issues in our own experiences?

Q. Are there any similar story schemas?

Explicit teaching of cognitive protocols and thinking skills

There are general rules and procedures which can usefully be followed when engaging in decision-making and problem solving. When these protocols are made explicit students can use them in a variety of new and different situations to improve their learning and problem solving. Some current models are as follows:

Teaching of thinking. This involves direct instruction in thinking in non curricular contexts. This includes bolt-on provision – see de Bono (1983) – CoRT Thinking Programme; Feuerstein *et al.* (1980) – Instrumental Enrichment (IE); and Blagg *et al.* (1993) – Somerset Thinking Skills Project ref. IE.

Teaching for thinking. This involves the use of methods which promote thinking in curricular contexts, e.g. Kerry and Kerry (2000); Eyre (1997); and Fisher (1994) etc. See also Adey and Shayer (1994) – Cognitive Acceleration through Science Education (CASE), also CAME and CAGE; Lipman (1991) – Philosophy for children; and Wallace and Adams (1993), Wallace (2000) – Thinking Actively in a Social Context.

Infusion. This involves restructuring content lessons for direct instruction in thinking: see Swartz and Parks (1994) – Infusion techniques, lessons; McGuinness (1999) – Activating Children's Thinking Skills using S and P's methods.

Pedagogy. This involves modest changes in teaching method: Cognitive process strategies, developmental differentiation, PCI and CBC (Montgomery 1990, 1996, 1998a, b).

Asking pupils to think about a topic does not teach them to become skilful thinkers. The first task would be to discuss with them the nature, for example, of *skilful decision-making* and a graphic organiser can be provided to show where they should arrive but it can be in their own words:

Skilful decision-making

1. What makes a decision necessary?
2. What are my options?
3. What are the likely consequences?
4. How important are the consequences?
5. Which option is best in the light of the consequences.

(Swartz and Parks 1994: 39)

An example science lesson might be about renewable energy sources and what a country should rely upon for the future. Pupils will have developed their plan for taking good decisions and are asked to review their previous knowledge on energy sources in the thinking actively section. Here the teacher uses reflective questioning techniques and explicit prompts, such as asking why people today are concerned about energy; what are some of the optional sources available; what information might the pupils need to research. They make lists of known information with factors such as cost of production which might need to be taken into account. Groups then pick two sources of energy to research and fill in a data matrix with headings such as, Options – Relevant Consequences, under this the Factors to Consider, e.g. ease of production; environment; cost; availability. From this each group decides which is the best source of energy and discusses why. They then have to prepare an oral or written recommendation giving the reasons for their choice.

In the next phase they are encouraged to think about their thinking, describe it and draw a flow chart to represent it. The flow charts should all contain the five key questions. They then discuss any difficulties experienced, the pros and cons of the procedure and compare it to the ways they ordinarily take decisions.

In the final phase they apply the strategy to a decision they are dealing with at the present, they consider other imaginary issues and later in the school year reinforcement activities are introduced and examples are given on pollution, endangered species, immigration and so on. Skill extension activities are also suggested, such as work on determining the reliability of sources for decision-making.

Skilful problem solving

In their approach to this Swartz and Parks (1994) make the argument that good problem solving can improve the quality of the lives it affects. Advances in science, medicine and technology have improved the standards of living of people today because problems were identified and solved. Everyday life as well as curriculum topics can present problems to be solved such as what to do when we get lost, cannot start the car, develop a rash, become too hot and so on. They then identify shortcomings in problem solving such as we do not recognise the situation as a problem, we make hasty choices or consider too narrow a band of solutions, we may fail to consider the consequences of our choices or the feasibility of them and the result is a poor solution.

They show how the pupil can learn to be a skilful problem solver and by the same method as before go through the problem solving protocol beginning with the *advance organiser*:

1. Why is there a problem?
2. What is the problem?
3. What are the possible solutions to the problem?
4. What would happen if you solved the problem in each of these ways?
5. What is the best solution to the problem?

Swartz and Parks (1994: 76)

The curriculum for infusion of critical and creative thinking which they identify and give detailed treatment is:

Skilfully managing thinking tasks
- decision-making
- problem solving.

Understanding and retention: clarifying ideas
a. Analysing ideas:
  - comparing and contrasting
  - classification
  - determining parts–whole relationships
  - sequencing.

b. Analysing arguments:
  - finding reasons and conclusions
  - uncovering assumptions.

Creative thinking: generating ideas

a. Alternative possibilities:
  - generating possibilities
b. Composition:
  - creating metaphors.

Critical thinking: assessing the reasonableness of ideas

a. Assessing basic information:
  - determining the reliability of sources
b. Well-founded inference:
  - i) Use of evidence
  - causal explanation
  - prediction
  - generalisation
  - reasoning by analogy
  - ii) Deduction
  - conditional reasoning.

Of special interest is their approach to creative thinking. They use the brainstorming technique first and then generate further possibilities by listing and considering aspects of the topic and recombining ideas to form new ones. They illustrate the use of concept maps as another way of generating possibilities and suggest that in asking the question, 'Are any of these original ideas?', this too promotes further and more original suggestions. The examples on metaphors shows how they may be constructed by considering among other things the key characteristics which the object, person or event has in common with other things which might indeed make the metaphor, e.g. 'All the world's a stage.' Throughout the pupil is helped to understand what are the errors or defaults in our thinking in order that they can be avoided.

Examples of similar protocols and sets of lessons may be found in de Bono (1983) in his Thinking Action programme. Although it is run as a separate course of thinking lessons the strategies and example lessons can be fitted into the normal lessons based in the NC. Fisher (1994) also gives examples of problem solving and curriculum thinking activities. He advocates the SCAMPER protocol for creative thinking.

Creativity training

Creativity refers to an innovative, ingenious and productive response to ordinary problems. This is often characterised by a flexible approach to thinking, the capacity for induction and use of analogies and models in new and productive ways. According to Simonton (1988) the creative person is particularly good at producing associations and then recognising the significance of the new configuration which has occurred. There is hence a need for inclusion of flexibility and creativity training and experience in education if the country is to maintain its economic position and even improve it.

In this area there are also protocols which can be followed to facilitate opportunities for creativity, as well as giving more open ended problems and activities to 'capture' any creative notions that might be presented. It is more difficult to ensure there will be a truly 'creative' response or outcome. Something truly creative has to be not only new in terms of the individual but also in terms of the society at large and be a recognisable product. Teachers who fostered creativity (de Alencar 1995) encouraged pupils to:

- be independent learners and thinkers;
- formulate their own ideas;
- be motivated to think and reason;
- cultivate their interest in new knowledge and discoveries;
- ask challenging questions.

The teachers presented them with:

- challenging tasks;
- stimulated analyses of different aspects of a problem;
- respected pupils' ideas (so that they could risk sharing them);
- were enthusiastic;
- accepted their students as equals;
- rewarded them for creative behaviour.

Reflective teaching and learning

Whenever we reflect upon our learning process and what we have learned this provides an opportunity for us to extend our schemata and scripts making connections between learned contents and processes across different areas. It is this reflective time which permits the brain to engage in analogical thinking and think in more creative ways. It also offers time for mental rehearsal of events so learning can be more deeply embedded and understood when connected to prior learning.

Even during learning and teaching it is noticeable that learners look away into the distance as though day dreaming when the teaching input reminds them of some personal experience which they try to integrate with the new information to give it personal relevance. It is essential to give time for this type of reflection and not move on too quickly or fill the time with rapid teacher talk. This is beginning to be discovered in interview and individual tutorial time. If not, the learner does not have pause to integrate the incoming information, especially if it is new and complex, and so learns less.

Cognitive process pedagogies

These are the core of developmental differentiation and PCI and they enable it to be achieved. Cognitive process teaching methods are based in Critical Thinking Theory

(Paul 1990; Resnick 1989) and are the means by which higher order thinking and metacognitive skills can be developed through the ordinary curriculum. These are given more detailed treatment in a later section.

In order to adjust to teaching the cognitive curriculum, the teacher's own theory or theories about teaching need to be changed. Without change in the guiding perceptions, the resultant lesson plans and teaching methods will not really change. The teacher will use the appropriate vocabulary but teach in the same old ways or lapse back into them very quickly.

The *central objectives in teaching* need to be redefined as follows:

- To enable students to think efficiently, and
- to express those thoughts succinctly.

This reframing can be represented in the form of a model (see Figure 5.3).

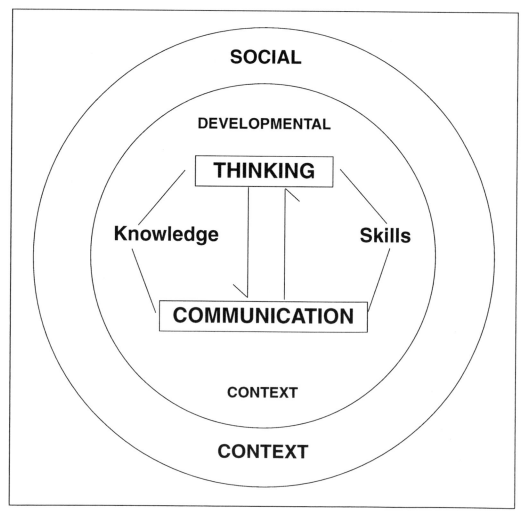

Figure 5.3 A model of modern teaching (Montgomery 1981)

Teaching for learning using cognitive process strategies

Games and simulations

In the non simulation game students work in groups and have to know certain facts, perform skills or demonstrate mastery of specific concepts to win or be successful. The participants agree objectives and there are sets of rules to obey. Typical of this form is the card game which can be adapted to educational purposes such as 'Phonic Rummy', 'Alphabet Snap' and so on.

Simulation games contain the elements of real situations and students individually or in groups interact with and become part of the reality. Role playing is often an important feature of the game. For example, in working with a class of children on the problems of bullying or stealing, it is often very useful to organise small group work role play so that individuals can practise expressing their own and other's feelings about the subject as well as analyse the issues and suggest solutions or resolutions of the problem. Characteristic of all games is that they must be followed by a discussion-debriefing session to discuss what transpired so that emotional, educational and metacognitive objectives can be achieved.

The castle task below is not only an example of problem solving it is also a simulation game in which roles are played.

Cognitive study skills

The following examples can apply to textual, visual and performance material: locating the main points and subordinate ones; flow charting; completion activities; prediction activities; sequencing; comparing and contrasting; drafting and editing; organising – tabulating, classifying, ordering, diagramming, categorising; drawing inferences and abstractions; recognising intent, bias and propaganda. Some of these have been exemplified in Chapter 4.

Cognitive study skills are a form of self directed learning and involve active work on textual and other material. Although reading skills are taught it is not usual to teach higher order reading and cognitive skills although they are considered to be essential to the educated person and a requirement for success in higher education. Even able children do not automatically develop them. It is important to incorporate study skills into ALL curriculum subject areas rather than try to teach them in a separate skills course. Bolt-on provision has been shown to be ineffective and non-transferrable.

Real problem solving and investigative learning

Human nature is such that if you present a person with an open ended situation in which the answer to a problem is not given the mind automatically tries to solve it. This notion of the human as scientific problem solver and investigator from birth was put forward by Kelly (1955). Although not everything can be converted into a problem, there is considerable scope for doing so across the curriculum.

Characteristic of the approach is that there needs to be plenty of content material around to research to help develop ideas and strategies or verify solutions. Because the activities start from the children's own ideas and knowledge each is building up their own cognitive structures and knowledge hierarchies and can interrogate the various sources. The teacher is not only a resource but is also the manager and facilitator of learning.

The essentials of *real problem solving* (RPS) and *problem based learning* (PBL) are that the initial problem is *'fuzzy'*. According to Gallagher (1997) PBL has been around for more than two decades and its evolution has resulted in four elements: an ill-structured problem; substantial content; student apprenticeship; and self directed learning. He confirms that research supports the view that PBL is better than traditional instructional methods for:

- long-term retention of information;
- conceptual understanding;
- self directed learning.

The research of Dods (1997) showed that didactic methods tended to widen the content coverage while understanding and retention were promoted by PBL. However, because of their previous training, it was found that students frequently demanded more information. Teachers and pupils on our courses behaved in a similar fashion (Montgomery 1993) until we were able to prove to them that our methods were powerful inducers of learning. The crucial concept was that if they had to spend a lot of time revising then they probably had not learned and understood the material the first time. Only a minimal amount of revision as a reminder should be necessary, even for those who lack very good or photographic methods. Verbal instructions from the teacher, direct teaching, can set the scene and define a structure or a procedure in a quick way but only those with gifted memories will retain it. Even then they may not be able to use it efficiently, i.e. transfer their learning.

The real problem solving approach in relation to an NC topic such as Saxon Settlement might be to start with the 'fuzzy' problem. In pairs the pupils should look at a map to note where settlements occurred and in pairs put themselves in the position of the settlers and try to hypothesise why they might choose those spots. They should try to form a description of each from the map details and find any common factors. This task should occupy 5–10 minutes and then they should share their ideas with the rest of the class and agree a best fit hypothesis.

In phase two new information should be presented and this can consist of a page or two of information so they can employ some study skills. Pictures of artifacts, and drawings of the life of the Saxons could now be presented. The pupils are asked to consider the following questions working in pairs or small groups of three. First they should raise an hypothetical answer to each question before looking at the study materials.

a. How did they come?
b. Why did they come?

c. Why were they permitted to settle?

d. Given the tools and materials available what sort of settlement could they build?

At intervals for a change of activity the pupils can share their findings and hypotheses with the rest of the class.

The key topic of what sort of site they will need to find can then be addressed now that they have the background. They can be given different maps and should identify in their groups five or six essentials which a site they now choose for settlement should fulfil and then apply these to their study of the map to decide on the best site. In the final session groups should explain which site they have chosen and give reasons for their choice. This procedure will take slightly longer but the final section could be set for individual homework.

As a follow-up they might focus on a particular aspect of Saxon life such as boats, tools, clothes, food for research. Thus not every lesson must be problem based but it is helpful to begin a series with such a lesson to excite interest and motivation, treating it all perhaps like a big detective story. There are a wide range of resources which can be used to reinforce the learning once they know something and they can learn more from a video tape with such advance organisers than if it is used as the primary and initial source of information. Preparing the mind for the new information is important if deep learning is to take place. Ensuring there is pupil discussion before more public sharing of ideas will help them to be clarified and expressed more succinctly.

Comparisons of real settlement sites with modern maps can bring it into the present and careers in archeology, history and geography can be mentioned as well as using such knowledge as a backcloth to novels. The idea of introducing these things is to extend the pupils' interests and experiences beyond the school walls.

Other PBL example topics

When the subject of Homes in different environments, in history and in different countries is considered the subject of Homes on Stilts may become a focus. Instead of giving the title, the pupils are given details about climate, monsoons, terrain, general physical geography, flora and fauna and tools available, in groups of three they arc asked to examine the resource materials and slides etc. and then discuss and design the sort of home which would take account of the setting. They usually come up with homes on boats and homes on stilts. They should then be asked to present their arguments for and against their chosen designs. At the conclusion of the session they can be shown pictures of how the locals solve the problems.

In a study of the local area pupils seldom have an overview or an understanding of how others may view it. Even in a historical study it can be important to start from the here and now before probing into the local past. A collection of holiday brochures can be brought in of pupils' ideal locations for a vacation. Pairs should then research the brochures to identify the types of information and the language register in which they are written. Using similar headings, they should then apply these to a selected part of their home area and document it with Polaroid photographs and cut-outs from local newspapers and magazines. At intervals the teacher can call them all together to share aspects and to develop points. They can paste up their four-page leaflets and word processing for homework and then hold an exhibition in which they can offer to do verbal presentations of their holiday offers. Follow-up work on other people's views and comparative studies of the photographs can lead into further work on the same area in the Victorian era, plus a new brochure and language register and interviews with their oldest relatives born in the area. It can also lead to the usual work on local survey and to visits to the local museums and libraries for research.

As a 20-minute problem-based introduction to mediaeval castles pupils can be shown a pictorial map on which five or six sites are under consideration for building a castle – a hilly area; a high circular plateau; an island in the middle of the river; a plot of land near a village in the fork of the river; a plot near the forest and some quarries and so on.

In groups of five pupils have to imagine that they are the site agent for the place designated for their group and then have to produce a marketing brief to try to persuade the teacher (now titled the Lord or Lady of the Manor) in AD 1200 to purchase their particular site. After about ten minutes' discussion (some may like to record a few notes), one of each group with the help of the rest has to make a presentation. When these are over the teacher can then help them to develop the criteria for a good castle site and then by comparing and contrasting the features of each site they can decide on the best one. The teacher can then factor in such things as cost and give details of the actual period labour charges for walls, slits, crenelations and so on, plus the master mason's rates and those of the work people. As the work proceeds they can begin to compare their hypothetical site and castle with some of those in existence and then select one to study in further depth. This should preferably be one close by so that a visit can be arranged for more intensive study and some measurements. This links PBL to experiential learning. Pictures and ground plans of some of the more important castles of the period can be studied together with their owners and how and why they came to be where they were.

In science it is usual for pupils to study separation as a set of scientific processes culminating in pupils being given a mixture of sand and salt to separate. As they are frequently given the diagram to draw first and then get out the apparatus and set up the 'experiment', there is little experimentation or problem about it except the enjoyment of doing it all. It was found to be far more memorable as a learning experience when the pupils after studying various forms of separation entered the laboratory one day to be given little piles of an unknown mixture which they were asked to separate. There were two substances in it which someone had stirred up together.

In pairs the pupils are asked to hypothesise what the substances might be and to design some apparatus to finish up with two piles of dry clean substances. Ask them to consider what the dangers might be in not knowing what the substances are and how they would avoid them. When they have designed their apparatus and it has been checked to see if it is safe, they should then set it up, even if it is wrong, and try it out. At the end of the session in the review a number will have modified their designs and now have semi-separated substances but know what they should have done to clean it. A few who went off on the wrong tack will want to set it up again in the lunch hour so that they can have the satisfaction of completing the task successfully. They remember this lesson very well.

A mathematical example of this sort of thinking is illustrated in the following:

Three numbers 3, 6 and 9 represent a rule which I have in my head. In order to find out what my rule is you can generate some numbers too and each time I will tell you either – 'Yes, that is an example of my rule', or, 'No, that is not an example of it.' As soon as you feel you know what the rule is you can propose it and you will be told whether or not you are correct. If you are incorrect you can go on and propose more examples. This can prove to be a useful exercise in examining metacognitive events in relation to number work.

Experiential learning

Experiential learning involves learning by doing or *action learning* but the learning is not circular, returning the learner to the same point each time. Instead, at each turn, the experience, the talking about the experience and the reflecting upon the learning and doing adds to the sum of knowledge and changes the processes and the understanding in an additive way. The result is a *learning spiral* (Montgomery 1994), progressing from surface to deep learning (Marton and Saljo 1976) often with the mediation of the teacher (Feuerstein 1995). (See Figure 5.4.)

Experiential learning can be based on a wide range of activities from visits to the local fish market or quay, the farm, church, and castle, to town centre visits. They can equally include theatre and cinema visits and the study of TV and radio programmes as well as journeys and holidays.

On return from one of these experiences it is not enough to simply talk and write about them recording the events. It is essential to talk about and reflect upon the thinking and learning experiences and processes which were engaged during and after the event.

Collaborative learning

Collaboration means that students work with each other towards the framing and design of problems and strategies as well as in their resolution or solution. Each contributes some part to the whole. Quite often the process is called 'cooperative learning'. *Think – pair and share* is a powerful vehicle for promoting learning. Pupils are frequently arranged in groups at tables but are only doing their own individual work (Bennett 1986). In real group work they are sharing the tasks, questioning and negotiating with each other and sometimes teaching each other. Collaborative work can be most effective when pairs work is arranged. It is more

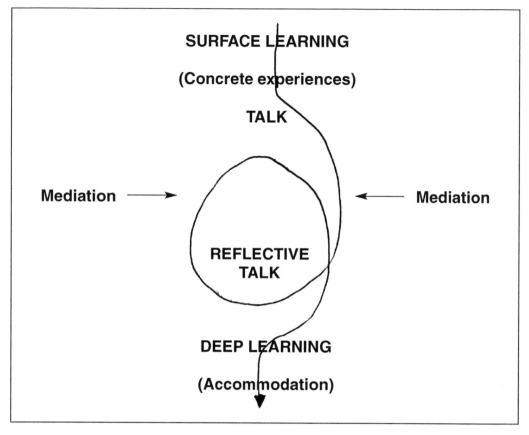

Figure 5.4 The Cognitive Learning Spiral (Montgomery 1994)

difficult to have groups of three or five with everyone contributing although some tasks need the larger groups.

The collaborative pairs Thinkback strategy has already been exemplified in Chapter 4.

Language experience methods

These involve the pupils composing and compiling their own textual materials. It began as a method of creating reading books for poor readers in which they would discuss topics and experiences with a tutor and then the tutor acted as a scribe and wrote down the story which the pupil told. This was then word processed and used as reading material. More recently pupils in pairs can work together at the word processor, composing stories and writing up reports. Equally they can work alone with the support of the word processor, drafting and editing their own material.

It will be seen that the various forms offered in the cognitive process methodologies have the objective of training in metacognition and in organising what one knows to take account of new knowledge and skills. The objective of training in metacognition is thus to make one a skilful user of knowledge. Nickerson *et al.* (1985) concluded that if training in metacognitive skills is done effectively it should have considerable pay off so that learners learn better and begin to behave like experts. The learners also take on different roles during the activities as many of them are collaborative. Collaborative work by pupils stimulates their thinking processes. As there is an element of open endedness to the tasks there is also a large amount of creativity involved both for learners and teachers.

Planning and managing one's learning and keeping it on task and on schedule

There are many activities which can be designed to help pupils learn and develop these skills. They need to start with small projects in which they have autonomy to try things out and to learn from their mistakes. Some of the activities already described can provide the initial training ground. An intermediate-sized project might be to set small groups to design and develop a school handbook on study skills for Year 7 pupils. They can begin by discussing in their groups their first two weeks in their new school and how they felt and what they needed to know. They can review what they know of study skills across the subjects so far and draw up a checklist of skills cross-matched with subjects. This can form the basis of a small-scale research project using presentational skills of various kinds including statistics. It can form the basis of a useful audit of the degree of permeation of study skills.

A *newspaper project*. Designing a class or year newspaper using PBL and modelling the processes and roles in a newspaper office can be undertaken with pupils across the age ranges. A full description of how to set this up has already appeared in Montgomery (1985b, 1996) and illustrated with pupils' work some five years old and some much older.

Over a period of ten years, more than 200 experienced teachers on two MA Distance Learning programmes have been given a range of different teaching techniques to evaluate with their pupils. These were methods such as games and simulations, real problem solving, experiential and collaborative learning. None of them was using these techniques prior to the programme. The tasks were to use the set materials or design and implement similar tasks of their own within NC content.

They then evaluated the learning outcomes for themselves and with the direct help of the students. In every case they were able to obtain better learning outcomes from the students than with their traditional methods and the pupils behaviour improved and they became highly motivated and interested. This is ongoing research for the Learning Difficulties Research Project (Montgomery 1998c).

Summary and conclusions

In this chapter the subjects of effective and good teaching have been grappled with. To some extent it is still a personal construction for there is a flood of influential official publications presenting a different view. However, this does not make the official view correct and the didactic mode it presents is in direct contradiction to the research on how people, especially children, are best enabled to learn.

An outline has been presented of what is effective teaching and how teachers may plan their teaching using a variety of different methods. The assumption is that if we teach, the pupils are automatically learning. They will learn effectively only if the methods we use help them to get below surface issues to the deeper levels. Each learner has to be enabled to construct their own knowledge and it is here that the cognitive curriculum becomes essential.

It is when thinking, reflection, decision-making and problem solving are built into daily teaching that learning the subject curriculum becomes relevant and effectively learned.

Seven key elements in teaching the cognitive curriculum were identified and exemplified. These were – developmental differentiation, positive cognitive interventions, cognitively challenging questioning, cognitive process pedagogies, and explicit teaching of cognitive protocols, teaching for creativity, and reflective teaching, all within the subject contents of the ordinary curriculum by every teacher in the school.

Epilogue

In performance management, classroom observation appraisal can take two main forms: one is summative to assess or grade a teacher's performance and the other is formative and diagnostic to promote development. In earlier decades three main purposes of appraisal were identified. These were for staff or professional development, for reward and for promotion. From the earliest times researchers and practitioners had agreed that the most effective use of classroom observation was for development rather than for payment by results and promotion. Nevertheless at intervals since, attempts have been made to make the system one for reward and accountability. In this most recent form – performance management – classroom observation and pupils' achievements have been linked and a staff development process has been endorsed as well as reward and promotion objectives.

However, at present one instrument, a summative one, has been recommended for all three purposes. Difficulties can arise when a school elects to use one form of assessment such as the checklist for all three purposes. It can be used summatively and it may even be used diagnostically to identify strengths and weaknesses. However, it has been shown in the appraisal researches that it cannot be used effectively for intervention to improve classroom performance or formatively, although users claim to use it for this purpose.

This book has set out to challenge this notion and provide a theory and practice of teacher development through the use of a formative classroom observation strategy.

The method uses a factual running record of events related to a specific sampling frame because everything in classrooms cannot be recorded. The record couched in positive and neutral terms is simply read to the teacher and points are raised by both observer and teacher and discussed all the way through. It acts as a detailed evidence-based system of what went on.

For helping schools with their development and teachers with their professional development, this sampling frame method of classroom observation was developed. It can be used in both primary and secondary schools and has produced evidence-based research in quantitaive and qualitative terms that it is an effective tool for the job.

Because of its detailed approach the method can be used as a coaching system to improve teaching performance across all subject disciplines, at all levels of education and training and also can contribute to identifying general and specific inservice training needs.

The method can be used in nursery classrooms and in further and higher education. With modifications to the classroom management section it has been shown to be equally effective in these settings although these results have not been included in this book.

Whole-school appraisals have been undertaken using the method and the results revealed that the majority of schools had similar general inservice needs. These were significant areas for whole-school approaches and three common targets for development were:

Target One
To address the cognitive curriculum and engage in its systematic development in all subject areas and coordinated across years by year teams.

Target Two
To address the behaviour management of classes as large groups and to increase the amount of CBG and the use of 3Ms to promote a more positive school ethos.

Target Three
To address the individual needs of learners, in particular the issues of handwriting and spelling. All pupils entering secondary school should be able to write at the speed of at least 15 words per minute and preferably 20 if they are to cope with the curriculum recording demands made upon them. This must include teaching a full cursive writing form where necessary and a cognitive approach to correcting and developing spelling. All pupils in Year 1 should be able to write simple sentences using a full cursive style unless they have mild handwriting coordination difficulties when they must be taught cursive but will take longer to become fluent. Those with the most severe and intractable difficulties must be given a laptop to work with.

Further details of how these targets may be addressed and a fuller rationale for positive behaviour management, cursive writing and cognitive approaches to spelling may be found in the companion text to this, *Reversing Lower Attainment* (Montgomery 1998a).

References

ACAS (1986) *Teachers' Dispute: ACAS Independent Panel.* Report of the Appraisal and Training Working Group. London: ACAS.

ACAS (1990) *Appraisal Related Pay.* Advisory Booklet, No. 11. London: ACAS.

Adelman, C. (1990) 'Teacher appraisal, collaborative research and teacher consortia', in Simons, H. and Elliott, J. *Rethinking Appraisal and Assessment.* Milton Keynes: Open University, 36–43.

Adey, P. and Shayer, M. (1991) *The Cognitive Acceleration through Science Education Programme (CASE).* London: Kings College.

Adey, P.S. and Shayer, M. (1994) *Really Raising Standards: Cognitive Interventions and Academic Achievement.* London: Routledge.

Alexander, C. (1998) 'An investigation into the voluntary reading practices and attitudes towards teaching of year 8 pupils in a London Secondary School'. Unpublished MA dissertation. London: Middlesex University.

Allen, R.M. and Casbergus, R.M. (1995) *Evolution of Novice through Expert Teachers' Recall.* San Francisco, CA: American Research Associates. (ERIC Document Reproduction Service no. ED387 681.)

Anderson, J.R. (1980) *Cognitive Psychology and its Implications* (3rd edn). San Francisco: Freeman.

Anderson, T.H. (1979) 'Study strategies and adjunct aids', in Anderson, R.C., Osborn, J. and Tierney, R.J. (eds) *Learning to Read in American Schools.* Hillsdale, NJ: Erlbaum, 483–502.

Ausubel, D.P. and Robinson, R.G. (1969) *School Learning: An Introduction to Educational Psychology.* New York: Holt Rinehart & Winston.

Ausubel, D.P. (1968) *Educational Psychology. A Cognitive View.* New York: Holt Rinehart & Winston.

Ausubel, D.P., Novak, J.D. and Hanesian, H. (1978) *Educational Psychology: A Cognitve View* (2nd edn). New York: Holt, Rinehart & Winston.

AVA News (1985) 'Table of percentage learning times'. *AVA News*, p. 23.

Bandura, A. and Walters, R.H. (1963) *Social Learning and Personality Development.* London: Holt, Rinehart & Winston.

Bannathan, M. and Boxall, M. (1998) 'The boxall profiles and underpinning research'. Speech by M. Bannathan at the November Conference of the European Association for Special Education (EASE). Prague: Benesov.

Barker, J. (1998) 'A study of ways of developing professional skills and literacy teaching through cross phase inservice training'. Unpublished MA SEN dissertation. London: Middlesex University.

Baron, S., Stalker, K., Wilkinson, H. and Riddell, S. (1998) 'The learning society: the highest stage of human capitalism?', in Cotfield, F. (ed.) *Learning at Work*. Bristol: Policy Press, 49–59.

Batteson, C. (1998) 'Empowering or enslaving? Speculations on the mentoring of trainee teachers'. *Management in Education*, 12(1), 28–30.

Becker, W.C., Madsen, C.H., Arnold, C.R. and Thomas, D.P. (1967) 'The contingent use of teacher reinforcement and praise in reducing classroom behaviour problems', *Journal of Special Education*, 1, 287–307.

Bennett, N. (1986) 'Cooperative learning: children do it in groups, or do they?' *Educational Child Psychology*, 4, 7–18.

Bennett, N. (1998) 'Learning to teach, the development of peadagogical reasoning', in McBride *op. cit.*, 130–42.

Bennett, N. and Desforges, C. (1984) *The Quality of Pupil Learning Experiences*. London: Erlbaum.

Bennett, N. and Jordan, A. (1975) 'A typology of teaching styles'. *British Journal of Educational Psychology*, 45(1), 20–8.

Beyer, B.K. (1997) *Improving Student Thinking: A Comprehensive Approach*. New York: Allyn & Bacon.

Biggs, J.B. (1987) *Student Approaches to Learning and Studying*. Melbourne: Australian Council for Educational Research.

Biggs, J.B. (ed.) (1991) *Teaching for Learning: The Viewpoint from Cognitive Psychology*. Hawthorn: Australian Council for Educational Research.

Blackham, G.J. and Silberman, A. (1971) *Modification of Child Behaviour*. Belmont, CA: Wadsworth.

Blagg, N., Lewis, R.E., and Ballinger, M.P. (1993) *Thinking and Learning at Work: A Report on the Development and Evaluation of the Thinking Skills at Work Modules*. Research Series. Sheffield: The Employment Department.

Bloom, B.S. (ed.) (1956) *Taxonomy of Educational Objectives, Vol. 1*. London: Longmans.

Bloom, B.S. (1976) *Human Characteristics and School Learning*. New York: McGraw-Hill.

Blum, E. (1999) 'An investigation into the effects of recent legislation on the process of integration of pupils with SEN at the H. high school'. Unpublished MA Thesis. London: Middlesex University.

Bogen, J.E. and Bogen, G.M. (1969) 'The other side of the brain. III The corpus callosum and creativity', *Bulletin of the Los Angeles Neurological Society*, 34(4), 191–220.

Borich, G. (1977) *The Appraisal of Teaching*. Reading: Mass.: Addison Wesley.

Bradley, H.W. *et al.* (1989) *Report on the Evaluation of the School Teacher Appraisal Pilot Study*. Cambridge: Cambridge Institute.

Britzman, D. (1991) *Practice Makes Practice: A Critical Study of Learning to Teach*. Albany: State University of NY Press.

Broadhead, P. (1987) 'A blueprint for the good teacher the HMI/DES model of good primary practice', *British Journal of Educational Studies*, 35(1), 37–71.

Brown, A.L. and Palinscar, A.S. (1984) Teaching and practising thinking skills to promote comprehension in the context of group problem solving', *Remedial and Special Education*, 9(1) 53–9.

Brown, A.L., Bransford, J.D., Ferrara, R.A. and Campione, J.C. (1983) 'Learning, remembering and understanding', in Flavell, J.H. and Markham, E. (eds) *Carmichael's Manual of Child Psychology: Vol. 1*. New York: Wiley.

Bruner, J. (1960/1977) *The Process of Education*. Cambridge, MA: Harvard University Press.

Bubb, S. and Hoare, P. (2001) *Performance Management: Monitoring Teaching in the Primary School.* London: David Fulton.

Bunnell, S. (ed.) (1987) *Teacher Appraisal in Practice.* London: Heinemann.

Burgess, R.G. (1990) 'A problem in search of a method or a method in search of a problem? A critique of teacher appraisal', in Simons, H, and Elliott, J. (eds) *Rethinking Appraisal and Assessment.* Milton Keynes: Open University, 24–35.

Buzzing, P. (1992) *An Effective Return to Secondary Teaching.* West Sussex County Council Print Unit.

Callaghan, J. (1976) Prime Ministerial Speech. Oxford, Ruskin College.

Canter, L. (1976) *Assertive Discipline.* Santa Monica, CA: Lee Canter Associates.

Canter, L. and Canter, M. (1976) *Assertive Discipline.* London: Behaviour Management Products.

Canter, L. and Canter, M. (1991) *Assertive Discipline.* London: Positive Behaviour Management Products.

Canter, L. and Canter, M. (1999) *Assertive Discipline: Positive Behaviour Management for Today's Classroom.* Bristol: Positive Behaviour Management Ltd.

Carnine, D.W. and Englemann, S. (1982) *Theory of Instruction: Principles and Practice.* New York: Irvington.

CATE (1983) CATENOTE 1. London: DES.

CATE (1991) *Teacher Competencies.* London: DfEE.

CBI (1990) *Towards a Skills Revolution.* London: CBI.

Cheeseman, P. and Watts, P. (1985) *Positive Behaviour Management: A Manual for Teachers.* Beckenham: Croom Helm.

Chisholm, B., Kearney, D., Knight, G., Little, H., Morris, S. and Tweddle, D. (1986) *Preventive Approaches to Disruption: Developing Teaching Skills.* London: Macmillan.

Clift, P. (1982) cited in Turner, G. and Clift, P. (1985) *A First Review and Register of School and College Based Teacher Appraises Schemes.* Milton Keynes: Open University Press.

Commonwealth of Australia (1997) *National Competency Framework for Beginning Teaching.* Canberra: Australian Government Publishing Service.

Cuban, L. (1984) *How Teachers Taught. Constancy and Change in American Classrooms 1890–1980.* New York: Longmans.

Curzon, L.B. (1992) *Teaching in Further Education* 4th edn. London: Cassell.

Dadds, M. (1987) 'Researching teacher appraisal'. Paper presented at the BERA Conference, Manchester Polytechnic, September.

Dansereau, D.F. (1988) 'Co-operative learning strategies', in Weinstein, C.F., Goetz, E.T. and Alexander, P.A. (eds) *Learning and Study Strategies.* New York: Academic Press, Chapter 7, 103–20.

Dare, C. (1982) 'Techniques of consultation', *Association of Child Psychology and Psychiatry; Newsletter,* No. 11, 5–9.

Darling-Hammond, L. (1985) 'Valuing teachers. The making of a profession', *Teachers' College Record,* 87, 205–18.

DE (1993) See Blagg *et al.* (1993) *op. cit.*

de Alencar, E.M.L. Soriano (1995) 'Developing creative abilities at the university level', *Journal of High Ability,* 6, 82–90.

de Bono, E. (1976) *Lateral Thinking.* Harmondsworth: Penguin.

de Bono, E. (1983) *CoRT Thinking Programme.* Oxford: Pergamon.

De Corte, E. (1995) 'Learning and high ability. A perspective from research in instructional psychology', in Katzko, M.W. and Monks, F.J. (eds). *Nurturing Talent.* Assen, The Netherlands: Van Gorcum, 148–61.

Dearing, Sir Ron (1994) *The Final Report. National Curriculum and its Assessment.* London: School Curriculum and Assessment Authority (SCAA).

Deci, E.L. (1988) 'Motivating the highly able to learn'. Lecture to the 10th International Symposium, Plovdiv, Bulgaria, October.

Deci, E.L. and Ryan, R.M. (1983) *Intrinsic Motivation and Human Behaviour.* New York: Plenum Press.

DES (1983) *Teaching Quality.* Command Paper 8835. London: HMSO.

DES (1984) *The CATE Criteria.* London: HMSO.

DES (1985a) *Better Schools.* Command Paper 9469. London: HMSO.

DES (1985b) *Education Observed 3. Good Teachers.* London: HMSO.

DES (1987) *The National Curriculum 5–16. A Consultation Document.* London: HMSO.

DES (1989) *The National Curriculum. From Policy into Practice.* London: HMSO.

DFE (1991) *Education (School Teacher Appraisal) Regulations.* London: HMSO.

DfEE (1994) *Code of Practice.* London: DfEE.

DfEE (1997) *Excellence for All. Meeting Special Needs.* London: DfEE.

DfEE (1998a) *The National Literacy Strategy: A Guide for Teachers.* London: DfEE.

DfEE (1998b) *Teaching: High Status High Standards* 4/98. London: DfEE.

DfEE (1999) *The National Numeracy Strategy: A Guide for Teachers.* London: DfEE.

DfEE (1999a) *Teachers, Meeting the Challenge of Change.* London: DfEE.

DfEE (1999b) *Getting the Most from Your Data.* London: DfEE AUTLEAF 3–4.

DfEE (1999c) *Performance Management.* London: DfEE.

DfEE (1999d) *Excellence in Cities.* London: DfEE Publications.

DfEE (2000a) *The Education (School Teacher Appraisal) (England) Regulations.* London: DfEE.

DfEE (2000b) *Performance Management in Schools: Model Performance Management Policy.* London: DfEE.

DfEE (2000c) *Threshold Assessment.* London: DfEE.

Desforges, G. (1998) 'Learning and teaching: current views and perspectives', in Shorrocks-Taylor, D. *Directions in Educational Psychology.* London: Whurr, 5–18.

Dods, R.F. (1997) 'An action research study of the effectiveness of PBL in promoting acquisition and retention of knowledge', *Journal of the Education of the Gifted,* 21(1), 18–25.

Edge, A. and Stokes, E. (1997) *Quality and Assessment in Secondary Education. An Exploration of Curriculum and Examinations Year 1.* London: LSE Centre for Educational Research.

Edwards, A. and Collison J. (1997) 'Partnerships in school-based teacher training. A new vision?', *Teaching and Teacher Education,* 13(5), 555–61.

Eisner, E. (1983) 'Can educational research inform educational practice?'. Paper presented to the annual meeting of AERA, Montreal, Canada.

Elliott, J. (1990a) 'Teachers as researchers: Implications for supervision and for teacher education', *Teaching and Teacher Education,* 6(1), 11–26.

Elliott, J. (1990b) 'Appraisal of performance or appraisal of persons?' in Simons, H. and Elliott, J. *Rethinking Appraisal and Assessment.* Milton Keynes: Open University, 80–99.

Elliott, J. (1990c) 'Conclusion, rethinking appraisal', in Simons, H. and Elliott, J. *Rethinking Appraisal and Assessment.* Milton Keynes: Open University, 180–93

Elliott, J. and Labett, B. (1974) *Teacher Research and Teacher Education.* Norwich: University of East Anglia CARE. Mimeo.

Englemann, S. and Carnine, D.W. (1982) *Theory of instruction: Principles and Practice.* New York: Irvington.

Entwistle, N.J. (1998) 'Understanding academic performance at University. A research retrospective', in Shorrocks-Taylor, D. (ed.) *Directions in Educational Psychology.* London:

Whurr, 106–27.

Eraut, M. (1990) 'Teacher appraisal and/or teacher development: friends or foes?', in Simons, H. and Elliott, J. *Rethinking Appraisal and Assessment*. Milton Keynes: Open University, 20–3.

Evans, A. and Tomlinson, J. (1990) *Teacher Appraisal*. London: Jessica Kingsley.

Eyre, D. (1997) *Able Children in Ordinary Schools*. London: NACE/Fulton.

Feller, M. (1994) 'Open book testing and education for the future', *Studies in Educational Evaluation*, 20(2), 225–38.

Fenstermacher, G.D. (1986) 'Philosophy of research on teaching. Three aspects', in Wittrock, M.C. (ed.) *Handbook of Research on Teaching* (3rd edn). New York: Macmillan, 37–49.

FEU (1987) *Behaviour and Motivation: Disruption in Further Education*. London: Longman.

Feuerstein. R. (1995) *Mediated Learning Experience Training Conference*. London: Regents College.

Feuerstein, R., Rand, Y., Hoffman, M.B., and Mitter, B. (1980) *Instrumental Enrichment*. Baltimore M.D.: University Park Press.

Fisher, R. (1994) *Teaching Children to Think*. Hemel Hempstead: Simon & Schuster.

Flanders, N. (1970) *Analysing Teacher Behaviour*. Reading, Mass.: Addison-Wesley.

Flavell, J.H. (1979) 'Metacognition and cognitive monitoring', *American Psychologist*, 34, 906–11.

Freeman, J. (1998) *Educating the Very Able: Current International Research*. OFSTED Reviews of Research. London: The Stationery Office.

Furlong, L. (1996) 'From integration to partnership. Changing structures in initial teacher education', in McBride *op. cit.*, 121–9.

Gagné, R.L. (1975) *The Essentials of Learning*. London: Holt, Rinehart & Winston.

Gagné, R., Briggs, L. and Wagner, L. (1988) *Principles of Instructional Design* (4th edn). New York. Holt, Rinehart & Winston.

Gallagher, S.A. (1997) 'PBL. Where did it come from? What does it do and where is it going?', *Journal for the Education of the Gifted*, 21(1), 3–18.

Galloway, D. and Goodwin, C. (1987) *The Education of Disturbing Children*. London: Longmans.

Gardner, H. (1993) *Frames of Mind*. London: Fontana.

Gazzaniga, R. (1967) 'Split brain in man', *Scientific American*, 217, 24–9.

Gibbs, G. (1990) *Information Sheet*. Summary of Courses and Contents. Oxford: Oxford Polytechnic Centre for Staff Development.

Gibbs, G. (ed.) (1994) *Improving Student Learning: Theory and Research*. Oxford: Oxford Brookes University Staff Development Centre Publication.

Gibbs, G. (ed.) (1995) *Improving Student Learning through Evaluation and Assessment*. Oxford: Oxford Brookes University Staff Development Centre Publication.

Glaser, B.G. (1977) *Adaptive Education: Individual Diversity and Learning*. New York: Holt, Rinehart & Winston.

Glaser, B.G. (1978) *Theoretical Sensitivity*. Mill Valley CA: Sociology Press.

Goodlad, J. (1984) *Teachers for our Nations' Schools*. San Francisco, CA: Jossey-Bass.

Graham, D. (1985) *Those having Torches: Teacher Appraisal, a Study*. Ipswich: Suffolk Education Department.

Graham, D. (1987) *In the Light of Torches: Teacher Appraisal, a Further Study*. London: Industrial Society.

Hadfield, N. (1990) 'Survey of probationary teachers' experience of ITT in one LEA': Unpublished Report. Learning Difficulties Research Project. Kingston Polytechnic.

Hadfield, N. (1999) Personal Communication.

Handy, C. (1972) in Handy, C. and Aitken, R. (1986) *Understanding Schools as Organisations*. London: Penguin Books.

Hargreaves, D. (1984) *Improving Secondary Schools.* London: ILEA.

Harrop, A. (1984) *Behaviour modification in the Classroom.* London: Unibooks.

Hay McBer (2000) *Research into Teacher Effectiveness: A Model of Teacher Effectiveness: Report to DfEE.* London: DfEE.

Hebb, D.O. (1958) *The Organisation of Behaviour.* New York: Prentice Hall.

Hilgard, A.H. and Bower, G. (1981) *Theories of Behaviour.* New York: Prentice Hall.

Hirst, P.H. (1968) 'The contribution of philosophy to the study of the curriculum', in Kerr, J.F. (ed.) *Changing the Curriculum.* London: University of London Press.

Hohmann, M., Banet, B. and Weikart, D.P. (1979) *Young Children in Action: A Manual for Preschool Educators.* Ypsilanti, Mich.: Highscope Press.

Honey, P. and Mumford, A. (1986) *A Manual of Learning Styles.* London: Honey.

House, E.R. and Lapan, S.D. (1990) 'Teacher appraisal', in Simons, H. and Elliott, J. *Rethinking Appraisal and Assessment.* Milton Keynes: Open University, 55–63.

Husbands, C. (1996) 'Change management in ITT. National contexts, local circumstances and dynamics'. Chapter 1 in McBride, R. (ed.) *Teacher Education Policy. Some Issues Arising from Research and Practice.* London: Falmer.

ILEA (1977) *Keeping the School Under Review.* London: ILEA.

Jackson, P. (1968) *The Practice of Teaching.* New York: Teachers College Press.

James, N. (1984/1989) Report on appraisal research in an LEA, cited in Montgomery, D. and Hadfield, N. (eds) (1989) *Practical Teacher Appraisal.* London: Kogan Page.

Johnson, G. (1997) 'Reframing teacher education and teaching: From personalism to post personalism', *Teaching and Teacher Education,* **13**(8), 815–29.

Jones, J. (2001) *Performance Management for School Improvement.* London: David Fulton.

Jones, S. (1998) 'Whole class teaching, democratic skills and improving performance', *Mangement in Education,* **12**(1), 22–4.

Joseph, Sir K. (1984) Speech at the North of England Conference, Sheffield January 6th.

Joseph, Sir K. (1985a) Speech at the North of England Conference, Sheffield January 4th.

Joseph, Sir K. (1985b) Speech at the 'Better Schools' Conference, Birmingham November 15th.

Joyce, B. and Shower, B. (1988) *Student Achievement Through Staff Development.* New York: Longman.

Joyce, B. and Weil, M. (1986) *Models of Teaching* (3rd edn). Englewood Cliffs N.J.: Prentice Hall.

Kelly, G. (1955) *The Psychology of Personal Constructs, Vols 1 and 2.* New York: Norton.

Kennedy, D. (1987) Draft of letter to College Principals.

Kerry, T. and Kerry, C. (2000) 'The centrality of teaching skills to improving able pupil education', *Educating Able Children,* **4**(2), 13–9.

Knight, B.A. (1999) 'Towards inclusion of students with special needs in the regular classroom', *Support for Learning,* **14**(1), 3–7.

Knight, B.A., Paterson, D. and Mulcahy, R. (1998) *SPELT: A Cognitive and Metacognitive Approach to Instruction.* Melbourne: Hawker Brownlow Education.

Kolb, D.A. (1984) *Experiential Learning: Experiences as a Source of Learning and Development.* New York: Prentice Hall.

Kounin, J. (1970) *Discipline and Group Management in Schools.* New York: Holt, Rinehart & Winston.

Lawrence, R., Steed, D. and Young, P. (1984) *Disruptive Children, Disruptive Schools?* London: Routledge and Kegan Paul.

Lawrence, R., Steed, D., and Young P. (1989) *Disruptive Children – Disruptive Schools?* London: Routledge and Kegan Paul.

Lipman, M. (1991) *Thinking in Education.* Cambridge: Cambridge University Press.

Lockhead, J. (2001) *THINKBACK: A User's Guide to Minding the Mind.* London: Lawrence Erlbaum Associates.

Luton, K. and Booth, A. (1991) *Positive Strategies for Behavioural Mangement.* Windsor: NFER-Nelson.

Maier, N.R. (1976) *The Appraisal Interview: Three Basic Approaches.* New York: University Associates.

Makins, V. (1991) 'Five steps to peace in the classroom', *TES* 1 November, p. 23.

Marton, F. and Saljo, R. (1976) 'On qualitative differences in learning I. Outcome as a function of the learner's conception of the task', *British Journal of Educational Psychology*, 46, 4–11.

McBride, R. (ed.) (1996) *Teacher Education Policy. Some Issues Arising from Research and Practice.* London: Falmer.

McGuinness, C. (1999) *From Thinking Schools to Thinking Classrooms. DfEE Research Report No. 115.* London: DfEE.

McIntyre, A. (1980) 'The contribution of research to quality in teaching education', in Hoyle, E. and McGarry, J. (eds) *Professional Development of Teachers.* World Yearbook of Education. London: Kogan Page, 295–307.

McIntyre, A. (1990) 'Criterion-referenced assessment of teaching', in Simon, H. and Elliott, J. (eds) *Rethinking Appraisal and Assessment.* Milton Keynes: Open University Press, 64–71.

Mellanby, J., Anderson, R., Campbell, B. and Westwood, E. (1996) 'Cognitive determinants of verbal underachievement at secondary school level', *British Journal of Educational Psychology*, 66, 483–500.

Mongon, D. and Hart, S. (1989) *Improving Classroom Behaviour: New Directions for Pupils.* London: Cassell.

Montgomery, D. (1981) 'Education comes of age. A modern theory of teaching', *School Psychology International*, 1, 1–3.

Montgomery, D. (1982) 'Teaching thinking skills in the school curriculum', *School Psychology International*, 3, pp. 105–12.

Montgomery, D. (1983) 'Teaching thinking skills in the school curriculum', *School Psychology International*, 3, 108–12.

Montgomery, D. (1984) *Evaluation and Enhancement of Teaching Performance.* Kingston: Learning Difficulties Research Project.

Montgomery, D. (1985a) 'Appraisal: The nub is credibility', *Education*, 22 March, 259.

Montgomery, D. (1985b) *The Special Needs Able Children in Ordinary Classrooms.* Kingston: Learning Difficulties Research Project.

Montgomery, D. (1985c) 'A positive approach to appraisal', *Inspection and Advice*, 2(1), 16–19.

Montgomery, D. (1986) 'Oxbridge's influences', *Education*, February, 127.

Montgomery, D. (1988) 'Appraisal', *New Era in Education*, 68(3), 85–90.

Montgomery, D. (1989) *Managing Behaviour Problems.* Sevenoaks: Hodder & Stoughton.

Montgomery, D. (1990) *Children with Learning Difficulties.* London: Cassell.

Montgomery, D. (1991) 'Appraisal: A review of 10 years work', *Management in Education*, 5(3), pp. 41–5.

Montgomery, D. (1993) 'Fostering learner managed learning in teacher education', in Graves, N. (ed.) *Learner Managed Learning.* Leeds: Higher Education for Capability/World Education Fellowship, pp. 59–70.

Montgomery, D. (1994) The role of metacognition and metalearning in teacher education', in Gibbs, G. (ed.) *Improving Student Learning.* Oxford: Oxford Centre for Staff Development, Chapter 8, 227–33.

Montgomery, D. (1995) 'Critical theory and practice in evaluation and assessment', in Gibbs,

G. (ed.) *Improving Student Learning*. Oxford: Oxford Brookes University Staff Development Center.

Montgomery, D. (1996) *Educating the Able*. London: Cassell.

Montgomery, D. (1997a) *Spelling: Remedial Strategies*. London: Cassell.

Montgomery, D. (1997b) *Developmental Spelling. A Handbook of 100 Spelling Lessons*. Maldon: Learning Difficulties Research Project.

Montgomery, D. (1998a) *Reversing Lower Attainment*. London: David Fulton.

Montgomery, D. (1998b) 'Teacher education and distance learning', *Education Today*, **48**(4), 39–46.

Montgomery, D. (1998c) *Appraisal and Staff Development (2nd edn) MA SEN and MA SpLD Module Ten*. London: Middlesex University (1994 1st edn).

Montgomery, D. (1999) *Positive Appraisal Through Classroom Observation*. London: David Fulton.

Montgomery, D. (ed.) (2000) *Able Underachievers*. London: Whurr.

Montgomery, D. (2001) 'Double exceptionality: gifted and dyslexic'. Paper presented at the British Psychological Society, Education and Development Sections. Worcester, 6–9 September.

Montgomery, D. and Hadfield, N. (1989) *Practical Teacher Appraisal*. London: Kogan Page.

Montgomery, D. and Hadfield, N. (1990) *Appraisal in the Primary Classroom*. Leamington Spa: Scholastic.

Moriarty, M. (1999) 'An hour a day helps them spell, read (and play!)', *Teachers*, **1**, Spring, 6–7.

Mortimore, P., Sammon, P. and Stoll, L. (1988) *School Matters*. London: ILEA.

Munro, J. (1996) *Gifted Students' Learning. Basing the Teaching of Gifted Students on a Model of Learning*. Melbourne: Educational Assistance.

NAHT (1999) An interview with the national President of the NAHT, on Radio 4, *News*, February.

Neagley, R.L. and Evans, N.D. (1967) *Handbook for Effective Curriculum Development*. Englewood Cliffs, N.J.: Prentice Hall.

Neill, A.S. (1883–1973) Founded Summerhill School in 1929 in Suffolk. A self styled 'Progressive School'.

Neville, M. and Pugh, A. (1977) 'Ability to use a book: the effect of teaching', *Reading* **11**(3), 13–8.

NAPH (1999) 'Survey of marking of SATs at Key Stage One'. Reported on Radio 4, *You and Yours*, 22nd February.

Nickerson, R.S., Perkins, D.N. and Smith, E.E. (eds) (1985) *The Teaching of Thinking*. Hillsdale, N.J.: Erlbaum.

Nisbet, J. (1986) 'Appraisal for improvement', *Appraising Appraisal*. London: BERA Publications.

Norman, D.A. (1977) 'Notes towards a complex theory of learning', in Lesgold, A.M., Pellargino, J.W., Fokkema, S.D. and Glaser, R. (eds) *Cognitive Psychology and Instruction*. New York: Plenum.

NUT (1997) Statement by Director of NUT, reported in *Times Educational Supplement*, 26 October, 1.

OFSTED (1997) *OFSTED Report*. London: HMSO.

OFSTED (1999) *Raising the Attainment of Minority Ethnic Pupils: School and LEA Responses*. OFSTED Reviews of Research. London: The Stationary Office.

OFSTED (2000) *Educational Inequality: Mapping Race, Class and Gender*. London: OFSTED Publications Centre, HMI 232.

Ornstein, R. (1982) *The Psychology of Thinking* (2nd edn). San Francisco: Freeman.

Osborn, M. (1997) 'When being top is not seen as best', *Time Educational Supplement*, 10 Jan, 14.

Pascal, L. (1998) Study Skills Training Course leaflet. Stafford: NASEN.

Patterson, W. (1985) 'Appraisal of schoolteachers. An Industrialist's perspective from

HAY/MSL', NUT Conference. London: NUT.

Paul, R. (1990) 'Critical thinking', in *Critical Thinking Handbook*. Sonoma: Sonoma State University Centre for Critical Thinking and Moral Critique, Chapter 3.

Perry, P. (1984) 'Preface', in Montgomery, D. (1984).

Piaget, J. (1952) *Origins of Intelligence in Children* (2nd edn). New York: International Universities Press.

Race, P. (1992) 'Developing competence', in *Professorial Inaugural Lectures*. Glamorgan: University of Glamorgan, 1–53.

Rawlings, A. (1996) *Ways and Means Today*. Conflict Resolution; Training and Resources. Kingston: Kingston Friends, 78 Eden Street, Kingston KT1 1DG.

Resnick, L.B. (1987) 'Learning in schools and out', *Educational Researcher*, 16(9), 13–20.

Resnick, L.B. (ed.) (1989) *Knowing, Learning and Instruction Essays in Honour of Robert Glaser*. Hillsdale, N.J.: Erlbaum, 1–23.

Reynolds, A. (1992) 'What is competent beginning teaching? A review of literature', *Review of Educational Research*, 62, 1–36.

Reynolds, D. (1995) 'The effective schools. An Inaugural lecture', *Evaluation and Research in Education*, 9(2), 57–73.

Reynolds, D. and Farrell, S. (1996) *Worlds Apart? A Review of International Surveys of Educational Achievement Involving England*. London: OFSTED.

Riding, R. and Rayner, S. (1998) *Cognitive Styles and Learning Strategies*. London: David Fulton.

Roberts, M. (1986) The education of preschool and nursery children'. Seminar given at the *World Education Fellowship Conference (GB Section)*. London: Kingston Polytechnic.

Rogers, W. (1994a) 'Teaching positive behaviour to behaviourally disordered students in primary schools', *Support for Learning*, 9(4), 166–70.

Rogers, W. (1994b) *Behavioural Recovery: A Whole School Approach for Behaviour Disordered Children*. Melbourne: Australian Council for Educational Research.

Rogers, W. (2000) *Behaviour Management: A Whole School Approach*. London: Paul Chapman.

Rose, J. (1995) *OFSTED Inspections Report*. London: OFSTED.

Rosenshine, B. (1979) 'Content, time and direction instruction', in Peterson, P.L. and Walberg, H.J. (eds) *Research on Teaching*. Berkeley, CA: McCutchan.

Ruddock, J. (1995) 'The effective teacher', *Evaluation and Research in Education*, 9(2), 74–83.

Rutter, M.L. (1989) 'Pathways from childhood to adult life', *Journal of Child Psychiatry*, 30(1), 23–51.

Rutter, M.L., Maugham, M., Mortimore, P. and Ouston, J. (1979) *Fifteen Thousand Hours*. London: Longman.

Ryan, M.L., Connell, J.P. and Deci, E.L. (1985) 'A motivational analysis of self determination and self regulation in education', in Ames, C. and Ames, R. (eds) *Vol. 2: Research on Motivation in Education: the Classroom Milieu*. New York: Academic Press, Chapter 1.

Samuel, G. (1983) 'Evaluation as a way of life', *Education*, 162(14), 296.

Savage, J. and Desforges, C. (1995) 'The role of informal assessment in teacher practical action', *Educational Studies*, 21(3), 433–46.

Scheerens, Y. and Barnes, D. (1991) *School Writing: Discovering the Ground Rules*. Milton Keynes: Open University Press.

Schon, D.A. (1983) *The Reflective Practitioner*. New York: Basic Books.

Schools Council (1980) *Study Skills in the Secondary School: Project Handbook*. London: Schools Council.

Scott MacDonald, W. (1971) *Battle in the Classroom*. Brighton: Intext.

Scriven, M. (1986) 'New functions of evaluations', *Evaluation Practice*, 7(1), 21–30.

SED (1978) *The Education of Pupils with Learning Difficulties in Primary and Secondary Schools: A Progress Report*. Edinburgh: HMSO.

SHA (1998) Secondary Heads Association Conference, March, Birmingham.

Sharpe, R. and Green, A. (1975) *Education and Social Control: A Study in Progressive Primary Education.* London: Routledge & Kegan Paul.

Silva, K. (1998) 'Report of an international comparative study of pre school education'. *24 Hour World News*, Strasbourg, 4 June.

Simons, H. and Elliott, J. (eds) (1990) *Rethinking Appraisal and Assessment.* Milton Keynes: Open University.

Simonton, D.K. (1988) *Scientific Genius. A Psychology of Science.* Cambridge: Cambridge University Press.

Skinner, B.F. (1958) *Science and Human Behaviour.* New York: Macmillan.

Smyth, J. (1989) 'Developing and maintaining critical reflection in teacher education', *Journal of Teacher Education*, **40**(2), 2–9.

Snow, R.E. (1973) 'Theory construction for research on teaching', in Travers, R.M.W. (ed.) *Second Handbook of Research on Teaching.* New York: Rand McNally, 77–112.

Southgate-Booth, V. (1986) 'Teachers of reading. Planning the most effective use of their time', in Root, B. (ed.) *Resources for Reading. Does Quality Count?* London: UKRA/MacMillan, 80–98.

Southgate-Booth, V., Arnold, H. and Johnson, S. (1982) *Extending Beginning Reading.* London: Heinemann.

Stephenson, J. and Weil, S. (1988) 'Launch of Higher Education for Capability'. London: Royal Society of Arts.

Stodolsky, S. (1984) 'Teacher evaluation: The limits of looking', *Educational Research*, **13**(9), 11–8.

Stopper, M.J. (ed.) (2000) *Meeting the Social and Emotional Needs of the Gifted and Talented.* London: NACE/Fulton.

Strauss, A.L. and Corbin, J. (1990) *Basics of Qualitative Research.* Newbury Park: Sage.

Swartz, R.J. and Parks, S. (1994) *Infusing the Teaching of Critical and Creative Thinking into Elementary Instruction.* Pacific Grove, CA: Critical Thinking Press and Software.

Taba, H. (1963) 'Learning by discovery: Psychological and educational rationale', *Elementary School Journal*, **63**, 308–16.

Thomas, L. (1976) 'Learning to learn', *Personnel Management*, **37**, 22–4.

Thomas, L. and Augstein, S. (1975) *Reading to Learn: Report of Research Study.* London: Brunel Centre for Human Learning.

Thomas, L. and Harri-Augstein, S. (1984) 'The self organised learner: A conversational science for teaching and learning'. SCEDSIP/COPOL Conference Paper, Kingston Polytechnic.

Thorndike, R.L., Hagen, E. and France, N. (1986) *The Cognitive Abilities Tests* (Rev. edn). Windsor: NFER-Nelson.

TIMSS (1997) *Third International Maths and Science Study.* TIMSS International Study Centre, Campion Hall Boston College, Cheshunt Hill, M.A.

Tom, A. (1984) *Teaching as a Moral Craft.* New York: Longman.

Torgeson, J.K. (1982) 'The learning disabled child as inactive learner. Educational implications', *Topics for Learning Disabilities*, **2**, 45–52.

Trethowan, D.M. (1987) *Appraisal and Target Setting.* London: Harper & Row.

Tufnell, R. (2001) Personal Communication as Dean of School Lifelong Learning and Education. London: Middlesex University.

Tuxworth, E.N. (1982) *Competency in Teaching.* London: FEU.

Van Manen, M. (1991) *Researching Lived Experience.: Human Science Research for an Active Sensitive Pedagogy.* London, Ontario: Althouse Press.

Vygotsky, L.S. (1978) *Mind in Society: The Development of Higher Pyschological Processes.* Cambridge,

M.A.: Harvard University Press.

Wallace, B. (2000) *Teaching the Very Able Child.* London: NACE/Fulton.

Wallace, B. and Adams, H.B. (1993) *TASC: Thinking Actively in a Social Context.* Oxford: AB Academic Publishers.

Wang, M.C. and Lindvall, C.M. (1984) 'Individual differences and school environments', in Gordon, I.F.W. (ed.) *Review of Research in Education II.* Washington, D.C.: American Education Research Association.

Watson, J. (1996) *Reflection Through Instruction.* London: Falmer.

Weikart, D. (1967) *Preschool Intervention: A Preliminary Report from the Preschool Project.* Michigan: Ann Arbor.

Weikart, D. (1998) 'Report of an international comparative study of pre school education'. *24 Hour World News,* Strasbourg, 4 June.

Weinstein, C.E., Goetz, E.T. and Alexander, P.A. (1988) *Learning and Study Strategies.* New York: Academic Press.

Wheldall, K. and Merritt, F. (1984) *BATPACK, Positive Products.* Birmingham: Birmingham University Press.

Wheldall, K. and Merritt, F. (1985) *Positive Teaching: A Behavioural Approach.* London: Unwin.

Whimbey, A. (1975) *Intelligence Can Be Taught.* Cary, NC: Innovative Sciences.

Wildman, T.M., Nites, J.S., Magharo, S.G. and McLaughlin, R.A. (1990) 'Prompting reflective change among beginning and experienced teachers', in Clift, K., Houston, T., Pugach, W.R. and Pugach, M.C. (eds) *Encouraging Reflective Practice in Education.* New York: Teachers College Press, 139–62.

Winter, R. (1990) 'Problems in teacher appraisal: an action-research solution', in *Rethinking Appraisal and Assessment.* Milton Keynes: Open University, 44–54.

Wise, A.E., Darling Hammond, L., McLaughlin, M.W. and Bernstein, H.T. (1984) *Teacher Evaluation: A Study of Effective Practices.* Santa Monica, CA: Rand Corp.

Woodhead, C. (1997) *The Annual Report of Her Majesty's Chief Inspector of Schools in England: Standards and Quality in Education 1995–96.* London: OFSTED/HMSO.

Woodhead, C. (1998) *The Chief Inspector's Report on English Schools.* London: DfEE.

Wragg, E., Wikely, F., Wragg, C. and Haynes, G. (1996) *Teacher Appraisal Observed.* London: Routledge.

Wragg, E. (1987) *Teacher Appraisal: A Practical Guide.* London: Macmillan.

Yorke, M. (ed.) (1995) *Capability in Higher Education. Conference Procedures.* Liverpool: John Moores University.

Zahorik, J.A. (1990) 'Stability and flexibility in teaching', *Teaching and Teacher Education,* 6(1), 69–80.

Index

Printed in the United Kingdom
by Lightning Source UK Ltd.
112939UKS00002B/77-410